Nigerian Folk Stories Collected From
The Efik, Ibibio & People of Ikom

Nigerian Folk Stories Collected From The Efik, Ibibio & People of Ikom
Two Volumes
Author: Elphinstone Dayrell

Cover image: Ju Ju mask from Ibo Country, Southern Nigeria
Lay-out: www.burokd.nl

ISBN 978-94-92355-48-5

© 2021 Revised publication by:

VAMzzz Publishing
P.O. Box 3340
1001 AC Amsterdam
The Netherlands
www.vamzzz.com
vamzzz@protonmail.com

NIGERIAN

FOLK STORIES COLLECTED FROM THE EFIK, IBIBIO & PEOPLE OF IKOM

Elphinstone Dayrell

— TWO VOLUMES —

VAMzzz PUBLISHING

CONTENTS VOLUME TWO

— VOLUME ONE —

FOLK STORIES FROM SOUTHERN NIGERIA

I

The Tortoise with a Pretty Daughter

There was once a king who was very powerful. He had great influence over the wild beasts and animals. Now the tortoise was looked upon as the wisest of all beasts and men. This king had a son named Ekpenyon, to whom he gave fifty young girls as wives, but the prince did not like any of them. The king was very angry at this, and made a law that if any man had a daughter who was finer than the prince's wives, and who found favour in his son's eyes, the girl herself and her father and mother should be killed.

Now about this time the tortoise and his wife had a daughter who was very beautiful. The mother thought it was not safe to keep such a fine child, as the prince might fall in love with her, so she told her husband that her daughter ought to be killed and thrown away into the bush. The tortoise, however, was unwilling, and hid her until she was three years old. One day, when both the tortoise and his wife were away on their farm, the king's son happened to be hunting near their house, and saw a bird perched on the top of the fence round the house. The bird was watching the little girl, and was so entranced with her beauty that he did not notice the prince coming. The prince shot the bird with his bow and arrow, and it dropped inside the fence, so the prince sent his servant to gather it. While the servant was looking for the bird he came across the little girl, and was so struck with her form, that he immediately returned to his master and told him what he had seen. The prince then broke down the fence and found the child, and fell in love with her at once. He stayed and talked with her for a long time, until at last she agreed to become his wife. He then went home, but concealed from his father the fact that he had fallen in love with the beautiful daughter of the tortoise.

But the next morning he sent for the treasurer, and got sixty pieces of cloth[2] and three hundred rods,[3] and sent them to the tortoise. Then in the early afternoon he went down to the tortoise's house, and told him that he wished to marry his daughter. The tortoise saw at once that what he had dreaded had come to pass, and that his life was in danger, so he told the prince that if the king knew, he would kill not only himself (the tortoise), but also his wife and daughter. The prince replied that he would be killed himself before he allowed the tortoise and his wife and daughter to be killed. Eventually, after much argument, the tortoise consented, and agreed to hand his daughter to the prince as his wife when she arrived at the proper age. Then the prince went home and told his mother what he had done. She was in great distress at the thought that she would lose her son, of whom she was very proud, as she knew that when

---

2　A piece of cloth is generally about 8 yards long by 1 yard broad, and is valued at 5s.

3　A rod is made of brass, and is worth 3d. It is in the shape of a narrow croquet hoop, about 16 inches long and 6 inches across. A rod is native currency on the Cross River.

the king heard of his son's disobedience he would kill him. However, the queen, although she knew how angry her husband would be, wanted her son to marry the girl he had fallen in love with, so she went to the tortoise and gave him some money, clothes, yams, and palm-oil as further dowry on her son's behalf in order that the tortoise should not give his daughter to another man. For the next five years the prince was constantly with the tortoise's daughter, whose name was Adet, and when she was about to be put in the fatting house,[4] the prince told his father that he was going to take Adet as his wife. On hearing this the king was very angry, and sent word all round his kingdom that all people should come on a certain day to the market-place to hear the palaver. When the appointed day arrived the market-place was quite full of people, and the stones belonging to the king and queen were placed in the middle of the market-place.

When the king and queen arrived all the people stood up and greeted them, and they then sat down on their stones. The king then told his attendants to bring the girl Adet before him. When she arrived the king was quite astonished at her beauty. He then told the people that he had sent for them to tell them that he was angry with his son for disobeying him and taking Adet as his wife without his knowledge, but that now he had seen her himself he had to acknowledge that she was very beautiful, and that his son had made a good choice. He would therefore forgive his son.

When the people saw the girl they agreed that she was very

---

4   The fatting house is a room where a girl is kept for some weeks previous to her marriage. She is given plenty of food, and made as fat as possible, as fatness is looked upon as a great beauty by the Efik people.

fine and quite worthy of being the prince's wife, and begged the king to cancel the law he had made altogether, and the king agreed; and as the law had been made under the "Egbo" law, he sent for eight Egbos,[5] and told them that the order was cancelled throughout his kingdom, and that for the future no one would be killed who had a daughter more beautiful than the prince's wives, and gave the Egbos palm wine and money to remove the law, and sent them away. Then he declared that the tortoise's daughter, Adet, should marry his son, and he made them marry the same day. A great feast was then given which lasted for fifty days, and the king killed five cows and gave all the people plenty of foo-foo[6] and palm-oil chop, and placed a large number of pots of palm wine in the streets for the people to drink as they liked. The women brought a big play to the king's compound, and there was singing and dancing kept up day and night during the whole time. The prince and his companions also played in the market square. When the feast was over the king gave half of his kingdom to the tortoise to rule over, and three hundred slaves to work on his

---

5   The Egbo Society has many branches, extending from Calabar up the Cross River as far as the German Cameroons. Formerly this society used to levy blackmail to a certain extent and collect debts for people. The head Ju Ju, or fetish man, of each society is disguised, and frequently wears a hideous mask. There is a bell tied round his waist, hanging behind and concealed by feathers; this bell makes a noise as he runs. When the Egbo is out no women are allowed outside their houses, and even at the present time the women pretend to be very frightened. The Egbo very often carries a whip in his hand, and hits out blindly at any one he comes across. He runs round the town, followed by young men of his society beating drums and firing off guns. There is generally much drinking going on when the Egbo is playing. There is an Egbo House in most towns, the end part of which is screened off for the Egbo to change in. Inside the house are hung human skulls and the skulls of buffalo, or bush cow, as they are called; also heads of the various antelopes, crocodiles, apes, and other animals which have been killed by the members. The skulls of cows and goats killed by the society are also hung up. A fire is always kept in the Egbo House; and in the morning and late afternoon, the members of the society frequently meet there to drink gin and palm wine.

6   Foo-foo=yams boiled and mashed up.

farm. The prince also gave his father-in-law two hundred women and one hundred girls to work for him, so the tortoise became one of the richest men in the kingdom. The prince and his wife lived together for a good many years until the king died, when the prince ruled in his place. And all this shows that the tortoise is the wisest of all men and animals.

Moral.—Always have pretty daughters, as no matter how poor they may be, there is always the chance that the king's son may fall in love with them, and they may thus become members of the royal house and obtain much wealth.

II

How a Hunter obtained Money from his Friends the Leopard, Goat, Bush Cat, and Cock, and how he got out of repaying them

Many years ago there was a Calabar hunter called Effiong, who lived in the bush, killed plenty of animals, and made much money. Every one in the country knew him, and one of his best friends was a man called Okun, who lived near him. But Effiong was very extravagant, and spent much money in eating and drinking with every one, until at last he became quite poor, so he had to go out hunting again; but now his good luck seemed to have deserted him, for although he worked hard, and hunted day and night, he could not succeed in killing anything. One day, as he was very hungry, he went to his friend Okun and borrowed two hundred rods from him, and told him to come to his house on a certain day to get his money, and he told him to bring his gun, loaded, with him.

Now, some time before this Effiong had made friends with a leopard and a bush cat, whom he had met in the forest whilst on one of his hunting expeditions; and he had also made friends with a goat and a cock at a farm where he had stayed for the night. But though Effiong had borrowed the money from Okun, he could not think how he was to repay it on the day he had promised. At last, however, he thought of a plan, and on the next day he went to his friend the leopard, and asked him to lend him two hundred rods, promising to return the amount to him on the same day as he had promised to pay Okun; and he also told the leopard, that if he were absent when he came for his money, he could kill anything he saw in the house and eat it. The leopard was then to wait until the hunter arrived, when he would pay him the money; and to this the leopard agreed. The hunter then went to his friend the goat, and borrowed two hundred rods from him in the same way. Effiong also went to his friends the bush cat and the cock, and borrowed two hundred rods from each of them on the same conditions, and told each one of them that if he were absent when they arrived, they could kill and eat anything they found about the place.

When the appointed day arrived the hunter spread some corn on the ground, and then went away and left the house deserted. Very early in the morning, soon after he had begun to crow, the cock remembered what the hunter had told him, and walked over to the hunter's house, but found no one there. On looking round, however, he saw some corn on the ground, and, being hungry, he commenced to eat. About this time the bush cat also arrived, and not finding the hunter at home, he, too, looked about, and very soon he espied the cock, who was busy picking up the grains of corn. So the bush cat went up very softly behind and pounced on the cock and killed him at once, and began to eat him. By this time the goat had come for his money; but not finding his friend, he walked about until he came upon the bush cat, who was so intent upon his meal off the cock, that he did not notice the goat approaching; and the goat, being in rather a bad temper at not getting his money, at once charged at the bush cat and knocked him over, butting him with his horns. This the bush cat did not like at all, so, as he was not big enough to fight the goat, he picked up the remains of the cock and ran off with it to the bush, and so lost his money, as he did not await the arrival of the hunter. The goat was thus left master of the situation and started bleating, and this noise attracted the attention of the leopard, who was on his way to receive payment from the hunter. As he got nearer the smell of goat became very strong, and being hungry, for he had not eaten anything for some time, he approached the goat very carefully. Not seeing any one about he stalked the goat and got nearer and nearer, until he was within springing distance. The goat, in the meantime, was grazing quietly, quite unsuspicious of any danger, as he was in his friend the hunter's compound. Now and then he would say Ba!! But most of the time he was busy eating the young grass, and picking up the leaves which had fallen from a tree of which he was very fond. Suddenly the leopard sprang at the goat, and with one crunch at the neck brought him down. The goat was dead almost at once, and the leopard started on his meal.

It was now about eight o'clock in the morning, and Okun, the hunter's friend, having had his early morning meal, went out with his gun to receive payment of the two hundred rods he had lent to the hunter. When he got close to the house he heard a crunching sound, and, being a hunter himself, he approached very cautiously, and looking over the fence saw the leopard only a few yards off busily engaged eating the goat. He took careful aim at the leopard and fired, whereupon the leopard rolled over dead. The death of the leopard meant that four of the hunter's creditors were now disposed of, as the bush cat had killed the cock, the goat had driven the bush cat away (who thus forfeited his claim), and in his turn the goat had been killed by the leopard, who had just been slain by Okun. This meant a saving of eight hundred rods to Effiong; but he was not content with this, and directly he heard the report of the gun he ran out from where he had been hiding all the time, and found the leopard lying dead with Okun standing over it. Then in very strong language Effiong began to upbraid his friend, and asked him why he had killed his old friend the leopard, that nothing would satisfy him but that he should report the whole matter to the king, who would no doubt deal with him as he thought fit. When Effiong said this Okun was frightened, and begged him not to say anything more about the matter, as the king would be angry; but the hunter was obdurate, and refused to listen to him; and at last Okun said, "If you will allow the whole thing to drop and will say no more about it, I will make you a present of the two hundred rods you borrowed from me." This was just what Effiong wanted, but still he did not give in at once; eventually, however, he agreed, and told Okun he might go, and that he would bury the body of his friend the leopard.

Directly Okun had gone, instead of burying the body Effiong dragged it inside the house and skinned it very carefully. The skin he put out to dry in the sun, and covered it with wood ash, and the body he ate. When the skin was well cured the hunter took it to a distant market, where he sold it for much money. And now, whenever a bush cat sees a cock he always kills it, and does so by right, as he takes the cock in part payment of the two hundred rods which the hunter never paid him.

Moral.—Never lend money to people, because if they cannot pay they will try to kill you or get rid of you in some way, either by poison or by setting bad Ju Ju's for you.

The Woman with Two Skins

Eyamba l. of Calabar was a very powerful king. He fought and conquered all the surrounding countries, killing all the old men and women, but the able-bodied men and girls he caught and brought back as slaves, and they worked on the farms until they died.

This king had two hundred wives, but none of them had borne a son to him. His subjects, seeing that he was becoming an old man, begged him to marry one of the spider's daughters, as they always had plenty of children. But when the king saw the spider's daughter he did not like her, as she was ugly, and the people said it was because her mother had had so many children at the same time. However, in order to please his people he married the ugly girl, and placed her among his other wives, but they all complained because she was so ugly, and said she could not live with them. The king, therefore, built her a separate house for herself, where she was given food and drink the same as the other wives. Every one jeered at her on account of her ugliness; but she was not really ugly, but beautiful, as she was born with two skins, and at her birth her mother was made to promise that she should never remove the ugly skin until a certain time arrived save only during the night, and that she must put it on again before dawn. Now the king's head wife knew this, and was very fearful lest the king should find it out and fall in love with the spider's daughter; so she went to a Ju Ju man and offered him two hundred rods to make a potion that would make the king forget altogether that the spider's daughter was his wife. This the Ju Ju man finally consented to do, after much haggling over the price, for three hundred and fifty rods; and he made up some "medicine," which the head wife mixed with the king's food. For some months this had the effect of making the king forget the spider's daughter, and he used to pass quite close to her without recognising her in any way. When four months had elapsed and the king had not once sent for Adiaha (for that was the name of the spider's daughter), she began to get tired, and went back to her parents. Her father, the spider, then took her to another Ju Ju man, who, by making spells and casting lots, very soon discovered that it was the king's head wife who had made the Ju Ju and had enchanted the king so that he would not look at Adiaha. He therefore told the spider that Adiaha should give the king some medicine which he would prepare, which would make the king remember her. He prepared the medicine, for which the spider had to pay a large sum of money; and that very day Adiaha made a small dish of food, into which she had placed the medicine, and presented it to the king. Directly he had eaten the dish his eyes were opened and he recognised his wife, and told her to come to him that very evening. So in the afternoon, being very joyful, she went down to the river and washed, and when she returned she put on her best cloth and went to the king's palace.

Directly it was dark and all the lights were out she pulled off her ugly skin, and the king saw how beautiful she was, and was very pleased with her; but when the cock crowed Adiaha pulled on her ugly skin again, and went back to her own house.

This she did for four nights running, always taking the ugly skin off in the dark, and leaving before daylight in the morning. In course of time, to the great surprise of all the people, and particularly of the king's two hundred wives, she gave birth to a son; but what surprised them most of all was that only one son was born, whereas her mother had always had a great many children at a time, generally about fifty.

The king's head wife became more jealous than ever when Adiaha had a son; so she went again to the Ju Ju man, and by giving him a large present induced him to give her some medicine which would make the king sick and forget his son. And the medicine would then make the king go to the Ju Ju man, who would tell him that it was his son who had made him sick, as he wanted to reign instead of his father. The Ju Ju man would also tell the king that if he wanted to recover he must throw his son away into the water.

And the king, when he had taken the medicine, went to the Ju Ju man, who told him everything as had been arranged with the head wife. But at first the king did not want to destroy his son. Then his chief subjects begged him to throw his son away, and said that perhaps in a year's time he might get another son. So the king at last agreed, and threw his son into the river, at which the mother grieved and cried bitterly.

Then the head wife went again to the Ju Ju man and got more

medicine, which made the king forget Adiaha for three years, during which time she was in mourning for her son. She then returned to her father, and he got some more medicine from his Ju Ju man, which Adiaha gave to the king. And the king knew her and called her to him again, and she lived with him as before. Now the Ju Ju who had helped Adiaha's father, the spider, was a Water Ju Ju, and he was ready when the king threw his son into the water, and saved his life and took him home and kept him alive. And the boy grew up very strong.

After a time Adiaha gave birth to a daughter, and her the jealous wife also persuaded the king to throw away. It took a longer time to persuade him, but at last he agreed, and threw his daughter into the water too, and forgot Adiaha again. But the Water Ju Ju was ready again, and when he had saved the little girl, he thought the time had arrived to punish the action of the jealous wife; so he went about amongst the head young men and persuaded them to hold a wrestling match in the market-place every week. This was done, and the Water Ju Ju told the king's son, who had become very strong, and was very like to his father in appearance, that he should go and wrestle, and that no one would be able to stand up before him. It was then arranged that there should be a grand wrestling match, to which all the strongest men in the country were invited, and the king promised to attend with his head wife.

On the day of the match the Water Ju Ju told the king's son that he need not be in the least afraid, and that his Ju Ju was so powerful, that even the strongest and best wrestlers in the country would not be able to stand up against him for even a few minutes. All the people of the country came to see the great contest, to the winner of which the king had promised to present prizes of cloth and money, and all the strongest men came. When they saw the king's son, whom nobody knew, they laughed and said, "Who is this small boy? He can have no chance against us." But when they came to wrestle, they very soon found that they were no match for him. The boy was very strong indeed, beautifully made and good to look upon, and all the people were surprised to see how like he was to the king.

After wrestling for the greater part of the day the king's son was declared the winner, having thrown every one who had stood up against him; in fact, some of his opponents had been badly hurt, and had their arms or ribs broken owing to the tremendous strength of the boy. After the match was over the king presented him with cloth and money, and invited him to dine with him in the evening. The boy gladly accepted his father's invitation; and after he had had a good wash in the river, put on his cloth and went up to the palace, where he found the head chiefs of the country and some of the king's most favoured wives. They then sat down to their meal, and the king had his own son, whom he did not know, sitting next to him. On the other side of the boy sat the jealous wife, who had been the cause of all the trouble. All through the dinner this woman did her best to make friends with the boy, with whom she had fallen violently in love on account of his beautiful appearance, his strength, and his being the best wrestler in the country. The woman thought to herself, "I will have this boy as my husband, as my husband is now an old man and will surely soon die." The boy, however, who was as wise as he was strong, was quite aware of everything the jealous woman had done, and although he pretended to be very flattered at the advances of the king's head wife, he did not respond very readily, and went home as soon as he could.

When he returned to the Water Ju Ju's house he told him everything that had happened, and the Water Ju Ju said—

"As you are now in high favour with the king, you must go to him to-morrow and beg a favour from him. The favour you will ask is that all the country shall be called together, and that a certain case shall be tried, and that when the case is finished, the man or woman who is found to be in the wrong shall be killed by the Egbos before all the people."

So the following morning the boy went to the king, who readily granted his request, and at once sent all round the country appointing a day for all the people to come in and hear the case tried. Then the boy went back to the Water Ju Ju, who told him to go to his mother and tell her who he was, and that when the day of the trial arrived, she was to take off her ugly skin and appear in all her beauty, for the time had come when she need no longer wear it. This the son did.

When the day of trial arrived, Adiaha sat in a corner of the square, and nobody recognised the beautiful stranger as the spider's daughter. Her son then sat down next to her, and brought his sister with him. Immediately his mother saw her she said—

"This must be my daughter, whom I have long mourned as dead," and embraced her most affectionately.

The king and his head wife then arrived and sat on their stones in the middle of the square, all the people saluting them with the usual greetings. The king then addressed the people, and said that he had called them together to hear a strong palaver at the request of the young man who had been the victor of the wrestling, and who had promised that if the case went against him he would offer up his life to the Egbo. The king also said that if, on the other hand, the case was decided in the boy's favour, then the other party would be killed, even though it were himself or one of his wives; whoever it was would have to take his or her place on the killing-stone and have their heads cut off by the Egbos. To this all the people agreed, and said they would like to hear what the young man had to say. The young man then walked round the square, and bowed to the king and the people, and asked the question, "Am I not worthy to be the son of any chief in the country?" And all the people answered "Yes!"

The boy then brought his sister out into the middle, leading her by the hand. She was a beautiful girl and well made. When every one had looked at her he said, "Is not my sister worthy to be any chief's daughter?" And the people replied that she was worthy of being any one's daughter, even the king's. Then he called his mother Adiaha, and she came out, looking very beautiful with her best cloth and beads on, and all the people cheered, as they had never seen a finer woman. The boy then asked them, "Is this woman worthy of being the king's wife?" And a shout went up from every one present that she would be a proper wife for the king, and looked as if she would be the mother of plenty of fine healthy sons.

Then the boy pointed out the jealous woman who was sitting next to the king, and told the people his story, how that his mother, who had two skins, was the spider's daughter; how she had married the king, and how the head wife was jealous and had made a bad Ju Ju for the king, which made him forget his wife; how she had persuaded the king to throw himself and his sister into the river, which, as they all knew, had been done, but the Water Ju Ju had saved both of them, and had brought them up.

Then the boy said: "I leave the king and all of you people to judge my case. If I have done wrong, let me be killed on the stone by the Egbos; if, on the other hand, the woman has done evil, then let the Egbos deal with her as you may decide."

When the king knew that the wrestler was his son he was very glad, and told the Egbos to take the jealous woman away, and punish her in accordance with their laws. The Egbos decided that the woman was a witch; so they took her into the forest and tied her up to a stake, and gave her two hundred lashes with a whip made from hippopotamus hide, and then burnt her alive, so that she should not make any more trouble, and her ashes were thrown into the river. The king then embraced his wife and daughter, and told all the people that she, Adiaha, was his proper wife, and would be the queen for the future.

When the palaver was over, Adiaha was dressed in fine clothes and beads, and carried back in state to the palace by the king's servants.

That night the king gave a big feast to all his subjects, and told them how glad he was to get back his beautiful wife whom he had never known properly before, also his son who was stronger than all men, and his fine daughter. The feast continued for a hundred and sixty-six days; and the king made a law that if any woman was found out getting medicine against her husband, she should be killed at once. Then the king built three new compounds, and placed many slaves in them, both men and women. One compound he gave to his wife, another to his son, and the third he gave to his daughter. They all lived together quite happily for some years until the king died, when his son came to the throne and ruled in his stead.

IV.

The King's Magic Drum

Efriam Duke was an ancient king of Calabar. He was a peaceful man, and did not like war. He had a wonderful drum, the property of which, when it was beaten, was always to provide plenty of good food and drink. So whenever any country declared war against him, he used to call all his enemies together and beat his drum; then to the surprise of every one, instead of fighting the people found tables spread with all sorts of dishes, fish, foo-foo, palm-oil chop, soup, cooked yams and ocros, and plenty of palm wine for everybody. In this way he kept all the country quiet, and sent his enemies away with full stomachs, and in a happy and contented frame of mind. There was only one drawback to possessing the drum, and that was, if the owner of the drum walked over any stick on the road or stept over a fallen tree, all the food would immediately go bad, and three hundred Egbo men would appear with sticks and whips and beat the owner of the drum and all the invited guests very severely.

Efriam Duke was a rich man. He had many farms and hundreds of slaves, a large store of kernels on the beach, and many puncheons of palm-oil. He also had fifty wives and many children.

The wives were all fine women and healthy; they were also good mothers, and all of them had plenty of children, which was good for the king's house.

Every few months the king used to issue invitations to all his subjects to come to a big feast, even the wild animals were invited; the elephants, hippopotami, leopards, bush cows, and antelopes used to come, for in those days there was no trouble, as they were friendly with man, and when they were at the feast they did not kill one another. All the people and the animals as well were envious of the king's drum and wanted to possess it, but the king would not part with it.

One morning Ikwor Edem, one of the king's wives, took her little daughter down to the spring to wash her, as she was covered with yaws, which are bad sores all over the body. The tortoise happened to be up a palm tree, just over the spring, cutting nuts for his midday meal; and while he was cutting, one of the nuts fell to the ground, just in front of the child. The little girl, seeing the good food, cried for it, and the mother, not knowing any better, picked up the palm nut and gave it to her daughter. Directly the tortoise saw this he climbed down the tree, and asked the woman where his palm nut was. She replied that she had given it to her child to eat. Then the tortoise, who very much wanted the king's drum, thought he would make plenty palaver over this and force the king to give him the drum, so he said to the mother of the child—

"I am a poor man, and I climbed the tree to get food for myself and my family. Then you took my palm nut and gave it to your child. I shall tell the whole matter to the king, and see what he has to say when he hears that one of his wives has stolen my food," for this, as every one knows, is a very serious crime according to native custom.

Ikwor Edem then said to the tortoise—

"I saw your palm nut lying on the ground, and thinking it had fallen from the tree, I gave it to my little girl to eat, but I did not steal it. My husband the king is a rich man, and if you have any complaint to make against me or my child, I will take you before him."

So when she had finished washing her daughter at the spring she took the tortoise to her husband, and told him what had taken place. The king then asked the tortoise what he would accept as compensation for the loss of his palm nut, and offered him money, cloth, kernels or palm-oil, all of which things the tortoise refused one after the other.

The king then said to the tortoise, "What will you take? You may have anything you like."

And the tortoise immediately pointed to the king's drum, and said that it was the only thing he wanted.

In order to get rid of the tortoise the king said, "Very well, take the drum," but he never told the tortoise about the bad things that would happen to him if he stept over a fallen tree, or walked over a stick on the road.

The tortoise was very glad at this, and carried the drum home in triumph to his wife, and said, "I am now a rich man, and shall do no more work. Whenever I want food, all I have to do is to beat this drum, and food will immediately be brought to me, and plenty to drink."

His wife and children were very pleased when they heard this, and asked the tortoise to get food at once, as they were all hungry. This the tortoise was only too pleased to do, as he wished to show off his newly acquired wealth, and was also rather hungry himself, so he beat the drum in the same way as he had seen the king do when he wanted something to eat, and immediately plenty of food appeared, so they all sat down and made a great feast. The tortoise did this for three days, and everything went well; all his children got fat, and had as much as they could possibly eat. He was therefore very proud of his drum, and in order to display his riches he sent invitations to the king and all the people and animals to come to a feast. When the people received their invitations they laughed, as they knew the tortoise was very poor, so very few attended the feast; but the king, knowing about the drum, came, and when the tortoise beat the drum, the food was brought as usual in great profusion, and all the people sat down and enjoyed their meal very much. They were much astonished that the poor tortoise should be able to entertain so many people, and told all their friends what fine dishes had been placed before them, and that they had never had a better dinner. The people who had not gone were very sorry when they heard this, as a good feast, at somebody else's expense, is not provided every day. After the feast all the people looked upon the tortoise as one of the richest men in the kingdom, and he was very much respected in consequence. No one, except the king, could understand how the poor tortoise could suddenly entertain so lavishly, but they all made up their minds that if the tortoise ever gave another feast, they would not refuse again.

When the tortoise had been in possession of the drum for a few weeks he became lazy and did no work, but went about the country boasting of his riches, and took to drinking too much. One day after he had been drinking a lot of palm wine at a distant farm, he started home carrying his drum; but having had too much to drink, he did not notice a stick in the path. He walked over the stick, and of course the Ju Ju was broken at once. But he did not know this, as nothing happened at the time, and eventually he arrived at his house very tired, and still not very well from having drunk too much. He threw the drum into a corner and went to sleep. When he woke up in the morning the tortoise began to feel hungry, and as his wife and children were calling out for food, he beat the drum; but instead of food being brought, the house was filled with Egbo men, who beat the tortoise, his wife and children, badly. At this the tortoise was very angry, and said to himself—

"I asked every one to a feast, but only a few came, and they had plenty to eat and drink. Now, when I want food for myself and my family, the Egbos come and beat me. Well, I will let the other people share the same fate, as I do not see why I and my family should be beaten when I have given a feast to all people."

He therefore at once sent out invitations to all the men and animals to come to a big dinner the next day at three o'clock in the afternoon.

When the time arrived many people came, as they did not wish to lose the chance of a free meal a second time. Even the sick men, the lame, and the blind got their friends to lead them to the feast. When they had all arrived, with the exception of the king and his wives, who sent excuses, the tortoise beat his drum as usual, and then quickly hid himself under a bench, where he could not be seen. His wife and children he had sent away before the feast, as he knew what would surely happen. Directly he had beaten the drum three hundred Egbo men appeared with whips, and started flogging all the guests, who could not escape, as the doors had been fastened. The beating went on for two hours, and the people were so badly punished, that many of them had to be carried home on the backs of their friends. The leopard was the only one who escaped, as directly he saw the Egbo men arrive he knew that things were likely to be unpleasant, so he gave a big spring and jumped right out of the compound.

When the tortoise was satisfied with the beating the people had received he crept to the door and opened it. The people then ran away, and when the tortoise gave a certain tap on the drum all the Egbo men vanished. The people who had been beaten were so angry, and made so much palaver with the tortoise, that he made up his mind to return the drum to the king the next day. So in the morning the tortoise went to the king and brought the drum with him. He told the king that he was not satisfied with the drum, and wished to exchange it for something else; he did not mind so much what the king gave him so long as he got full value for the drum, and he was quite willing to accept a certain number of slaves, or a few farms, or their equivalent in cloth or rods.

The king, however, refused to do this; but as he was rather sorry for the tortoise, he said he would present him with a magic foo-foo tree, which would provide the tortoise and his family with food, provided he kept a certain condition. This the tortoise gladly consented to do. Now this foo-foo tree only bore fruit once a year, but every day it dropped foo-foo and soup on the ground. And the condition was, that the owner should gather sufficient food for the day, once, and not return again for more. The tortoise, when he had thanked the king for his generosity, went home to his wife and told her to bring her calabashes to the tree. She did so, and they gathered plenty of foo-foo and soup quite sufficient for the whole family for that day, and went back to their house very happy.

That night they all feasted and enjoyed themselves. But one of the sons, who was very greedy, thought to himself—

"I wonder where my father gets all this good food from? I must ask him."

So in the morning he said to his father—

"Tell me where do you get all this foo-foo and soup from?"

But his father refused to tell him, as his wife, who was a cunning woman, said—

"If we let our children know the secret of the foo-foo tree, some day when they are hungry, after we have got our daily supply, one of them may go to the tree and gather more, which will break the Ju Ju."

But the envious son, being determined to get plenty of food for himself, decided to track his father to the place where he obtained the food. This was rather difficult to do, as the tortoise always went out alone, and took the greatest care to prevent any one following him. The boy, however, soon thought of a plan, and got a calabash with a long neck and a hole in the end. He filled the calabash with wood ashes, which he obtained from the fire, and then got a bag which his father always carried on his back when he went out to get food. In the bottom of the bag the boy then made a small hole, and inserted the calabash with the neck downwards, so that when his father walked to the foo-foo tree he would leave a small trail of wood ashes behind him. Then when his father, having slung his bag over his back as usual, set out to get the daily supply of food, his greedy son followed the trail of the wood ashes, taking great care to hide himself and not to let his father perceive that he was being followed. At last the tortoise arrived at the tree, and placed his calabashes on the ground and collected the food for the day, the boy watching him from a distance. When his father had finished and went home the boy also returned, and having had a good meal, said nothing to his parents, but went to bed. The next morning he got some of his brothers, and after his father had finished getting the daily supply, they went to the tree and collected much foo-foo and soup, and so broke the Ju Ju.

At daylight the tortoise went to the tree as usual, but he could not find it, as during the night the whole bush had grown up, and the foo-foo tree was hidden from sight. There was nothing to be seen but a dense mass of prickly tie-tie palm. Then the tortoise at once knew that some one had broken the Ju Ju, and had gathered foo-foo from the tree twice in the same day; so he returned very sadly to his house, and told his wife. He then called all his family together and told them what had happened, and asked them who had done this evil thing. They all denied having had anything to do with the tree, so the tortoise in despair brought all his family to the place where the foo-foo tree had been, but which was now all prickly tie-tie palm, and said—

"My dear wife and children, I have done all that I can for you, but you have broken my Ju Ju; you must therefore for the future live on the tie-tie palm."

So they made their home underneath the prickly tree, and from that day you will always find tortoises living under the prickly tie-tie palm, as they have nowhere else to go to for food.

V.

Ituen and the King's Wife

Ituen was a young man of Calabar. He was the only child of his parents, and they were extremely fond of him, as he was of fine proportions and very good to look upon. They were poor people, and when Ituen grew up and became a man, he had very little money indeed, in fact he had so little food, that every day it was his custom to go to the market carrying an empty bag, into which he used to put anything eatable he could find after the market was over.

At this time Offiong was king. He was an old man, but he had plenty of wives. One of these women, named Attem, was quite young and very good-looking. She did not like her old husband, but wished for a young and handsome husband. She therefore told her servant to go round the town and the market to try and find such a man and to bring him at night by the side door to her house, and she herself would let him in, and would take care that her husband did not discover him.

That day the servant went all round the town, but failed to find any young man good-looking enough. She was just returning to report her ill-success when, on passing through the market-place, she saw Ituen picking up the remains of corn and other things which had been left on the ground. She was immediately struck with his fine appearance and strength, and saw that he was just the man to make a proper lover for her mistress, so she went up to him, and said that the queen had sent for him, as she was so taken with his good looks. At first Ituen was frightened and refused to go, as he knew that if the King discovered him he would be killed. However, after much persuasion he consented, and agreed to go to the queen's side door when it was dark.

When night came he went with great fear and trembling, and knocked very softly at the queen's door. The door was opened at once by the queen herself, who was dressed in all her best clothes, and had many necklaces, beads, and anklets on. Directly she saw Ituen she fell in love with him at once, and praised his good looks and his shapely limbs. She then told her servant to bring water and clothes, and after he had had a good wash and put on a clean cloth, he rejoined the queen. She hid him in her house all the night.

In the morning when he wished to go she would not let him, but, although it was very dangerous, she hid him in the house, and secretly conveyed food and clothes to him. Ituen stayed there for two weeks, and then he said that it was time for him to go and see his mother, but the queen persuaded him to stay another week, much against his will.

When the time came for him to depart, the queen got together fifty carriers with presents for Ituen's mother who, she knew, was a poor woman. Ten slaves carried three hundred rods; the other forty carried yams, pepper, salt, tobacco, and cloth. When all the presents arrived Ituen's mother was very pleased and embraced her son, and noticed with pleasure that he was looking well, and was dressed in much finer clothes than usual; but when she heard that he had attracted the queen's attention she was frightened, as she knew the penalty imposed on any one who attracted the attention of one of the king's wives.

Ituen stayed for a month in his parents' house and worked on the farm; but the queen could not be without her lover any longer, so she sent for him to go to her at once. Ituen went again, and, as before, arrived at night, when the queen was delighted to see him again.

In the middle of the night some of the king's servants, who had been told the story by the slaves who had carried the presents to Ituen's mother, came into the queen's room and surprised her there with Ituen. They hastened to the king, and told him what they had seen. Ituen was then made a prisoner, and the king sent out to all his people to attend at the palaver house to hear the case tried. He also ordered eight Egbos to attend armed with machetes. When the case was tried Ituen was found guilty, and the king told the eight Egbo men to take him into the bush and deal with him according to native custom. The Egbos then took Ituen into the bush and tied him up to a tree; then with a sharp knife they cut off his lower jaw, and carried it to the king.

When the queen heard the fate of her lover she was very sad, and cried for three days. This made the king angry, so he told the Egbos to deal with his wife and her servant according to their law. They took the queen and the servant into the bush, where Ituen was still tied up to the tree dying and in great pain. Then, as the queen had nothing to say in her defence, they tied her and the girl up to different trees, and cut the queen's lower jaw off in the same way as they had her lover's. The Egbos then put out both the eyes of the servant, and left all three to die of starvation. The king then made an Egbo law that for the future no one belonging to Ituen's family was to go into the market on market day, and that no one was to pick up the rubbish in the market. The king made an exception to the law in favour of the vulture and the dog, who were not considered very fine people, and would not be likely to run off with one of the king's wives, and that is why you still find vultures and dogs doing scavenger in the market-places even at the present time.

VI.

Of the Pretty Stranger who Killed the King

Mbotu was a very famous king of Old Town, Calabar. He was frequently at war, and was always successful, as he was a most skilful leader. All the prisoners he took were made slaves. He therefore became very rich, but, on the other hand, he had many enemies. The people of Itu in particular were very angry with him and wanted to kill him, but they were not strong enough to beat Mbotu in a pitched battle, so they had to resort to craft. The Itu people had an old woman who was a witch and could turn herself into whatever she pleased, and when she offered to kill Mbotu, the people were very glad, and promised her plenty of money and cloth if she succeeded in ridding them of their worst enemy. The witch then turned herself into a young and pretty girl, and having armed herself with a very sharp knife, which she concealed in her bosom, she went to Old Town, Calabar, to seek the king.

It happened that when she arrived there was a big play being held in the town, and all the people from the surrounding country had come in to dance and feast. Oyaikan, the witch, went to the play, and walked about so that every one could see her. Directly she appeared the people all marvelled at her beauty, and said that she was as beautiful as the setting sun when all the sky was red. Word was quickly brought to king Mbotu, who, it was well known, was fond of pretty girls, and he sent for her at once, all the people agreeing that she was quite worthy of being the king's wife. When she appeared before him he fancied her so much, that he told her he would marry her that very day. Oyaikan was very pleased at this, as she had never expected to get her opportunity so quickly. She therefore prepared a dainty meal for the king, into which she placed a strong medicine to make the king sleep, and then went down to the river to wash.

When she had finished it was getting dark, so she went to the king's compound, carrying her dish on her head, and was at once shown in to the king, who embraced her affectionately. She then offered him the food, which she said, quite truly, she had prepared with her own hands. The king ate the whole dish, and immediately began to feel very sleepy, as the medicine was strong and took effect quickly.

They retired to the king's chamber, and the king went to sleep at once. About midnight, when all the town was quiet, Oyaikan drew her knife from her bosom and cut the king's head off. She put the head in a bag and went out very softly, shutting and barring the door behind her. Then she walked through the town without any one observing her, and went straight to Itu, where she placed king Mbotu's head before her own king.

When the people heard that the witch had been successful and that their enemy was dead, there was great rejoicing, and the king of Itu at once made up his mind to attack Old Town, Calabar.

He therefore got his fighting men together and took them in canoes by the creeks to Old Town, taking care that no one carried word to Calabar that he was coming.

The morning following the murder of Mbotu his people were rather surprised that he did not appear at his usual time, so his head wife knocked at his door. Not receiving any answer she called the household together, and they broke open the door. When they entered the room they found the king lying dead on his bed covered in blood, but his head was missing. At this a great shout went up, and the whole town mourned. Although they missed the pretty stranger, they never connected her in their minds with the death of their king, and were quite unsuspicious of any danger, and were unprepared for fighting. In the middle of the mourning, while they were all dancing, crying, and drinking palm wine, the king of Itu with all his soldiers attacked Old Town, taking them quite by surprise, and as their leader was dead, the Calabar people were very soon defeated, and many killed and taken prisoners.

Moral.—Never marry a stranger, no matter how pretty she may be.

VII.

Why the Bat flies by Night

A bush rat called Oyot was a great friend of Emiong, the bat; they always fed together, but the bat was jealous of the bush rat. When the bat cooked the food it was always very good, and the bush rat said, "How is it that when you make the soup it is so tasty?"

The bat replied, "I always boil myself in the water, and my flesh is so sweet, that the soup is good."

He then told the bush rat that he would show him how it was done; so he got a pot of warm water, which he told the bush rat was boiling water, and jumped into it, and very shortly afterwards came out again. When the soup was brought it was as strong and good as usual, as the bat had prepared it beforehand.

The bush rat then went home and told his wife that he was going to make good soup like the bat's. He therefore told her to boil some water, which she did. Then, when his wife was not looking, he jumped into the pot, and was very soon dead.

When his wife looked into the pot and saw the dead body of her husband boiling she was very angry, and reported the matter to the king, who gave orders that the bat should be made a prisoner.

Every one turned out to catch the bat, but as he expected trouble he flew away into the bush and hid himself. All day long the people tried to catch him, so he had to change his habits, and only came out to feed when it was dark, and that is why you never see a bat in the daytime.

VIII.

The Disobedient Daughter who Married a Skull

Effiong Edem was a native of Cobham Town. He had a very fine daughter, whose name was Afiong. All the young men in the country wanted to marry her on account of her beauty; but she refused all offers of marriage in spite of repeated entreaties from her parents, as she was very vain, and said she would only marry the best-looking man in the country, who would have to be young and strong, and capable of loving her properly. Most of the men her parents wanted her to marry, although they were rich, were old men and ugly, so the girl continued to disobey her parents, at which they were very much grieved. The skull who lived in the spirit land heard of the beauty of this Calabar virgin, and thought he would like to possess her; so he went about amongst his friends and borrowed different parts of the body from them, all of the best. From one he got a good head, another lent him a body, a third gave him strong arms, and a fourth lent him a fine pair of legs. At last he was complete, and was a very perfect specimen of manhood.

He then left the spirit land and went to Cobham market, where he saw Afiong, and admired her very much.

About this time Afiong heard that a very fine man had been seen in the market, who was better-looking than any of the natives. She therefore went to the market at once, and directly she saw the Skull in his borrowed beauty, she fell in love with him, and invited him to her house. The Skull was delighted, and went home with her, and on his arrival was introduced by the girl to her parents, and immediately asked their consent to marry their daughter. At first they refused, as they did not wish her to marry a stranger, but at last they agreed.

He lived with Afiong for two days in her parents' house, and then said he wished to take his wife back to his country, which was far off. To this the girl readily agreed, as he was such a fine man, but her parents tried to persuade her not to go. However, being very headstrong, she made up her mind to go, and they started off together. After they had been gone a few days the father consulted his Ju Ju man, who by casting lots very soon discovered that his daughter's husband belonged to the spirit land, and that she would surely be killed. They therefore all mourned her as dead.

After walking for several days, Afiong and the Skull crossed the border between the spirit land and the human country. Directly they set foot in the spirit land, first of all one man came to the Skull and demanded his legs, then another his head, and the next his body, and so on, until in a few minutes the skull was left by itself in all its natural ugliness. At this the girl was very frightened, and wanted to return home, but the skull would not allow this, and ordered her to go with him. When they arrived at the skull's house they found his mother, who was a very old woman quite incapable of doing any work, who could only creep about. Afiong tried her best to help her, and cooked her food, and brought water and firewood for the old woman. The old creature was very grateful for these attentions, and soon became quite fond of Afiong.

One day the old woman told Afiong that she was very sorry for her, but all the people in the spirit land were cannibals, and when they heard there was a human being in their country, they would come down and kill her and eat her. The skull's mother then hid Afiong, and as she had looked after her so well, she promised she would send her back to her country as soon as possible, providing that she promised for the future to obey her parents. This Afiong readily consented to do. Then the old woman sent for the spider, who was a very clever hairdresser, and made him dress Afiong's hair in the latest fashion. She also presented her with anklets and other things on account of her kindness. She then made a Ju Ju and called the winds to come and convey Afiong to her home. At first a violent tornado came, with thunder, lightning and rain, but the skull's mother sent him away as unsuitable. The next wind to come was a gentle breeze, so she told the breeze to carry Afiong to her mother's house, and said good-bye to her. Very soon afterwards the breeze deposited Afiong outside her home, and left her there.

When the parents saw their daughter they were very glad, as they had for some months given her up as lost. The father spread soft animals' skins on the ground from where his daughter was standing all the way to the house, so that her feet should not be soiled. Afiong then walked to the house, and her father called all the young girls who belonged to Afiong's company to come and dance, and the feasting and dancing was kept up for eight days and nights. When the rejoicing was over, the father reported what had happened to the head chief of the town. The chief then passed a law that parents should never allow their daughters to marry strangers who came from a far country. Then the father told his daughter to marry a friend of his, and she willingly consented, and lived with him for many years, and had many children.

IX.

The King who Married the Cock's Daughter

King Effiom of Duke Town, Calabar, was very fond of pretty maidens, and whenever he heard of a girl who was unusually good-looking, he always sent for her, and if she took his fancy, he made her one of his wives. This he could afford to do, as he was a rich man, and could pay any dowry which the parents asked, most of his money having been made by buying and selling slaves.

Effiom had two hundred and fifty wives, but he was never content, and wanted to have all the finest women in the land. Some of the king's friends, who were always on the look-out for pretty girls, told Effiom that the Cock's daughter was a lovely virgin, and far superior to any of the king's wives. Directly the king heard this he sent for the Cock, and said he intended to have his daughter as one of his wives. The Cock, being a poor man, could not resist the order of the king, so he brought his daughter, who was very good-looking and pleased the king immensely. When the king had paid the Cock a dowry of six puncheons of palm-oil, the Cock told Effiom that if he married his daughter he must not forget that she had the natural instincts of a hen, and that he should not blame Adia unen (his daughter) if she picked up corn whenever she saw it. The king replied that he did not mind what she ate so long as he possessed her.

The king then took Adia unen as his wife, and liked her so much, that he neglected all his other wives, and lived entirely with Adia unen, as she suited him exactly and pleased him more than any of his other wives. She also amused the king, and played with him and enticed him in so many different ways that he could not live without her, and always had her with him to the exclusion of his former favourites, whom he would not even speak to or notice in any way when he met them. This so enraged the neglected wives that they met together, and although they all hated one another, they agreed so far that they hated the Cock's daughter more than any one, as now that she had come to the king none of them ever had a chance with him. Formerly the king, although he always had his favourites, used to favour different girls with his attentions when they pleased him particularly. That was very different in their opinion to being excluded from his presence and all his affections being concentrated on one girl, who received all his love and embraces. In consequence of this they were very angry, and determined if possible to disgrace Adia unen. After much discussion, one of the wives, who was the last favourite, and whom the arrival of the Cock's daughter had displaced, said: "This girl, whom we all hate, is, after all, only a Cock's daughter, and we can easily disgrace her in the king's eyes, as I heard her father tell the king that she could not resist corn, no matter how it was thrown about."

Very shortly after the king's wives had determined to try and disgrace Adia unen, all the people of the country came to pay homage to the king. This was done three times a year, the people bringing yams, fowls, goats, and new corn as presents, and the king entertained them with a feast of foo-foo, palm-oil chop, and tombo.[7] A big dance was also held, which was usually kept up for several days and nights. Early in the morning the king's head wife told her servant to wash one head of corn, and when all the people were present she was to bring it in a calabash and throw it on the ground and then walk away. The corn was to be thrown in front of Adia unen, so that all the people and chiefs could see.

About ten o'clock, when all the chiefs and people had assembled, and the king had taken his seat on his big wooden chair, the servant girl came and threw the corn on the ground as she had been ordered. Directly she had done this Adia unen started towards the corn, picked it up, and began to eat. At this all the people laughed, and the king was very angry and ashamed. The king's wives and many people said that they thought the king's finest wife would have learnt better manners than to pick up corn which had been thrown away as refuse. Others said: "What can you expect from a Cock's daughter? She should not be blamed for obeying her natural instincts." But the king was so vexed, that he told one of his servants to pack up Adia unen's things and take them to her father's house. And this was done, and Aida unen returned to her parents.

That night the king's third wife, who was a friend of Adia unen's, talked the whole matter over with the king, and explained to

---

7   Tombo is an intoxicating drink made from the juice which is extracted from the tombo palm, and which ferments very quickly. It is drawn from the tree twice a day—in the morning very early, and again in the afternoon.

him that it was entirely owing to the jealousy of his head wife that Adia unen had been disgraced. She also told him that the whole thing had been arranged beforehand in order that the king should get rid of Adia unen, of whom all the other wives were jealous. When the king heard this he was very angry, and made up his mind to send the jealous woman back to her parents empty-handed, without her clothes and presents. When she arrived at her father's house the parents refused to take her in, as she had been given as a wife to the king, and whenever the parents wanted anything, they could always get it at the palace. It was therefore a great loss to them. She was thus turned into the streets, and walked about very miserable, and after a time died, very poor and starving.

The king grieved so much at having been compelled to send his favourite wife Adia unen away, that he died the following year. And when the people saw that their king had died of a broken heart, they passed a law that for the future no one should marry any bird or animal.

X.

The Woman, the Ape, and the Child

Okun Archibong was one of King Archibong's slaves, and lived on a farm near Calabar. He was a hunter, and used to kill bush buck and other kinds of antelopes and many monkeys. The skins he used to dry in the sun, and when they were properly cured, he used to sell them in the market; the monkey skins were used for making drums, and the antelope skins were used for sitting mats. The flesh, after it had been well smoked over a wood fire, he also sold, but he did not make much money.

Okun Archibong married a slave woman of Duke's house named Nkoyo. He paid a small dowry to the Dukes, took his wife home to his farm, and in the dry season time she had a son. About four months after the birth of the child Nkoyo took him to the farm while her husband was absent hunting. She placed the little boy under a shady tree and went about her work, which was clearing the ground for the yams which would be planted about two months before the rains. Every day while the mother was working a big ape used to come from the forest and play with the little boy; he used to hold him in his arms and carry him up a tree, and when Nkoyo had finished her work, he used to bring the baby back to her. There was a hunter named Edem Effiong who had for a long time been in love with Nkoyo, and had made advances to her, but she would have nothing to do with him, as she was very fond of her husband. When she had her little child Effiong Edem was very jealous, and meeting her one day on the farm without her baby, he said: "Where is your baby?" And she replied that a big ape had taken it up a tree and was looking after it for her. When Effiong Edem saw that the ape was a big one, he made up his mind to tell Nkoyo's husband. The very next day he told Okun Archibong that he had seen his wife in the forest with a big ape. At first Okun would not believe this, but the hunter told him to come with him and he could see it with his own eyes. Okun Archibong therefore made up his mind to kill the ape. The next day he went with the other hunter to the farm and saw the ape up a tree playing with his son, so he took very careful aim and shot the ape, but it was not quite killed. It was so angry, and its strength was so great, that it tore the child limb from limb and threw it to the ground. This so enraged Okun Archibong that seeing his wife standing near he shot her also. He then ran home and told King Archibong what had taken place. This king was very brave and fond of fighting, so as he knew that King Duke would be certain to make war upon him, he immediately called in all his fighting men. When he was quite prepared he sent a messenger to tell King Duke what had happened. Duke was very angry, and sent the messenger back to King Archibong to say that he must send the hunter to him, so that he could kill him in any way he pleased. This Archibong refused to do, and said he would rather fight. Duke then got his men together, and both sides met and fought in the market square. Thirty men were killed of Duke's men, and twenty were killed on Archibong's side; there were also many wounded. On the whole King Archibong had the best of the fighting, and drove King Duke back. When the fighting was at its hottest the other chiefs sent out all the Egbo men with drums and stopped the fight, and the next day the palaver was tried in Egbo house. King Archibong was found guilty, and was ordered to pay six thousand rods to King Duke. He refused to pay this amount to Duke, and said he would rather go on fighting, but he did not mind paying the six thousand rods to the town, as the Egbos had decided the case. They were about to commence fighting again when the whole country rose up and said they would not have any more fighting, as Archibong said to Duke that the woman's death was not really the fault of his slave Okun Archibong, but of Effiong Edem, who made the false report. When Duke heard this he agreed to leave the whole matter to the chiefs to decide, and Effiong Edem was called to take his place on the stone. He was tried and found guilty, and two Egbos came out armed with cutting whips and gave him two hundred lashes on his bare back, and then cut off his head and sent it to Duke, who placed it before his Ju Ju. From that time to the present all apes and monkeys have been frightened of human beings; and even of little children. The Egbos also passed a law that a chief should not allow one of his men slaves to marry a woman slave of another house, as it would probably lead to fighting.

XI.

The Fish and the Leopard's Wife; or, Why the Fish lives in the Water

Many years ago, when King Eyo was ruler of Calabar, the fish used to live on the land; he was a great friend of the leopard, and frequently used to go to his house in the bush, where the leopard entertained him. Now the leopard had a very fine wife, with whom the fish fell in love. And after a time, whenever the leopard was absent in the bush, the fish used to go to his house and make love to the leopard's wife, until at last an old woman who lived near informed the leopard what happened whenever he went away. At first the leopard would not believe that the fish, who had been his friend for so long, would play such a low trick, but one night he came back unexpectedly, and found the fish and his wife together; at this the leopard was very angry, and was going to kill the fish, but he thought as the fish had been his friend for so long, he would not deal with him himself, but would report his behaviour to King Eyo. This he did, and the king held a big palaver, at which the leopard stated his case quite shortly, but when the fish was put upon his defence he had nothing to say, so the king addressing his subjects said, "This is a very bad case, as the fish has been the leopard's friend, and has been trusted by him, but the fish has taken advantage of his friend's absence, and has betrayed him." The king, therefore, made an order that for the future the fish should live in the water, and that if he ever came on the land he should die; he also said that all men and animals should kill and eat the fish whenever they could catch him, as a punishment for his behaviour with his friend's wife.

XII

Why the Bat is Ashamed
to be seen in the Daytime

There was once an old mother sheep who had seven lambs, and one day the bat, who was about to make a visit to his father-in-law who lived a long day's march away, went to the old sheep and asked her to lend him one of her young lambs to carry his load for him. At first the mother sheep refused, but as the young lamb was anxious to travel and see something of the world, and begged to be allowed to go, at last she reluctantly consented. So in the morning at daylight the bat and the lamb set off together, the lamb carrying the bat's drinking-horn. When they reached half-way, the bat told the lamb to leave the horn underneath a bamboo tree. Directly he arrived at the house, he sent the lamb back to get the horn. When the lamb had gone the bat's father-in-law brought him food, and the bat ate it all, leaving nothing for the lamb. When the lamb returned, the bat said to him, "Hullo! you have arrived at last I see, but you are too late for food; it is all finished." He then sent the lamb back to the tree with the horn, and when the lamb returned again it was late, and he went supperless to bed. The next day, just before it was time for food, the bat sent the lamb off again for the drinking-horn, and when the food arrived the bat, who was very greedy, ate it all up a second time. This mean behaviour on the part of the bat went on for four days, until at last the lamb became quite thin and weak. The bat decided to return home the next day, and it was all the lamb could do to carry his load. When he got home to his mother the lamb complained bitterly of the treatment he had received from the bat, and was baa-ing all night, complaining of pains in his inside. The old mother sheep, who was very fond of her children, determined to be revenged on the bat for the cruel way he had starved her lamb; she therefore decided to consult the tortoise, who, although very poor, was considered by all people to be the wisest of all animals. When the old sheep had told the whole story to the tortoise, he considered for some time, and then told the sheep that she might leave the matter entirely to him, and he would take ample revenge on the bat for his cruel treatment of her son.

Very soon after this the bat thought he would again go and see his father-in-law, so he went to the mother sheep again and asked her for one of her sons to carry his load as before. The tortoise, who happened to be present, told the bat that he was going in that direction, and would cheerfully carry his load for him. They set out on their journey the following day, and when they arrived at the half-way halting-place the bat pursued the same tactics that he had on the previous occasion. He told the tortoise to hide his drinking-horn under the same tree as the lamb had hidden it before; this the tortoise did, but when the bat was not looking he picked up the drinking-horn again and hid it in his bag. When they arrived at the house the tortoise hung the horn up out of sight in the back yard, and then sat down in the house. Just before it was time for food the bat sent the tortoise to get the drinking-horn, and the tortoise went outside into the yard, and waited until he heard that the beating of the boiled yams into foo-foo had finished; he then went into the house and gave the drinking-horn to the bat, who was so surprised and angry, that when the food was passed he refused to eat any of it, so the tortoise ate it all; this went on for four days, until at last the bat became as thin as the poor little lamb had been on the previous occasion. At last the bat could stand the pains of his inside no longer, and secretly told his mother-in-law to bring him food when the tortoise was not looking. He said, "I am now going to sleep for a little, but you can wake me up when the food is ready." The tortoise, who had been listening all the time, being hidden in a corner out of sight, waited until the bat was fast asleep, and then carried him very gently into the next room and placed him on his own bed; he then very softly and quietly took off the bat's cloth and covered himself in it, and lay down where the bat had been; very soon the bat's mother-in-law brought the food and placed it next to where the bat was supposed to be sleeping, and having pulled his cloth to wake him, went away. The tortoise then got up and ate all the food; when he had finished he carried the bat back again, and took some of the palm-oil and foo-foo and placed it inside the bat's lips while he was asleep; then the tortoise went to sleep himself. In the morning when he woke up the bat was more hungry than ever, and in a very bad temper, so he sought out his mother-in-law and started scolding her, and asked her why she had not brought his food as he had told her to do. She replied she had brought his food, and that he had eaten it; but this the bat denied, and accused the tortoise of having eaten the food. The woman then said she would call the people in and they should decide the matter; but the tortoise slipped out first and told the people that the best way to find out who had eaten the food was to make both the bat and himself rinse their mouths out with clean water into a basin. This they decided to do, so the tortoise got his tooth-stick which he always used, and having cleaned his teeth properly, washed his mouth out, and returned to the house.

When all the people had arrived the woman told them how the bat had abused her, and as he still maintained stoutly that he had had no food for five days, the people said that both he and the tortoise should wash their mouths out with clean water into two clean calabashes; this was done, and at once it could clearly be seen that the bat had been eating, as there were distinct traces of the palm-oil and foo-foo which the tortoise had put inside his lips floating on the water. When the people saw this they decided against the bat, and he was so ashamed that he ran away then and there, and has ever since always hidden himself in the bush during the daytime, so that no one could see him, and only comes out at night to get his food.

The next day the tortoise returned to the mother sheep and told her what he had done, and that the bat was for ever disgraced. The old sheep praised him very much, and told all her friends, in consequence of which the reputation of the tortoise for wisdom was greatly increased throughout the whole country.

XIII.

Why the Worms live Underneath the Ground

When Eyo III. was ruling over all men and animals, he had a very big palaver house to which he used to invite his subjects at intervals to feast. After the feast had been held and plenty of tombo had been drunk, it was the custom of the people to make speeches. One day after the feast the head driver ant got up and said he and his people were stronger than any one, and that no one, not even the elephant, could stand before him, which was quite true. He was particularly offensive in his allusions to the worms (whom he disliked very much), and said they were poor wriggling things.

The worms were very angry and complained, so the king said that the best way to decide the question who was the stronger was for both sides to meet on the road and fight the matter out between themselves to a finish. He appointed the third day from the feast for the contest, and all the people turned out to witness the battle.

The driver ants left their nest in the early morning in thousands and millions, and, as is their custom, marched in a line about one inch broad densely packed, so that it was like a dark-brown band moving over the country. In front of the advancing column they had out their scouts, advance guard, and flankers, and the main body followed in their millions close behind.

When they came to the battlefield the moving band spread out, and as the thousands upon thousands of ants rolled up, the whole piece of ground was a moving mass of ants and bunches of struggling worms. The fight was over in a very few minutes, as the worms were bitten in pieces by the sharp pincer-like mouths of the driver ants. The few worms who survived squirmed away and buried themselves out of sight.

King Eyo decided that the driver ants were easy winners, and ever since the worms have always been afraid and have lived underground; and if they happen to come to the surface after the rain they hide themselves under the ground whenever anything approaches, as they fear all people.

XlV.

The Elephant and the Tortoise;
or, Why the Worms are Blind and
Why the Elephant has Small Eyes

When Ambo was king of Calabar, the elephant was not only a very big animal, but he had eyes in proportion to his immense bulk. In those days men and animals were friends, and all mixed together quite freely. At regular intervals King Ambo used to give a feast, and the elephant used to eat more than any one, although the hippopotamus used to do his best; however, not being as big as the elephant, although he was very fat, he was left a long way behind.

As the elephant ate so much at these feasts, the tortoise, who was small but very cunning, made up his mind to put a stop to the elephant eating more than a fair share of the food provided. He therefore placed some dry kernels and shrimps, of which the elephant was very fond, in his bag, and went to the elephant's house to make an afternoon call.

When the tortoise arrived the elephant told him to sit down, so he made himself comfortable, and, having shut one eye, took one palm kernel and a shrimp out of his bag, and commenced to eat them with much relish.

When the elephant saw the tortoise eating, he said, as he was always hungry himself, "You seem to have some good food there; what are you eating?"

The tortoise replied that the food was "sweet too much," but was rather painful to him, as he was eating one of his own eyeballs; and he lifted up his head, showing one eye closed.

The elephant then said, "If the food is so good, take out one of my eyes and give me the same food."

The tortoise, who was waiting for this, knowing how greedy the elephant was, had brought a sharp knife with him for that very purpose, and said to the elephant, "I cannot reach your eye, as you are so big."

The elephant then took the tortoise up in his trunk and lifted him up. As soon as he came near the elephant's eye, with one quick scoop of the sharp knife he had the elephant's right eye out. The elephant trumpeted with pain; but the tortoise gave him some of the dried kernels and shrimps, and they so pleased the elephant's palate that he soon forgot the pain.

Very soon the elephant said, "That food is so sweet, I must have some more"; but the tortoise told him that before he could have any the other eye must come out. To this the elephant agreed; so the tortoise quickly got his knife to work, and very soon the elephant's left eye was on the ground, thus leaving the elephant quite blind. The tortoise then slid down the elephant's trunk on to the ground and hid himself. The elephant then began to make a great noise, and started pulling trees down and doing much damage, calling out for the tortoise; but of course he never answered, and the elephant could not find him.

The next morning, when the elephant heard the people passing, he asked them what the time was, and the bush buck, who was nearest, shouted out, "The sun is now up, and I am going to market to get some yams and fresh leaves for my food."

Then the elephant perceived that the tortoise had deceived him, and began to ask all the passers-by to lend him a pair of eyes, as he could not see, but every one refused, as they wanted their eyes themselves. At last the worm grovelled past, and seeing the big elephant, greeted him in his humble way. He was much surprised when the king of the forest returned his salutation, and very much flattered also.

The elephant said, "Look here, worm, I have mislaid my eyes. Will you lend me yours for a few days? I will return them next market-day."

The worm was so flattered at being noticed by the elephant that he gladly consented, and took his eyes out—which, as every one knows, were very small—and gave them to the elephant. When the elephant had put the worm's eyes into his own large eye-sockets, the flesh immediately closed round them so tightly that when the market-day arrived it was impossible for the elephant to get them out again to return to the worm; and although the worm repeatedly made applications to the elephant to return his eyes, the elephant always pretended not to hear, and sometimes used to say in a very loud voice, "If there are any worms about, they had better get out of my way, as they are so small I cannot see them, and if I tread on them they will be squashed into a nasty mess."

Ever since then the worms have been blind, and for the same

reason elephants have such small eyes, quite out of proportion to the size of their huge bodies.

XV

Why a Hawk kills Chickens

In the olden days there was a very fine young hen who lived with her parents in the bush.

One day a hawk was hovering round, about eleven o'clock in the morning, as was his custom, making large circles in the air and scarcely moving his wings. His keen eyes were wide open, taking in everything (for nothing moving ever escapes the eyes of a hawk, no matter how small it may be or how high up in the air the hawk may be circling). This hawk saw the pretty hen picking up some corn near her father's house. He therefore closed his wings slightly, and in a second of time was close to the ground; then spreading his wings out to check his flight, he alighted close to the hen and perched himself on the fence, as a hawk does not like to walk on the ground if he can help it.

He then greeted the young hen with his most enticing whistle, and offered to marry her. She agreed, so the hawk spoke to the parents, and paid the agreed amount of dowry, which consisted mostly of corn, and the next day took the young hen off to his home.

Shortly after this a young cock who lived near the hen's former home found out where she was living, and having been in love with her for some months—in fact, ever since his spurs had grown—determined to try and make her return to her own country. He therefore went at dawn, and, having flapped his wings once or twice, crowed in his best voice to the young hen. When she heard the sweet voice of the cock she could not resist his invitation, so she went out to him, and they walked off together to her parent's house, the young cock strutting in front crowing at intervals.

The hawk, who was hovering high up in the sky, quite out of sight of any ordinary eye, saw what had happened, and was very angry. He made up his mind at once that he would obtain justice from the king, and flew off to Calabar, where he told the whole story, and asked for immediate redress. So the king sent for the parents of the hen, and told them they must repay to the hawk the amount of dowry they had received from him on the marriage of their daughter, according to the native custom; but the hen's parents said that they were so poor that they could not possibly afford to pay. So the king told the hawk that he could kill and eat any of the cock's children whenever and wherever he found them as payment of his dowry, and, if the cock made any complaint, the king would not listen to him.

From that time until now, whenever a hawk sees a chicken he swoops down and carries it off in part-payment of his dowry.

XVI.

Why the Sun and the Moon live in the Sky

Many years ago the sun and water were great friends, and both lived on the earth together. The sun very often used to visit the water, but the water never returned his visits. At last the sun asked the water why it was that he never came to see him in his house, the water replied that the sun's house was not big enough, and that if he came with his people he would drive the sun out.

He then said, "If you wish me to visit you, you must build a very large compound; but I warn you that it will have to be a tremendous place, as my people are very numerous, and take up a lot of room."

The sun promised to build a very big compound, and soon afterwards he returned home to his wife, the moon, who greeted him with a broad smile when he opened the door. The sun told the moon what he had promised the water, and the next day commenced building a huge compound in which to entertain his friend.

When it was completed, he asked the water to come and visit him the next day.

When the water arrived, he called out to the sun, and asked him whether it would be safe for him to enter, and the sun answered,

"Yes, come in, my friend."

The water then began to flow in, accompanied by the fish and all the water animals.

Very soon the water was knee-deep, so he asked the sun if it was still safe, and the sun again said, "Yes," so more water came in.

When the water was level with the top of a man's head, the water said to the sun, "Do you want more of my people to come?" and the sun and moon both answered, "Yes," not knowing any better, so the water flowed on, until the sun and moon had to perch themselves on the top of the roof.

Again the water addressed the sun, but receiving the same answer, and more of his people rushing in, the water very soon overflowed the top of the roof, and the sun and moon were forced to go up into the sky, where they have remained ever since.

XVII

Why the Flies Bother the Cows

When Adiaha Umo was Queen of Calabar, being very rich and hospitable, she used to give big feasts to all the domestic animals, but never invited the wild beasts, as she was afraid of them.

At one feast she gave there were three large tables, and she told the cow to sit at the head of the table, as she was the biggest animal present, and share out the food. The cow was quite ready to do this, and the first course was passed, which the cow shared out amongst the people, but forgot the fly, because he was so small.

When the fly saw this, he called out to the cow to give him his share, but the cow said: "Be quiet, my friend, you must have patience."

When the second course arrived, the fly again called out to the cow, but the cow merely pointed to her eye, and told the fly to look there, and he would get food later.

At last all the dishes were finished, and the fly, having been given no food by the cow, went supperless to bed.

The next day the fly complained to the queen, who decided that, as the cow had presided at the feast, and had not given the fly his share, but had pointed to her eye, for the future the fly could always get his food from the cow's eyes wherever she went; and even at the present time, wherever the cows are, the flies can always be seen feeding off their eyes in accordance with the queen's orders.

XVIII.

Why the Cat kills Rats

Ansa was King of Calabar for fifty years. He had a very faithful cat as a housekeeper, and a rat was his house-boy. The king was an obstinate, headstrong man, but was very fond of the cat, who had been in his store for many years.

The rat, who was very poor, fell in love with one of the king's servant girls, but was unable to give her any presents, as he had no money.

At last he thought of the king's store, so in the night-time, being quite small, he had little difficulty, having made a hole in the roof, in getting into the store. He then stole corn and native pears, and presented them to his sweetheart.

At the end of the month, when the cat had to render her account of the things in the store to the king, it was found that a lot of corn and native pears were missing. The king was very angry at this, and asked the cat for an explanation. But the cat could not account for the loss, until one of her friends told her that the rat had been stealing the corn and giving it to the girl.

When the cat told the king, he called the girl before him and had her flogged. The rat he handed over to the cat to deal with, and dismissed them both from his service. The cat was so angry at this that she killed and ate the rat, and ever since that time whenever a cat sees a rat she kills and eats it.

XIX.

The Story of the Lightning and the Thunder

In the olden days the thunder and lightning lived on the earth amongst all the other people, but the king made them live at the far end of the town, as far as possible from other people's houses.

The thunder was an old mother sheep, and the lightning was her son, a ram. Whenever the ram got angry he used to go about and burn houses and knock down trees; he even did damage on the farms, and sometimes killed people. Whenever the lightning did these things, his mother used to call out to him in a very loud voice to stop and not to do any more damage; but the lightning did not care in the least for what his mother said, and when he was in a bad temper used to do a very large amount of damage. At last the people could not stand it any longer, and complained to the king.

So the king made a special order that the sheep (Thunder) and her son, the ram (Lightning), should leave the town and live in the far bush. This did not do much good, as when the ram got angry he still burnt the forest, and the flames sometimes spread to the farms and consumed them.

So the people complained again, and the king banished both

the lightning and the thunder from the earth and made them live in the sky, where they could not cause so much destruction. Ever since, when the lightning is angry, he commits damage as before, but you can hear his mother, the thunder, rebuking him and telling him to stop. Sometimes, however, when the mother has gone away some distance from her naughty son, you can still see that he is angry and is doing damage, but his mother's voice cannot be heard.

XX.

Why the Bush Cow and the Elephant
are bad Friends

The bush cow and the elephant were always bad friends, and as they could not settle their disputes between themselves, they agreed to let the head chief decide.

The cause of their unfriendliness was that the elephant was always boasting about his strength to all his friends, which made the bush cow ashamed of himself, as he was always a good fighter and feared no man or animal. When the matter was referred to the head chief, he decided that the best way to settle the dispute was for the elephant and bush cow to meet and fight one another in a large open space. He decided that the fight should take place in the market-place on the next market-day, when all the country people could witness the battle.

When the market-day arrived, the bush cow went out in the early morning and took up his position some distance from the town on the main road to the market, and started bellowing and tearing up the ground. As the people passed he asked them whether they had seen anything of the "Big, Big one," which was the name of the elephant.

A bush buck, who happened to be passing, replied, "I am only a small antelope, and am on my way to the market. How should I know anything of the movements of the 'Big, Big one?'" The bush cow then allowed him to pass.

After a little time the bush cow heard the elephant trumpeting, and could hear him as he came nearer breaking down trees and trampling down the small bush.

When the elephant came near the bush cow, they both charged one another, and a tremendous fight commenced, in which a lot of damage was done to the surrounding farms, and many of the people were frightened to go to the market, and returned to their houses.

At last the monkey, who had been watching the fight from a distance whilst he was jumping from branch to branch high up in the trees, thought he would report what he had seen to the head chief. Although he forgot several times what it was he wanted to do, which is a little way monkeys have, he eventually reached the chief's house, and jumped upon the roof, where he caught and ate a spider. He then climbed to the ground again, and commenced playing with a small stick. But he very soon got tired of this, and then, picking up a stone, he rubbed it backwards and forwards on the ground in an aimless sort of way, whilst looking in the opposite direction. This did not last long, and very soon he was busily engaged in a minute personal inspection.

His attention was then attracted by a large praying mantis, which had fluttered into the house, making much clatter with its wings. When it settled, it immediately assumed its usual prayerful attitude.

The monkey, after a careful stalk, seized the mantis, and having deliberately pulled the legs off one after the other, he ate the body, and sat down with his head on one side, looking very wise, but in reality thinking of nothing.

Just then the chief caught sight of him while he was scratching himself, and shouted out in a loud voice, "Ha, monkey, is that you? What do you want here?"

At the chief's voice the monkey gave a jump, and started chattering like anything. After a time he replied very nervously: "Oh yes, of course! Yes, I came to see you." Then he said to himself, "I wonder what on earth it was I came to tell the chief?" but it was no use, everything had gone out of his head.

Then the chief told the monkey he might take one of the ripe plantains hanging up in the verandah. The monkey did not want telling twice, as he was very fond of plantains. He soon tore off the skin, and holding the plantain in both hands, took bite after bite from the end of it, looking at it carefully after each bite.

Then the chief remarked that the elephant and the bush cow ought to have arrived by that time, as they were going to have a great fight. Directly the monkey heard this he remembered what it was he wanted to tell the chief; so, having swallowed the piece of plantain he had placed in the side of his cheek, he said: "Ah! that reminds me," and then, after much chattering and making all sorts of funny grimaces, finally made the chief understand that the elephant and bush cow, instead of fighting where they had been told, were having it out in the bush on the main road leading to the market, and had thus stopped most of the people coming in.

When the chief heard this he was much incensed, and called for his bow and poisoned arrows, and went to the scene of the combat. He then shot both the elephant and the bush cow, and throwing his bow and arrows away, ran and hid himself in the bush. About six hours afterwards both the elephant and bush cow died in great pain.

Ever since, when wild animals want to fight between themselves, they always fight in the big bush and not on the public roads; but as the fight was never definitely decided between the elephant and the bush cow, whenever they meet one another in the forest, even to the present time, they always fight.

XXI.

The Cock who caused a Fight between two Towns

Ekpo and Etim were half-brothers, that is to say they had the same mother, but different fathers. Their mother first of all had married a chief of Duke Town, when Ekpo was born; but after a time she got tired of him and went to Old Town, where she married Ejuqua and gave birth to Etim.

Both of the boys grew up and became very rich. Ekpo had a cock, of which he was very fond, and every day when Ekpo sat down to meals the cock used to fly on to the table and feed also. Ama Ukwa, a native of Old Town, who was rather poor, was jealous of the two brothers, and made up his mind if possible to bring about a quarrel between them, although he pretended to be friends with both.

One day Ekpo, the elder brother, gave a big dinner, to which Etim and many other people were invited. Ama Ukwa was also present. A very good dinner was laid for the guests, and plenty of palm wine was provided. When they had commenced to feed, the pet cock flew on to the table and began to feed off Etim's plate. Etim then told one of his servants to seize the cock and tie him up in the house until after the feast. So the servant carried the cock to Etim's house and tied him up for safety.

After much eating and drinking, Etim returned home late at night with his friend Ama Ukwa, and just before they went to bed, Ama Ukwa saw Ekpo's cock tied up. So early in the morning he went to Ekpo's house, who received him gladly.

About eight o'clock, when it was time for Ekpo to have his early morning meal, he noticed that his pet cock was missing. When he remarked upon its absence, Ama Ukwa told him that his brother had seized the cock the previous evening during the dinner, and was going to kill it, just to see what Ekpo would do. When Ekpo heard this, he was very vexed, and sent Ama Ukwa back to his brother to ask him to return the cock immediately. Instead of delivering the message as he had been instructed, Ama Ukwa told Etim that his elder brother was so angry with him for taking away his friend, the cock, that he would fight him, and had sent Ama Ukwa on purpose to declare war between the two towns.

Etim then told Ama Ukwa to return to Ekpo, and say he would be prepared for anything his brother could do. Ama Ukwa then advised Ekpo to call all his people in from their farms, as Etim would attack him, and on his return he advised Etim to do the same. He then arranged a day for the fight to take place between the two brothers and their people. Etim then marched his men to the other side of the creek, and waited for his brother; so Ama Ukwa went to Ekpo and told him that Etim had got all his people together and was waiting to fight. Ekpo then led his men against his brother, and there was a big battle, many men being killed on both sides. The fighting went on all day, until at last, towards evening, the other chiefs of Calabar met and determined to stop it; so they called the Egbo men together and sent them out with their drums, and eventually the fight stopped.

Three days later a big palaver was held, when each of the brothers was told to state his case. When they had done so, it was found that Ama Ukwa had caused the quarrel, and the chiefs ordered that he should be killed. His father, who was a rich man, offered to give the Egbos five thousand rods, five cows, and seven slaves to redeem his son, but they decided to refuse his offer.

The next day, after being severely flogged, he was left for twenty-four hours tied up to a tree, and the following day his head was cut off.

Ekpo was then ordered to kill his pet cock, so that it should not cause any further trouble between himself and his brother, and a law was passed that for the future no one should keep a pet cock or any other tame animal.

XXII

The Affair of the Hippopotamus and the Tortoise; or, Why the Hippopotamus lives in the Water

Many years ago the hippopotamus, whose name was Isantim, was one of the biggest kings on the land; he was second only to the elephant. The hippo had seven large fat wives, of whom he was very fond. Now and then he used to give a big feast to the people, but a curious thing was that, although every one knew the hippo, no one, except his seven wives, knew his name.

At one of the feasts, just as the people were about to sit down, the hippo said, "You have come to feed at my table, but none of you know my name. If you cannot tell my name, you shall all of you go away without your dinner."

As they could not guess his name, they had to go away and leave all the good food and tombo behind them. But before they left, the tortoise stood up and asked the hippopotamus what he would do if he told him his name at the next feast? So the hippo replied that he would be so ashamed of himself, that he and his whole family would leave the land, and for the future would dwell in the water.

Now it was the custom for the hippo and his seven wives to go down every morning and evening to the river to wash and have a drink. Of this custom the tortoise was aware. The hippo used to walk first, and the seven wives followed. One day when they had gone down to the river to bathe, the tortoise made a small hole in the middle of the path, and then waited. When the hippo and his wives returned, two of the wives were some distance behind, so the tortoise came out from where he had been hiding, and half buried himself in the hole he had dug, leaving the greater part of his shell exposed. When the two hippo wives came along, the first one knocked her foot against the tortoise's shell, and immediately called out to her husband, "Oh! Isantim, my husband, I have hurt my foot." At this the tortoise was very glad, and went joyfully home, as he had found out the hippo's name.

When the next feast was given by the hippo, he made the same condition about his name; so the tortoise got up and said, "You promise you will not kill me if I tell you your name?" and the hippo promised. The tortoise then shouted as loud as he was able, "Your name is Isantim," at which a cheer went up from all the people, and then they sat down to their dinner.

When the feast was over, the hippo, with his seven wives, in accordance with his promise, went down to the river, and they have always lived in the water from that day till now; and although they come on shore to feed at night, you never find a hippo on the land in the daytime.

XXIII.

Why Dead People are Buried

In the beginning of the world when the Creator had made men and women and the animals, they all lived together in the creation land. The Creator was a big chief, past all men, and being very kind-hearted, was very sorry whenever any one died. So one day he sent for the dog, who was his head messenger, and told him to go out into the world and give his word to all people that for the future whenever any one died the body was to be placed in the compound, and wood ashes were to be thrown over it; that the dead body was to be left on the ground, and in twenty-four hours it would become alive again.

When the dog had travelled for half a day he began to get tired; so as he was near an old woman's house he looked in, and seeing a bone with some meat on it he made a meal off it, and then went to sleep, entirely forgetting the message which had been given him to deliver.

After a time, when the dog did not return, the Creator called for a sheep, and sent him out with the same message. But the sheep was a very foolish one, and being hungry, began eating the sweet grasses by the wayside. After a time, however, he remembered that he had a message to deliver, but forgot what it was exactly; so as he went about among the people he told them that the message the Creator had given him to tell the people, was that whenever any one died they should be buried underneath the ground.

A little time afterwards the dog remembered his message, so he ran into the town and told the people that they were to place wood ashes on the dead bodies and leave them in the compound, and that they would come to life again after twenty-four hours. But the people would not believe him, and said, "We have already received the word from the Creator by the sheep, that all dead bodies should be buried." In consequence of this the dead bodies are now always buried, and the dog is much disliked and not trusted as a messenger, as if he had not found the bone in the old woman's house and forgotten his message, the dead people might still be alive.

XXIV.

Of the Fat Woman who Melted Away

There was once a very fat woman who was made of oil. She was very beautiful, and many young men applied to the parents for permission to marry their daughter, and offered dowry, but the mother always refused, as she said it was impossible for her daughter to work on a farm, as she would melt in the sun. At last a stranger came from a far-distant country and fell in love with the fat woman, and he promised if her mother would hand her to him that he would keep her in the shade. At last the mother agreed, and he took his wife away.

When he arrived at his house, his other wife immediately became very jealous, because when there was work to be done, firewood to be collected, or water to be carried, the fat woman stayed at home and never helped, as she was frightened of the heat.

One day when the husband was absent, the jealous wife abused the fat woman so much that she finally agreed to go and work on the farm, although her little sister, whom she had brought from home with her, implored her not to go, reminding her that their mother had always told them ever since they were born that she would melt away if she went into the sun. All the way to the farm the fat woman managed to keep in the shade, and when they arrived at the farm the sun was very hot, so the fat woman remained in the shade of a big tree. When the jealous wife saw this she again began abusing her, and asked her why she did not do her share of the work. At last she could stand the nagging no longer, and although her little sister tried very hard to prevent her, the fat woman went out into the sun to work, and immediately began to melt away. There was very soon nothing left of her but one big toe, which had been covered by a leaf. This her little sister observed, and with tears in her eyes she picked up the toe, which was all that remained of the fat woman, and having covered it carefully with leaves, placed it in the bottom of her basket. When she arrived at the house the little sister placed the toe in an earthen pot, filled it with water, and covered the top up with clay.

When the husband returned, he said, "Where is my fat wife?" and the little sister, crying bitterly, told him that the jealous woman had made her go out into the sun, and that she had melted away. She then showed him the pot with the remains of her sister, and told him that her sister would come to life again in three months' time quite complete, but he must send away the jealous wife, so that there should be no more trouble; if he refused to do this, the little girl said she would take the pot back to their mother, and when her sister became complete again they would remain at home.

The husband then took the jealous wife back to her parents, who sold her as a slave and paid the dowry back to the husband, so that he could get another wife. When he received the money, the husband took it home and kept it until the three months had elapsed, when the little sister opened the pot and the fat woman emerged, quite as fat and beautiful as she had been before. The husband was so delighted that he gave a feast to all his friends and neighbours, and told them the whole story of the bad behaviour of his jealous wife.

Ever since that time, whenever a wife behaves very badly the husband returns her to the parents, who sell the woman as a slave, and out of the proceeds of the sale reimburse the husband the amount of dowry which he paid when he married the girl.

XXV.

Concerning the Leopard, the Squirrel,
and the Tortoise

Many years ago there was a great famine throughout the land, and all the people were starving. The yam crop had failed entirely, the plantains did not bear any fruit, the ground-nuts were all shrivelled up, and the corn never came to a head; even the palm-oil nuts did not ripen, and the peppers and ocros also gave out.

The leopard, however, who lived entirely on "beef," did not care for any of these things; and although some of the animals who lived on corn and the growing crops began to get rather skinny, he did not mind very much. In order to save himself trouble, as everybody was complaining of the famine, he called a meeting of all the animals and told them that, as they all knew, he was very powerful and must have food, that the famine did not affect him, as he only lived on flesh, and as there were plenty of animals about he did not intend to starve. He then told all the animals present at the meeting that if they did not wish to be killed themselves they must bring their grandmothers to him for food, and when they were finished he would feed off their mothers. The animals might bring their grandmothers in succession, and he would take them in their turn; so that, as there were many different animals, it would probably be some time before their mothers were eaten, by which time it was possible that the famine would be over. But in any case, he warned them that he was determined to have sufficient food for himself, and that if the grandmothers or mothers were not forthcoming he would turn upon the young people themselves and kill and eat them.

This, of course, the young generation, who had attended the meeting, did not appreciate, and in order to save their own skins, agreed to supply the leopard with his daily meal.

The first to appear with his aged grandmother was the squirrel. The grandmother was a poor decrepit old thing, with a mangy tail, and the leopard swallowed her at one gulp, and then looked round for more. In an angry voice he growled out: "This is not the proper food for me; I must have more at once."

Then a bush cat pushed his old grandmother in front of the leopard, but he snarled at her and said, "Take the nasty old thing away; I want some sweet food."

It was then the turn of a bush buck, and after a great deal of hesitation a wretchedly poor and thin old doe tottered and fell in front of the leopard, who immediately despatched her, and although the meal was very unsatisfactory, declared that his appetite was appeased for that day.

The next day a few more animals brought their old grandmothers, until at last it became the tortoise's turn; but being very cunning, he produced witnesses to prove that his grandmother was dead, so the leopard excused him.

After a few days all the animals' grandmothers were exhausted, and it became the turn of the mothers to supply food for the ravenous leopard. Now although most of the young animals did not mind getting rid of their grandmothers, whom they had scarcely even known, many of them had very strong objections to providing their mothers, of whom they were very fond, as food for the leopard. Amongst the strongest objectors were the squirrel and the tortoise. The tortoise, who had thought the whole thing out, was aware that, as every one knew that his mother was alive (she being rather an amiable old person and friendly with all-comers), the same excuse would not avail him a second time. He therefore told his mother to climb up a palm tree, and that he would provide her with food until the famine was over. He instructed her to let down a basket every day, and said that he would place food in it for her. The tortoise made the basket for his mother, and attached it to a long string of tie-tie. The string was so strong that she could haul her son up whenever he wished to visit her.

All went well for some days, as the tortoise used to go at daylight to the bottom of the tree where his mother lived and place her food in the basket; then the old lady would pull the basket up and have her food, and the tortoise would depart on his daily round in his usual leisurely manner.

In the meantime the leopard had to have his daily food, and the squirrel's turn came first after the grandmothers had been finished, so he was forced to produce his mother for the leopard to eat, as he was a poor, weak thing and not possessed of any cunning. The squirrel was, however, very fond of his mother, and when she had been eaten he remembered that the tortoise had not produced his grandmother for the leopard's food. He therefore determined to set a watch on the movements of the tortoise.

The very next morning, while he was gathering nuts, he saw the tortoise walking very slowly through the bush, and being high up in the trees and able to travel very fast, had no difficulty in keeping the tortoise in sight without being noticed. When the tortoise arrived at the foot of the tree where his mother lived, he placed the food in the basket which his mother had let down already by the tie-tie, and having got into the basket and given a pull at the string to signify that everything was right, was hauled up, and after a time was let down again in the basket. The squirrel was watching all the time, and directly the tortoise had gone, jumped from branch to branch of the trees, and very soon arrived at the place where the leopard was snoozing.

When he woke up, the squirrel said:

"You have eaten my grandmother and my mother, but the tortoise has not provided any food for you. It is now his turn, and he has hidden his mother away in a tree."

At this the leopard was very angry, and told the squirrel to lead him at once to the tree where the tortoise's mother lived. But the squirrel said:

"The tortoise only goes at daylight, when his mother lets down a basket; so if you go in the morning early, she will pull you up, and you can then kill her."

To this the leopard agreed, and the next morning the squirrel came at cockcrow and led the leopard to the tree where the tortoise's mother was hidden. The old lady had already let down the basket for her daily supply of food, and the leopard got into it and gave the line a pull; but except a few small jerks nothing happened, as the old mother tortoise was not strong enough to pull a heavy leopard off the ground. When the leopard saw that he was not going to be pulled up, being an expert climber, he scrambled up the tree, and when he got to the top he found the poor old tortoise, whose shell was so tough that he thought she was not worth eating, so he threw her down on to the ground in a violent temper, and then came down himself and went home.

Shortly after this the tortoise arrived at the tree, and finding the basket on the ground gave his usual tug at it, but there was no answer. He then looked about, and after a little time came upon the broken shell of his poor old mother, who by this time was quite dead. The tortoise knew at once that the leopard had killed his mother, and made up his mind that for the future he would live alone and have nothing to do with the other animals.

XXVI.

Why the Moon Waxes and Wanes

There was once an old woman who was very poor, and lived in a small mud hut thatched with mats made from the leaves of the tombo palm in the bush. She was often very hungry, as there was no one to look after her.

In the olden days the moon used often to come down to the earth, although she lived most of the time in the sky. The moon was a fat woman with a skin of hide, and she was full of fat meat. She was quite round, and in the night used to give plenty of light. The moon was sorry for the poor starving old woman, so she came to her and said, "You may cut some of my meat away for your food." This the old woman did every evening, and the moon got smaller and smaller until you could scarcely see her at all. Of course this made her give very little light, and all the people began to grumble in consequence, and to ask why it was that the moon was getting so thin.

At last the people went to the old woman's house where there happened to be a little girl sleeping. She had been there for some little time, and had seen the moon come down every evening, and the old woman go out with her knife and carve her daily supply of meat out of the moon. As she was very frightened, she told the people all about it, so they determined to set a watch on the movements of the old woman.

That very night the moon came down as usual, and the old woman went out with her knife and basket to get her food; but before she could carve any meat all the people rushed out shouting, and the moon was so frightened that she went back again into the sky, and never came down again to the earth. The old woman was left to starve in the bush.

Ever since that time the moon has hidden herself most of the day, as she was so frightened, and she still gets very thin once a month, but later on she gets fat again, and when she is quite fat she gives plenty of light all the night; but this does not last very long, and she begins to get thinner and thinner, in the same way as she did when the old woman was carving her meat from her.

XXVII.

The Story of the Leopard, the Tortoise, and the Bush Rat

At the time of the great famine all the animals were very thin and weak from want of food; but there was one exception, and that was the tortoise and all his family, who were quite fat, and did not seem to suffer at all. Even the leopard was very thin, in spite of the arrangement he had made with the animals to bring him their old grandmothers and mothers for food.

In the early days of the famine (as you will remember) the leopard had killed the mother of the tortoise, in consequence of which the tortoise was very angry with the leopard, and determined if possible to be revenged upon him. The tortoise, who was very clever, had discovered a shallow lake full of fish in the middle of the forest, and every morning he used to go to the lake and, without much trouble, bring back enough food for himself and his family. One day the leopard met the tortoise and noticed how fat he was. As he was very thin himself he decided to watch the tortoise, so the next morning he hid himself in the long grass near the tortoise's house and waited very patiently, until at last the tortoise came along quite slowly, carrying a basket which appeared to be very heavy. Then the leopard sprang out, and said to the tortoise:

"What have you got in that basket?"

The tortoise, as he did not want to lose his breakfast, replied that he was carrying firewood back to his home. Unfortunately for the tortoise the leopard had a very acute sense of smell, and knew at once that there was fish in the basket, so he said:

"I know there is fish in there, and I am going to eat it."

The tortoise, not being in a position to refuse, as he was such a poor creature, said:

"Very well. Let us sit down under this shady tree, and if you will make a fire I will go to my house and get pepper, oil, and salt, and then we will feed together."

To this the leopard agreed, and began to search about for dry wood, and started the fire. In the meantime the tortoise waddled off to his house, and very soon returned with the pepper, salt, and oil; he also brought a long piece of cane tie-tie, which is very strong. This he put on the ground, and began boiling the fish. Then he said to the leopard:

"While we are waiting for the fish to cook, let us play at tying one another up to a tree. You may tie me up first, and when I say 'Tighten,' you must loose the rope, and when I say 'Loosen,' you must tighten the rope."

The leopard, who was very hungry, thought that this game would make the time pass more quickly until the fish was cooked, so he said he would play. The tortoise then stood with his back to the tree and said, "Loosen the rope," and the leopard, in accordance with the rules of the game, began to tie up the tortoise. Very soon the tortoise shouted out, "Tighten!" and the leopard at once unfastened the tie-tie, and the tortoise was free. The tortoise then said, "Now, leopard, it is your turn;" so the leopard stood up against the tree and called out to the tortoise to loosen the rope, and the tortoise at once very quickly passed the rope several times round the leopard and got him fast to the tree. Then the leopard said, "Tighten the rope;" but instead of playing the game in accordance with the rules he had laid down, the tortoise ran faster and faster with the rope round the leopard, taking great care, however, to keep out of reach of the leopard's claws, and very soon had the leopard so securely fastened that it was quite impossible for him to free himself.

All this time the leopard was calling out to the tortoise to let him go, as he was tired of the game; but the tortoise only laughed, and sat down at the fireside and commenced his meal. When he had finished he packed up the remainder of the fish for his family, and prepared to go, but before he started he said to the leopard:

"You killed my mother and now you want to take my fish. It is not likely that I am going to the lake to get fish for you, so I shall leave you here to starve."

He then threw the remains of the pepper and salt into the leopard's eyes and quietly went on his way, leaving the leopard roaring with pain.

All that day and throughout the night the leopard was calling out for some one to release him, and vowing all sorts of vengeance on the tortoise; but no one came, as the people and animals of the forest do not like to hear the leopard's voice.

In the morning, when the animals began to go about to get

their food, the leopard called out to every one he saw to come and untie him, but they all refused, as they knew that if they did so the leopard would most likely kill them at once and eat them. At last a bush rat came near and saw the leopard tied up to the tree and asked him what was the matter, so the leopard told him that he had been playing a game of "tight" and "loose" with the tortoise, and that he had tied him up and left him there to starve. The leopard then implored the bush rat to cut the ropes with his sharp teeth. The bush rat was very sorry for the leopard; but at the same time he knew that, if he let the leopard go, he would most likely be killed and eaten, so he hesitated, and said that he did not quite see his way to cutting the ropes. But this bush rat, being rather kind-hearted, and having had some experience of traps himself, could sympathise with the leopard in his uncomfortable position. He therefore thought for a time, and then hit upon a plan. He first started to dig a hole under the tree, quite regardless of the leopard's cries. When he had finished the hole he came out and cut one of the ropes, and immediately ran into his hole, and waited there to see what would happen; but although the leopard struggled frantically, he could not get loose, as the tortoise had tied him up so fast. After a time, when he saw that there was no danger, the bush rat crept out again and very carefully bit through another rope, and then retired to his hole as before. Again nothing happened, and he began to feel more confidence, so he bit several strands through one after the other until at last the leopard was free. The leopard, who was ravenous with hunger, instead of being grateful to the bush rat, directly he was free, made a dash at the bush rat with his big paw, but just missed him, as the bush rat had dived for his hole; but he was not quite quick enough to escape altogether, and the leopard's sharp claws scored his back and left marks which he carried to his grave.

Ever since then the bush rats have had white spots on their skins, which represent the marks of the leopard's claws.

XXVIII.

The King and the Ju Ju Tree

Udo Ubok Udom was a famous king who lived at Itam, which is an inland town, and does not possess a river. The king and his wife therefore used to wash at the spring just behind their house.

King Udo had a daughter, of whom he was very fond, and looked after her most carefully, and she grew up into a beautiful woman.

For some time the king had been absent from his house, and had not been to the spring for two years. When he went to his old place to wash, he found that the Idem Ju Ju tree had grown up all round the place, and it was impossible for him to use the spring as he had done formerly. He therefore called fifty of his young men to bring their matchets[8] and cut down the tree. They started cutting the tree, but it had no effect, as, directly they made a cut in the tree, it closed up again; so, after working all day, they found they had made no impression on it.

When they returned at night, they told the king that they had

---

8   A matchet is a long sharp knife in general use throughout the country. It has a wooden handle; it is about two feet six inches long and two inches wide.

been unable to destroy the tree. He was very angry when he heard this, and went to the spring the following morning, taking his own matchet with him.

When the Ju Ju tree saw that the king had come himself and was starting to try to cut his branches, he caused a small splinter of wood to go into the king's eye. This gave the king great pain, so he threw down his matchet and went back to his house. The pain, however, got worse, and he could not eat or sleep for three days.

He therefore sent for his witch men, and told them to cast lots to find out why he was in such pain. When they had cast lots, they decided that the reason was that the Ju Ju tree was angry with the king because he wanted to wash at the spring, and had tried to destroy the tree.

They then told the king that he must take seven baskets of flies, a white goat, a white chicken, and a piece of white cloth, and make a sacrifice of them in order to satisfy the Ju Ju.

The king did this, and the witch men tried their lotions on the king's eye, but it got worse and worse.

He then dismissed these witches and got another lot. When they arrived they told the king that, although they could do nothing themselves to relieve his pain, they knew one man who lived in the spirit land who could cure him; so the king told them to send for him at once, and he arrived the next day.

Then the spirit man said, "Before I do anything to your eye, what will you give me?" So King Udo said, "I will give you half my town with the people in it, also seven cows and some money." But the spirit man refused to accept the king's offer. As the king was in such pain, he said, "Name your own price, and I will pay you." So the spirit man said the only thing he was willing to accept as payment was the king's daughter. At this the king cried very much, and told the man to go away, as he would rather die than let him have his daughter.

That night the pain was worse than ever, and some of his subjects pleaded with the king to send for the spirit man again and give him his daughter, and told him that when he got well he could no doubt have another daughter but that if he died now he would lose everything.

The king then sent for the spirit man again, who came very quickly, and in great grief the king handed his daughter to the spirit.

The spirit man then went out into the bush, and collected some leaves, which he soaked in water and beat up. The juice he poured into the king's eye, and told him that when he washed his face in the morning he would be able to see what was troubling him in the eye.

The king tried to persuade him to stay the night, but the spirit man refused, and departed that same night for the spirit land, taking the king's daughter with him.

Before it was light the king rose up and washed his face, and found that the small splinter from the Ju Ju tree, which had been troubling him so much, dropped out of his eye, the pain disappeared, and he was quite well again.

When he came to his proper senses he realised that he had sacrificed his daughter for one of his eyes, so he made an order that there should be general mourning throughout his kingdom for three years.

For the first two years of the mourning the king's daughter

was put in the fatting house by the spirit man, and was given food; but a skull, who was in the house, told her not to eat, as they were fatting her up, not for marriage, but so that they could eat her. She therefore gave all the food which was brought to her to the skull, and lived on chalk herself.

Towards the end of the third year the spirit man brought some of his friends to see the king's daughter, and told them he would kill her the next day, and they would have a good feast off her.

When she woke up in the morning the spirit man brought her food as usual; but the skull, who wanted to preserve her life, and who had heard what the spirit man had said, called her into the room and told her what was going to happen later in the day. She handed the food to the skull, and he said, "When the spirit man goes to the wood with his friends to prepare for the feast, you must run back to your father."

He then gave her some medicine which would make her strong for the journey, and also gave her directions as to the road, telling her that there were two roads but that when she came to the parting of the ways she was to drop some of the medicine on the ground and the two roads would become one.

He then told her to leave by the back door, and go through the wood until she came to the end of the town; she would then find the road. If she met people on the road she was to pass them in silence, as if she saluted them they would know that she was a stranger in the spirit land, and might kill her. She was also not to turn round if any one called to her, but was to go straight on till she reached her father's house.

Having thanked the skull for his kind advice, the king's daughter started off, and when she reached the end of the town and found the road, she ran for three hours, and at last arrived at the branch roads. There she dropped the medicine, as she had been instructed, and the two roads immediately became one; so she went straight on and never saluted any one or turned back, although several people called to her.

About this time the spirit man had returned from the wood, and went to the house, only to find the king's daughter was absent. He asked the skull where she was, and he replied that she had gone out by the back door, but he did not know where she had gone to. Being a spirit, however, he very soon guessed that she had gone home; so he followed as quickly as possible, shouting out all the time.

When the girl heard his voice she ran as fast as she could, and at last arrived at her father's house, and told him to take at once a cow, a pig, a sheep, a goat, a dog, a chicken, and seven eggs, and cut them into seven parts as a sacrifice, and leave them on the road, so that when the spirit man saw these things he would stop and not enter the town. This the king did immediately, and made the sacrifice as his daughter had told him.

When the spirit man saw the sacrifice on the road, he sat down and at once began to eat.

When he had satisfied his appetite, he packed up the remainder and returned to the spirit land, not troubling any more about the king's daughter.

When the king saw that the danger was over, he beat his drum, and declared that for the future, when people died and went to the spirit land, they should not come to earth again as spirits to cure sick people.

XXIX.

How the Tortoise overcame the Elephant and the Hippopotamus

The elephant and the hippopotamus always used to feed together, and were good friends.

One day when they were both dining together, the tortoise appeared and said that although they were both big and strong, neither of them could pull him out of the water with a strong piece of tie-tie, and he offered the elephant ten thousand rods if he could draw him out of the river the next day. The elephant, seeing that the tortoise was very small, said, "If I cannot draw you out of the water, I will give you twenty thousand rods." So on the following morning the tortoise got some very strong tie-tie and made it fast to his leg, and went down to the river. When he got there, as he knew the place well, he made the tie-tie fast round a big rock, and left the other end on the shore for the elephant to pull by, then went down to the bottom of the river and hid himself. The elephant then came down and started pulling, and after a time he smashed the rope.

Directly this happened, the tortoise undid the rope from the rock and came to the land, showing all people that the rope was still fast to his leg, but that the elephant had failed to pull him out. The elephant was thus forced to admit that the tortoise was the winner, and paid to him the twenty thousand rods, as agreed. The tortoise then took the rods home to his wife, and they lived together very happily.

After three months had passed, the tortoise, seeing that the money was greatly reduced, thought he would make some more by the same trick, so he went to the hippopotamus and made the same bet with him. The hippopotamus said, "I will make the bet, but I shall take the water and you shall take the land; I will then pull you into the water."

To this the tortoise agreed, so they went down to the river as before, and having got some strong tie-tie, the tortoise made it fast to the hippopotamus' hind leg, and told him to go into the water. Directly the hippo had turned his back and disappeared, the tortoise took the rope twice round a strong palm-tree which was growing near, and then hid himself at the foot of the tree.

When the hippo was tired of pulling, he came up puffing and blowing water into the air from his nostrils. Directly the tortoise saw him coming up, he unwound the rope, and walked down towards the hippopotamus, showing him the tie-tie round his leg. The hippo had to acknowledge that the tortoise was too strong for him, and reluctantly handed over the twenty thousand rods.

The elephant and the hippo then agreed that they would take the tortoise as their friend, as he was so very strong; but he was not really so strong as they thought, and had won because he was so cunning.

He then told them that he would like to live with both of them, but that, as he could not be in two places at the same time, he said that he would leave his son to live with the elephant on the land, and that he himself would live with the hippopotamus in the water.

This explains why there are both tortoises on the land and tortoises who live in the water. The water tortoise is always much the bigger of the two, as there is plenty of fish for him to eat in the river, whereas the land tortoise is often very short of food.

XXX.

Of the Pretty Girl and the Seven Jealous Women

There was once a very beautiful girl called Akim. She was a native of Ibibio, and the name was given to her on account of her good looks, as she was born in the spring-time. She was an only daughter, and her parents were extremely fond of her. The people of the town, and more particularly the young girls, were so jealous of Akim's good looks and beautiful form—for she was perfectly made, very strong, and her carriage, bearing, and manners were most graceful—that her parents would not allow her to join the young girls' society in the town, as is customary for all young people to do, both boys and girls belonging to a company according to their age; a company consisting, as a rule, of all the boys or girls born in the same year.

Akim's parents were rather poor, but she was a good daughter, and gave them no trouble, so they had a happy home. One day as Akim was on her way to draw water from the spring she met the company of seven girls, to which in an ordinary way she would have belonged, if her parents had not forbidden her. These girls told her that they were going to hold a play in the town in three days' time, and asked her to join them. She said she was very sorry, but that her parents were poor, and only had herself to work for them, she therefore had no time to spare for dancing and plays. She then left them and went home.

In the evening the seven girls met together, and as they were very envious of Akim, they discussed how they should be revenged upon her for refusing to join their company, and they talked for a long time as to how they could get Akim into danger or punish her in some way.

At last one of the girls suggested that they should all go to Akim's house every day and help her with her work, so that when they had made friends with her they would be able to entice her away and take their revenge upon her for being more beautiful than themselves. Although they went every day and helped Akim and her parents with their work, the parents knew that they were jealous of their daughter, and repeatedly warned her not on any account to go with them, as they were not to be trusted.

At the end of the year there was going to be a big play, called the new yam play, to which Akim's parents had been invited. The play was going to be held at a town about two hours' march from where they lived. Akim was very anxious to go and take part in the dance, but her parents gave her plenty of work to do before they started, thinking that this would surely prevent her going, as she was a very obedient daughter, and always did her work properly.

On the morning of the play the jealous seven came to Akim and asked her to go with them, but she pointed to all the water-pots she had to fill, and showed them where her parents had told her to polish the walls with a stone and make the floor good; and after that was finished she had to pull up all the weeds round the house and clean up all round. She therefore said it was impossible for her to leave the house until all the work was finished. When the girls heard this they took up the water-pots, went to the spring, and quickly returned with them full; they placed them in a row, and then they got stones, and very soon had the walls polished and the floor made good; after that they did the weeding outside and the cleaning up, and when everything was completed they said to Akim, "Now then, come along; you have no excuse to remain behind, as all the work is done."

Akim really wanted to go to the play; so as all the work was done which her parents had told her to do, she finally consented to go. About half-way to the town, where the new yam play was being held, there was a small river, about five feet deep, which had to be crossed by wading, as there was no bridge. In this river there was a powerful Ju Ju, whose law was that whenever any one crossed the river and returned the same way on the return journey, whoever it was, had to give some food to the Ju Ju. If they did not make the proper sacrifice the Ju Ju dragged them down and took them to his home, and kept them there to work for him. The seven jealous girls knew all about this Ju Ju, having often crossed the river before, as they walked about all over the country, and had plenty of friends in the different towns. Akim, however, who was a good girl, and never went anywhere, knew nothing about this Ju Ju, which her companions had found out.

When the work was finished they all started off together, and crossed the river without any trouble. When they had gone a small distance on the other side they saw a small bird, perched on a high tree, who admired Akim very much, and sang in praise of her beauty, much to the annoyance of the seven girls; but they walked on without saying anything, and eventually arrived at the town where the play was being held. Akim had not taken the trouble to change her clothes, but when she arrived at the town, although her companions had on all their best beads and their finest clothes, the young men and people admired Akim far more than the other girls, and she was declared to be the finest and most beautiful woman at the dance. They gave her plenty of palm wine, foo-foo, and everything she wanted, so that the seven girls became more angry and jealous than before. The people danced and sang all that night, but Akim managed to keep out of the sight of her parents until the following morning, when they asked her how it was that she had disobeyed them and neglected her work; so Akim told them that the work had all been done by her friends, and they had enticed her to come to the play with them. Her mother then told her to return home at once, and that she was not to remain in the town any longer.

When Akim told her friends this they said, "Very well, we are just going to have some small meal, and then we will return with you." They all then sat down together and had their food, but each of the seven jealous girls hid a small quantity of foo-foo and fish in her clothes for the Water Ju Ju. However Akim, who knew nothing about this, as her parents had forgotten to tell her about the Ju Ju, never thinking for one moment that their daughter would cross the river, did not take any food as a sacrifice to the Ju Ju with her.

When they arrived at the river Akim saw the girls making their small sacrifices, and begged them to give her a small share so that she could do the same, but they refused, and all walked across the river safely. Then when it was Akim's turn to cross, when she arrived in the middle of the river, the Water Ju Ju caught hold of her and dragged her underneath the water, so that she immediately disappeared from sight. The seven girls had been watching for this, and when they saw that she had gone they went on their way, very pleased at the success of their scheme, and said to one another, "Now Akim is gone for ever, and we shall hear no more about her being better-looking than we are."

As there was no one to be seen at the time when Akim disappeared they naturally thought that their cruel action had escaped detection, so they went home rejoicing; but they never noticed the little bird high up in the tree who had sung of Akim's beauty when they were on their way to the play. The little bird was very sorry for Akim, and made up his mind that, when the proper time came, he would tell her parents what he had seen, so that perhaps they would be able to save her. The bird had heard Akim asking for a small portion of the food to make a sacrifice with, and had heard all the girls refusing to give her any.

The following morning, when Akim's parents returned home, they were much surprised to find that the door was fastened, and that there was no sign of their daughter anywhere about the place, so they inquired of their neighbours, but no one was able to give them any information about her. They then went to the seven girls, and asked them what had become of Akim. They replied that they did not know what had become of her, but that she had reached their town safely with them, and then said she was going home. The father then went to his Ju Ju man, who, by casting lots, discovered what had happened, and told him that on her way back from the play Akim had crossed the river without making the customary sacrifice to the Water Ju Ju, and that, as the Ju Ju was angry, he had seized Akim and taken her to his home. He therefore told Akim's father to take one goat, one basketful of eggs, and one piece of white cloth to the river in the morning, and to offer them as a sacrifice to the Water Ju Ju; then Akim would be thrown out of the water seven times, but that if her father failed to catch her on the seventh time, she would disappear for ever.

Akim's father then returned home, and, when he arrived there, the little bird who had seen Akim taken by the Water Ju Ju, told him everything that had happened, confirming the Ju Ju's words. He also said that it was entirely the fault of the seven girls, who had refused to give Akim any food to make the sacrifice with.

Early the following morning the parents went to the river, and made the sacrifice as advised by the Ju Ju. Immediately they had done so, the Water Ju Ju threw Akim up from the middle of the river. Her father caught her at once, and returned home very thankfully.

He never told any one, however, that he had recovered his daughter, but made up his mind to punish the seven jealous girls, so he dug a deep pit in the middle of his house, and placed dried palm leaves and sharp stakes in the bottom of the pit. He then covered the top of the pit with new mats, and sent out word for all people to come and hold a play to rejoice with him, as he had recovered his daughter from the spirit land. Many people came, and danced and sang all the day and night, but the seven jealous girls did not appear, as they were frightened. However, as they were told that everything had gone well on the previous day, and that there had been no trouble, they went to the house the following morning and mixed with the dancers; but they were ashamed to look Akim in the face, who was sitting down in the middle of the dancing ring.

When Akim's father saw the seven girls he pretended to welcome them as his daughter's friends, and presented each of them with a brass rod, which he placed round their necks. He also gave them tombo to drink.

He then picked them out, and told them to go and sit on mats on the other side of the pit he had prepared for them. When they walked over the mats which hid the pit they all fell in, and Akim's father immediately got some red-hot ashes from the fire and threw them in on top of the screaming girls, who were in great pain. At once the dried palm leaves caught fire, killing all the girls at once.

When the people heard the cries and saw the smoke, they all ran back to the town.

The next day the parents of the dead girls went to the head chief, and complained that Akim's father had killed their daughters, so the chief called him before him, and asked him for an explanation.

Akim's father went at once to the chief, taking the Ju Ju man, whom everybody relied upon, and the small bird, as his witnesses.

When the chief had heard the whole case, he told Akim's father that he should only have killed one girl to avenge his daughter, and not seven. So he told the father to bring Akim before him.

When she arrived, the head chief, seeing how beautiful she was, said that her father was justified in killing all the seven girls on her behalf, so he dismissed the case, and told the parents of the dead girls to go away and mourn for their daughters, who had been wicked and jealous women, and had been properly punished for their cruel behaviour to Akim.

Moral.—Never kill a man or a woman because you are envious of their beauty, as if you do, you will surely be punished.

XXXI.

How the Cannibals drove the People from Insofan Mountain to the Cross River (Ikom)

Very many years ago, before the oldest man alive at the present time can remember, the towns of Ikom, Okuni, Abijon, Insofan, Obokum, and all the other Injor towns were situated round and near the Insofan Mountain, and the head chief of the whole country was called Agbor. Abragba and Enfitop also lived there, and were also under King Agbor. The Insofan Mountain is about two days' march inland from the Cross River, and as none of the people there could swim, and knew nothing about canoes, they never went anywhere outside their own country, and were afraid to go down to the big river. The whole country was taken up with yam farms, and was divided amongst the various towns, each town having its own bush. At the end of each year, when it was time to dig the yams, there was a big play held, which was called the New Yam feast. At this festival there was always a big human sacrifice, fifty slaves being killed in one day. These slaves were tied up to trees in a row, and many drums were beaten; then a strong man, armed with a sharp matchet, went from one slave to another and cut their heads off. This was done to cool the new yams, so that they would not hurt the stomachs of the people. Until this sacrifice was made no one in the country would eat a new yam, as they knew, if they did so, they would suffer great pain in their insides.

When the feast was held, all the towns brought one hundred yams each as a present to King Agbor. When the slaves were all killed fires were lit, and the dead bodies were placed over the fires to burn the hair off. A number of plantain leaves were then gathered and placed on the ground, and the bodies, having been cut into pieces, were placed on the plantain leaves.

When the yams were skinned, they were put into large pots, with water, oil, pepper, and salt. The cut-up bodies were then put in on top, and the pots covered up with other clay pots and left to boil for an hour.

The king, having called all the people together, then declared the New Yam feast had commenced, and singing and dancing were kept up for three days and nights, during which time much palm wine was consumed, and all the bodies and yams, which had been provided for them, were eaten by the people.

The heads were given to the king for his share, and, when he had finished eating them, the skulls were placed before the Ju Ju with some new yams, so that there should be a good crop the following season.

But although these natives ate the dead bodies of the slaves at the New Yam feast, they did not eat human flesh during the rest of the year.

This went on for many years, until at last the Okuni people noticed that the graves of the people who had been buried were frequently dug open and the bodies removed. This caused great wonder, and, as they did not like the idea of their dead relations being taken away, they made a complaint to King Agbor. He at once caused a watch to be set on all newly dug graves, and that very night they caught seven men, who were very greedy, and used to come whenever a body was buried, dig it up, and carry it into the bush, where they made a fire, and cooked and ate it.

When they were caught, the people made them show where they lived, and where they cooked the bodies.

After walking for some hours in the forest, they came to a place where large heaps of human bones and skulls were found.

The seven men were then securely fastened up and brought before King Agbor, who held a large palaver of all the towns, and the whole situation was discussed.

Agbor said that this bad custom would necessitate all the towns separating, as they could not allow their dead relations to be dug up and eaten by these greedy people, and he could see no other way to prevent it. Agbor then gave one of the men to each of the seven towns, and told some of them to go on the far side of the big river and make their towns there. The others were to go farther down the river on the same side as Insofan Mountain, and when they found suitable places, they were each to kill their man as a sacrifice and then build their town.

All the towns then departed, and when they had found good sites, they built their towns there.

When they had all gone, after a time Agbor began to feel very lonely, so he left the site of his old town and also went to the Cross

River to live, so that he could see his friends.

After that the New Yam feast was held in each town, and the people still continued to kill and eat a few slaves at the feast, but the bodies of their relations and friends were kept for a long time above ground until they had become rotten, so that the greedy people should not dig them up and eat them.

This is why, even at the present time, the people do not like to bury their dead relations until they have become putrid.

XXXII.

The Lucky Fisherman

In the olden days there were no hooks or casting nets, so that when the natives wanted to catch fish they made baskets and set traps at the river side.

One man named Akon Obo, who was very poor, began to make baskets and traps out of bamboo palm, and then when the river went down he used to take his traps to a pool and set them baited with palm-nuts. In the night the big fish used to smell the palm-nuts and go into the trap, when at once the door would fall down, and in the morning Akon Obo would go and take the fish out. He was very successful in his fishing, and used to sell the fish in the market for plenty of money. When he could afford to pay the dowry he married a woman named Eyong, a native of Okuni, and had three children by her, but he still continued his fishing. The eldest son was called Odey, the second Yambi, and the third Atuk. These three boys, when they grew up, helped their father with his fishing, and he gradually became wealthy and bought plenty of slaves. At last he joined the Egbo society, and became one of the chiefs of the town. Even after he became a chief, he and his sons still continued to fish.

One day, when he was crossing the river in a small dug-out canoe, a tornado came on very suddenly, and the canoe capsized, drowning the chief. When his sons heard of the death of their father, they wanted to go and drown themselves also, but they were persuaded not to by the people. After searching for two days, they found the dead body some distance down the river, and brought it back to the town. They then called their company together to play, dance, and sing for twelve days, in accordance with their native custom, and much palm wine was drunk.

When the play was finished, they took their father's body to a hollowed-out cavern, and placed two live slaves with it, one holding a native lamp of palm-oil, and the other holding a matchet. They were both tied up, so that they could not escape, and were left there to keep watch over the dead chief, until they died of starvation.

When the cave was covered in, the sons called the chiefs together, and they played Egbo [9] for seven days, which used up a lot of their late father's money. When the play was over, the chiefs were surprised at the amount of money which the sons had been able to spend on the funeral of their father, as they knew how poor he had been as a young man. They therefore called him the lucky fisherman.

---

9   The Egbo society would meet together and would be provided with palm wine and food, as much as they could eat and drink, which frequently cost a lot of money. Dancing and singing would also be kept up and a band would play, consisting of drums made of hollowed-out trunks of trees, beaten with two pieces of soft wood, native made bells and rattles made of basket work, with stones inside, the bottom consisting of hard dried skin, and covered all over with long streamers of fibre. Other drums are also played by hand; these are made out of hollow wood, covered at one end with dried skin, the other end being left open. The drummer usually sits on two of these drums, which have a different note, one being a deep sound, and the other slightly higher.

XXXIII.

The Orphan Boy and the Magic Stone

A chief of Inde named Inkita had a son named Ayong Kita, whose mother had died at his birth.

The old chief was a hunter, and used to take his son out with him when he went into the bush. He used to do most of his hunting in the long grass which grows over nearly all the Inde country, and used to kill plenty of bush buck in the dry season.

In those days the people had no guns, so the chief had to shoot everything he got with his bow and arrows, which required a lot of skill.

When his little son was old enough, he gave him a small bow and some small arrows, and taught him how to shoot. The little boy was very quick at learning, and by continually practising at lizards and small birds, soon became expert in the use of his little bow, and could hit them almost every time he shot at them.

When the boy was ten years old his father died, and as he thus became the head of his father's house, and was in authority over all the slaves, they became very discontented, and made plans to kill him, so he ran away into the bush.

Having nothing to eat, he lived for several days on the nuts which fell from the palm trees. He was too young to kill any large animals, and only had his small bow and arrows, with which he killed a few squirrels, bush rats, and small birds, and so managed to live.

Now once at night, when he was sleeping in the hollow of a tree, he had a dream in which his father appeared, and told him where there was plenty of treasure buried in the earth, but, being a small boy, he was frightened, and did not go to the place.

One day, some time after the dream, having walked far and being very thirsty, he went to a lake, and was just going to drink, when he heard a hissing sound, and heard a voice tell him not to drink. Not seeing any one, he was afraid, and ran away without drinking.

Early next morning, when he was out with his bow trying to shoot some small animal, he met an old woman with quite long hair. She was so ugly that he thought she must be a witch, so he tried to run, but she told him not to fear, as she wanted to help him and assist him to rule over his late father's house. She also told him that it was she who had called out to him at the lake not to drink, as there was a bad Ju Ju in the water which would have killed him. The old woman then took Ayong to a stream some little distance from the lake, and bending down, took out a small shining stone from the water, which she gave to him, at the same time telling him to go to the place which his father had advised him to visit in his dream. She then said, "When you get there you must dig, and you will find plenty of money; you must then go and buy two strong slaves, and when you have got them, you must take them into the forest, away from the town, and get them to build you a house with several rooms in it. You must then place the stone in one of the rooms, and whenever you want anything, all you have to do is to go into the room and tell the stone what you want, and your wishes will be at once gratified."

Ayong did as the old woman told him, and after much difficulty and danger bought the two slaves and built a house in the forest, taking great care of the precious stone, which he placed in an inside room. Then for some time, whenever he wanted anything, he used to go into the room and ask for a sufficient number of rods to buy what he wanted, and they were always brought at once.

This went on for many years, and Ayong grew up to be a man, and became very rich, and bought many slaves, having made friends with the Aro men, who in those days used to do a big traffic in slaves. After ten years had passed Ayong had quite a large town and many slaves, but one night the old woman appeared to him in a dream and told him that she thought that he was sufficiently wealthy, and that it was time for him to return the magic stone to the small stream from whence it came. But Ayong, although he was rich, wanted to rule his father's house and be a head chief for all the Inde country, so he sent for all the Ju Ju men in the country and two witch men, and marched with all his slaves to his father's town. Before he started he held a big palaver, and told them to point out any slave who had a bad heart, and who might kill him when he came to rule the country. Then the Ju Ju men consulted together, and pointed out fifty of the slaves who, they said, were witches, and would try to kill Ayong. He at once had them made prisoners, and tried them by the ordeal of

Esere bean [10] to see whether they were witches or not. As none of them could vomit the beans they all died, and were declared to be witches. He then had them buried at once. When the remainder of his slaves saw what had happened, they all came to him and begged his pardon, and promised to serve him faithfully. Although the fifty men were buried they could not rest, and troubled Ayong very much, and after a time he became very sick himself, so he sent again for the Ju Ju men, who told him that it was the witch men who, although they were dead and buried, had power to come out at night and used to suck Ayong's blood, which was the cause of his sickness. They then said, "We are only three Ju Ju men; you must get seven more of us, making the magic number of ten." When they came they dug up the bodies of the fifty witches, and found they were quite fresh. Then Ayong had big fires made, and burned them one after the other, and gave the Ju Ju men a big present. He soon after became quite well again, and took possession of his father's property, and ruled over all the country.

Ever since then, whenever any one is accused of being a witch, they are tried by the ordeal of the poisonous Esere bean, and if they can vomit they do not die, and are declared innocent, but if they cannot do so, they die in great pain.

---

10   The Esere or Calabar bean is a strong poison, and was formerly much used by the natives. These beans are ground up in a stone mortar, and are then swallowed by the accused person. If the man dies he is considered guilty, but if he lives, he is supposed to have proved his innocence of whatever the charge may have been which was brought against him. Death generally ensues about two hours after the poison is administered. If the accused takes a sufficient amount of the ground-up beans to make him vomit it will probably save his life, otherwise he will die in great pain.

XXXIV.

The Slave Girl who tried to Kill her Mistress

A man called Akpan, who was a native of Oku, a town in the Ibibio country, admired a girl called Emme very much, who lived at Ibibio, and wished to marry her, as she was the finest girl in her company. It was the custom in those days for the parents to demand such a large amount for their daughters as dowry, that if after they were married they failed to get on with their husbands, as they could not redeem themselves, they were sold as slaves. Akpan paid a very large sum as dowry for Emme, and she was put in the fatting-house until the proper time arrived for her to marry.

Akpan told the parents that when their daughter was ready they must send her over to him. This they promised to do. Emme's father was a rich man, and after seven years had elapsed, and it became time for her to go to her husband, he saw a very fine girl, who had also just come out of the fatting-house, and whom the parents wished to sell as a slave. Emme's father therefore bought her, and gave her to his daughter as her handmaiden.

The next day Emme's little sister, being very anxious to go with her, obtained the consent of her mother, and they started off together, the slave girlcarrying a large bundle containing clothes and presents from Emme's father. Akpan's house was a long day's march from where they lived. When they arrived just outside the town they came to a spring, where the people used to get their drinking water from, but no one was allowed to bathe there. Emme, however, knew nothing about this. They took off their clothes to wash close to the spring, and where there was a deep hole which led to the Water Ju Ju's house. The slave girl knew of this Ju Ju, and thought if she could get her mistress to bathe, she would be taken by the Ju Ju, and she would then be able to take her place and marry Akpan. So they went down to bathe, and when they were close to the water the slave girl pushed her mistress in, and she at once disappeared. The little girl then began to cry, but the slave girl said, "If you cry any more I will kill you at once, and throw your body into the hole after your sister." And she told the child that she must never mention what had happened to any one, and particularly not to Akpan, as she was going to represent her sister and marry him, and that if she ever told any one what she had seen, she would be killed at once. She then made the little girl carry her load to Akpan's house.

When they arrived, Akpan was very much disappointed at the slave girl's appearance, as she was not nearly as pretty and fine as he had expected her to be; but as he had not seen Emme for seven years, he had no suspicion that the girl was not really Emme, for whom he had paid such a large dowry. He then called all his company together to play and feast, and when they arrived they were much astonished, and said, "Is this the fine woman for whom you paid so much dowry, and whom you told us so much about?" And Akpan could not answer them.

The slave girl was then for some time very cruel to Emme's little sister, and wanted her to die, so that her position would be more secure with her husband. She beat the little girl every day, and always made her carry the largest water-pot to the spring; she also made the child place her finger in the fire to use as firewood. When the time came for food, the slave girl went to the fire and got a burning piece of wood and burned the child all over the body with it. When Akpan asked her why she treated the child so badly, she replied that she was a slave that her father had bought for her. When the little girl took the heavy water-pot to the river to fill it there was no one to lift it up for her, so that she could not get it on to her head; she therefore had to remain a long time at the spring, and at last began calling for her sister Emme to come and help her.

When Emme heard her little sister crying for her, she begged the Water Ju Ju to allow her to go and help her, so he told her she might go, but that she must return to him again immediately. When the little girl saw her sister she did not want to leave her, and asked to be allowed to go into the hole with her. She then told Emme how very badly she had been treated by the slave girl, and her elder sister told her to have patience and wait, that a day of vengeance would arrive sooner or later. The little girl went back to Akpan's house with a glad heart as she had seen her sister, but when she got to the house, the slave girl said, "Why have you been so long getting the water?" and then took another stick from the fire and burnt the little girl again very badly, and starved her for the rest of the day.

This went on for some time, until, one day, when the child

went to the river for water, after all the people had gone, she cried out for her sister as usual, but she did not come for a long time, as there was a hunter from Akpan's town hidden near watching the hole, and the Water Ju Ju told Emme that she must not go; but, as the little girl went on crying bitterly, Emme at last persuaded the Ju Ju to let her go, promising to return quickly. When she emerged from the water, she looked very beautiful with the rays of the setting sun shining on her glistening body. She helped her little sister with her water-pot, and then disappeared into the hole again.

The hunter was amazed at what he had seen, and when he returned, he told Akpan what a beautiful woman had come out of the water and had helped the little girl with her water-pot. He also told Akpan that he was convinced that the girl he had seen at the spring was his proper wife, Emme, and that the Water Ju Ju must have taken her.

Akpan then made up his mind to go out and watch and see what happened, so, in the early morning the hunter came for him, and they both went down to the river, and hid in the forest near the water-hole.

When Akpan saw Emme come out of the water, he recognised her at once, and went home and considered how he should get her out of the power of the Water Ju Ju. He was advised by some of his friends to go to an old woman, who frequently made sacrifices to the Water Ju Ju, and consult her as to what was the best thing to do.

When he went to her, she told him to bring her one white slave, one white goat, one piece of white cloth, one white chicken, and a basket of eggs. Then, when the great Ju Ju day arrived, she would take them to the Water Ju Ju, and make a sacrifice of them on his behalf. The day after the sacrifice was made, the Water Ju Ju would return the girl to her, and she would bring her to Akpan.

Akpan then bought the slave, and took all the other things to the old woman, and, when the day of the sacrifice arrived, he went with his friend the hunter and witnessed the old woman make the sacrifice. The slave was bound up and led to the hole, then the old woman called to the Water Ju Ju and cut the slave's throat with a sharp knife and pushed him into the hole. She then did the same to the goat and chicken, and also threw the eggs and cloth in on top of them.

After this had been done, they all returned to their homes. The next morning at dawn the old woman went to the hole, and found Emme standing at the side of the spring, so she told her that she was her friend, and was going to take her to her husband. She then took Emme back to her own home, and hid her in her room, and sent word to Akpan to come to her house, and to take great care that the slave woman knew nothing about the matter.

So Akpan left the house secretly by the back door, and arrived at the old woman's house without meeting anybody.

When Emme saw Akpan, she asked for her little sister, so he sent his friend, the hunter, for her to the spring, and he met her carrying her water-pot to get the morning supply of water for the house, and brought her to the old woman's house with him.

When Emme had embraced her sister, she told her to return to the house and do something to annoy the slave woman, and then she was to run as fast as she could back to the old woman's house, where, no doubt, the slave girl would follow her, and would meet them all inside the house, and see Emme, who she believed she had killed.

The little girl did as she was told, and, directly she got into the house, she called out to the slave woman: "Do you know that you are a wicked woman, and have treated me very badly? I know you are only my sister's slave, and you will be properly punished." She then ran as hard as she could to the old woman's house. Directly the slave woman heard what the little girl said, she was quite mad with rage, and seized a burning stick from the fire, and ran after the child; but the little one got to the house first, and ran inside, the slave woman following close upon her heels with the burning stick in her hand.

Then Emme came out and confronted the slave woman, and she at once recognised her mistress, whom she thought she had killed, so she stood quite still.

Then they all went back to Akpan's house, and when they arrived there, Akpan asked the slave woman what she meant by pretending that she was Emme, and why she had tried to kill her. But, seeing she was found out, the slave woman had nothing to say.

Many people were then called to a play to celebrate the recovery of Akpan's wife, and when they had all come, he told them what the slave woman had done.

After this, Emme treated the slave girl in the same way as she had treated her little sister. She made her put her fingers in the fire, and burnt her with sticks. She also made her beat foo-foo with her head in a hollowed-out tree, and after a time she was tied up to a tree and starved to death.

Ever since that time, when a man marries a girl, he is always present when she comes out of the fatting-house and takes her home himself, so that such evil things as happened to Emme and her sister may not occur again.

XXXV.

The King and the 'Nsiat Bird

When 'Ndarake was King of Idu, being young and rich, he was very fond of fine girls, and had plenty of slaves. The 'Nsiat bird was then living at Idu, and had a very pretty daughter, whom 'Ndarake wished to marry. When he spoke to the father about the matter, he replied that of course he had no objection personally, as it would be a great honour for his daughter to marry the king, but, unfortunately, when any of his family had children, they always gave birth to twins, which, as the king knew, was not allowed in the country; the native custom being to kill both the children and throw them into the bush, the mother being driven away and allowed to starve. The king, however, being greatly struck with Adit, the bird's daughter, insisted on marrying her, so the 'Nsiat bird had to agree. A large amount of dowry was paid by the king, and a big play and feast was held. One strong slave was told to carry Adit 'Nsiat during the whole play, and she sat on his shoulders with her legs around his neck; this was done to show what a rich and powerful man the king was.

After the marriage, in due course Adit gave birth to twins,

as her mother had done before her. The king immediately became very fond of the two babies, but according to the native custom, which was too strong for any one to resist, he had to give them up to be killed. When the 'Nsiat bird heard this, he went to the king and reminded him that he had warned the king before he married what would happen if he married Adit, and rather than that the twins should be killed, he and the whole of his family would leave the earth and dwell in the air, taking the twins with them. As the king was so fond of Adit and the two children, and did not want them to be killed, he gladly consented, and the 'Nsiat bird took the whole of his family, as well as Adit and her two children, away, and left the earth to live and make their home in the trees; but as they had formerly lived in the town with all the people, they did not like to go into the forest, so they made their nests in the trees which grew in the town, and that is why you always see the 'Nsiat birds living and making their nests only in places where human beings are. The black birds are the cocks, and the golden-coloured ones are the hens. It was the beautiful colour of Adit which first attracted the attention of 'Ndarake and caused him to marry her.

XXXVI.

Concerning the Fate of Essido
and his Evil Companions

Chief Oborri lived at a town called Adiagor, which is on the right bank of the Calabar River. He was a wealthy chief, and belonged to the Egbo Society. He had many large canoes, and plenty of slaves to paddle them. These canoes he used to fill up with new yams—each canoe being under one head slave and containing eight paddles; the canoes were capable of holding three puncheons of palm-oil, and cost eight hundred rods each. When they were full, about ten of them used to start off together and paddle to Rio del Rey. They went through creeks all the way, which run through mangrove swamps, with palm-oil trees here and there. Sometimes in the tornado season it was very dangerous crossing the creeks, as the canoes were so heavily laden, having only a few inches above the water, that quite a small wave would fill the canoe and cause it to sink to the bottom. Although most of the boys could swim, it often happened that some of them were lost, as there are many large alligators in these waters. After four days' hard paddling they would arrive at Rio del Rey, where they had very little difficulty in exchanging their new yams for bags of dried shrimps and sticks with smoked fish on them.[11]

Chief Oborri had two sons, named Eyo I. and Essido. Their mother having died when they were babies, the children were brought up by their father. As they grew up, they developed entirely different characters. The eldest was very hard-working and led a solitary life; but the younger son was fond of gaiety and was very lazy, in fact, he spent most of his time in the neighbouring towns playing and dancing. When the two boys arrived at the respective ages of eighteen and twenty their father died, and they were left to look after themselves. According to native custom, the elder son, Eyo I., was entitled to the whole of his father's estate; but being very fond of his younger brother, he gave him a large number of rods and some land with a house. Immediately Essido became possessed of the money he became wilder than ever, gave big feasts to his companions, and always had his house full of women, upon whom he spent large sums. Although the amount his brother had given him on his father's death was very large, in the course of a few years Essido had spent it all. He then sold his house and effects, and spent the proceeds on feasting.

While he had been living this gay and unprofitable life, Eyo I.

---

11   A stick of fish consisted of two sticks with a big fish in the middle of each and small fish at each end, there being eight fish on each stick, making sixteen in all. These sticks were then tied together, and smoked over wood fires until they were quite dried. One stick of fish would sell at Calabar in the dry season time for from 3s. 6d. to 5s. a stick, and a stick would be got for five large yams which cost Chief Oborri only 1s., so a large profit was made on each canoe load—the canoes carrying about a thousand yams each. A bag of shrimps would be bartered for twenty-five large yams, and the shrimps would be sold for 15s., being a profit of 10s. on each bag. At the present time, however, the same sized bag of shrimps, in the wet season, would sell at Calabar for £3, 10s., and in the dry season for between £1, 10s. and £2.

had been working harder than ever at his father's old trade, and had made many trips to Rio del Rey himself. Almost every week he had canoes laden with yams going down river and returning after about twelve days with shrimps and fish, which Eyo I. himself disposed of in the neighbouring markets, and he very rapidly became a rich man. At intervals he remonstrated with Essido on his extravagance, but his warnings had no effect; if anything, his brother became worse. At last the time arrived when all his money was spent, so Essido went to his brother and asked him to lend him two thousand rods, but Eyo refused, and told Essido that he would not help him in any way to continue his present life of debauchery, but that if he liked to work on the farm and trade, he would give him a fair share of the profits. This Essido indignantly refused, and went back to the town and consulted some of the very few friends he had left as to what was the best thing to do.

The men he spoke to were thoroughly bad men, and had been living upon Essido for a long time. They suggested to him that he should go round the town and borrow money from the people he had entertained, and then they would run away to Akpabryos town, which was about four days' march from Calabar. This Essido did, and managed to borrow a lot of money, although many people refused to lend him anything. Then at night he set off with his evil companions, who carried his money, as they had not been able to borrow any themselves, being so well known. When they arrived at Akpabryos town they found many beautiful women and graceful dancers. They then started the same life again, until after a few weeks most of the money had gone. They then met and consulted together how to get more money, and advised Essido to return to his rich brother, pretending that he was going to work and give up his old life; he should then get poison from a man they knew of, and place it in his brother's food, so that he would die, and then Essido would become possessed of all his brother's wealth, and they would be able to live in the same way as they had formerly. Essido, who had sunk very low, agreed to this plan, and they left Akpabryos town the next morning. After marching for two days, they arrived at a small hut in the bush where a man who was an expert poisoner lived, called Okponesip. He was the head Ju Ju man of the country, and when they had bribed him with eight hundred rods he swore them to secrecy, and gave Essido a small parcel containing a deadly poison which he said would kill his brother in three months. All he had to do was to place the poison in his brother's food.

When Essido returned to his brother's house he pretended to be very sorry for his former mode of living, and said that for the future he was going to work. Eyo I. was very glad when he heard this, and at once asked his brother in, and gave him new clothes and plenty to eat.

In the evening, when supper was being prepared, Essido went into the kitchen, pretending he wanted to get a light from the fire for his pipe. The cook being absent and no one about, he put the poison in the soup, and then returned to the living-room. He then asked for some tombo, which was brought, and when he had finished it, he said he did not want any supper, and went to sleep. His brother, Eyo I., had supper by himself and consumed all the soup. In a week's time he began to feel very ill, and as the days passed he became worse, so he sent for his Ju Ju man.

When Essido saw him coming, he quietly left the house; but the Ju Ju man, by casting lots, very soon discovered that it was Essido who had given poison to his brother. When he told Eyo I. this, he would not believe it, and sent him away. However, when Essido returned, his elder brother told him what the Ju Ju man had said, but that he did not believe him for one moment, and had sent him away. Essido was much relieved when he heard this, but as he was anxious that no suspicion of the crime should be attached to him, he went to the Household Ju Ju,[12] and having first sworn that he had never administered poison to his brother, he drank out of the pot.

Three months after he had taken the poison Eyo I. died, much to the grief of every one who knew him, as he was much respected, not only on account of his great wealth, but because he was also an upright and honest man, who never did harm to any one.

Essido kept his brother's funeral according to the usual custom, and there was much playing and dancing, which was kept up for a long time. Then Essido paid off his old creditors in order to make himself popular, and kept open house, entertaining most lavishly, and spending his money in many foolish ways. All the bad women

---

12   Every compound has a small Ju Ju in the centre, which generally consists of a few curiously shaped stones and a small tree on which the 'Nsiat bird frequently builds. There is sometimes a species of cactus at the foot, an earthenware pot is supported on sticks against the tree, and tied on with tie-tie, or native rope. In this pot there is always a very foul-smelling liquid, with frequently some rotten eggs floating in it. Small sacrifices are made to these Ju Ju's of chickens, &c., and this Ju Ju is frequently appealed to. The liquid is sometimes taken as a specific against sickness or poison. In the dry season the author has often observed large spiders with their webs all over these Ju Ju's, but they are never touched. There is also frequently a roughly carved image of wood, and sometimes an old matchet and some broken earthenware on the ground, with a brass rod or manilla. It is generally a very dirty spot.

about collected at his house, and his old evil companions went on as they had done before.

Things got so bad that none of the respectable people would have anything to do with him, and at last the chiefs of the country, seeing the way Essido was squandering his late brother's estate, assembled together, and eventually came to the conclusion that he was a witch man, and had poisoned his brother in order to acquire his position. The chiefs, who were all friends of the late Eyo, and who were very sorry at the death, as they knew that if he had lived he would have become a great and powerful chief, made up their minds to give Essido the Ekpawor Ju Ju, which is a very strong medicine, and gets into men's heads, so that when they have drunk it they are compelled to speak the truth, and if they have done wrong they die very shortly. Essido was then told to dress himself and attend the meeting at the palaver house, and when he arrived the chiefs charged him with having killed his brother by witchcraft. Essido denied having done so, but the chiefs told him that if he were innocent he must prove it by drinking the bowl of Ekpawor medicine which was placed before him. As he could not refuse to drink, he drank the bowl off in great fear and trembling, and very soon the Ju Ju having got hold of him, he confessed that he had poisoned his brother, but that his friends had advised him to do so. About two hours after drinking the Ekpawor, Essido died in great pain.

The friends were then brought to the meeting and tied up to posts, and questioned as to the part they had taken in the death of Eyo. As they were too frightened to answer, the chiefs told them that they knew from Essido that they had induced him to poison his brother. They were then taken to the place where Eyo was buried, the grave having been dug open, and their heads were cut off and fell into the grave, and their bodies were thrown in after them as a sacrifice for the wrong they had done. The grave was then filled up again.

Ever since that time, whenever any one is suspected of being a witch, he is tried by the Ekpawor Ju Ju.

XXXVII.

Concerning the Hawk and the Owl

In the olden days when Effiong was king of Calabar, it was customary at that time for rulers to give big feasts, to which all the subjects and all the birds of the air and animals of the forest, also the fish and other things that lived in the water, were invited. All the people, birds, animals, and fish, were under the king, and had to obey him. His favourite messenger was the hawk, as he could travel so quickly.

The hawk served the king faithfully for several years, and when he wanted to retire, he asked what the king proposed to do for him, as very soon he would be too old to work any more. So the king told the hawk to bring any living creature, bird or animal, to him, and he would allow the hawk for the future to live on that particular species without any trouble. The hawk then flew over a lot of country, and went from forest to forest, until at last he found a young owl which had tumbled out of its nest. This the hawk brought to the king, who told him that for the future he might eat owls. The hawk then carried the owlet away, and told his friends what the king had said.

One of the wisest of them said, "Tell me when you seized

the young owlet, what did the parents say?" And the hawk replied that the father and mother owls kept quite quiet, and never said anything. The hawk's friend then advised him to return the owlet to his parents, as he could never tell what the owls would do to him in the night-time, and as they had made no noise, they were no doubt plotting in their minds some deep and cruel revenge.

The next day the hawk carried the owlet back to his parents and left him near the nest. He then flew about, trying to find some other bird which would do as his food; but as all the birds had heard that the hawk had seized the owlet, they hid themselves, and would not come out when the hawk was near. He therefore could not catch any birds.

As he was flying home he saw a lot of fowls near a house, basking in the sun and scratching in the dust. There were also several small chickens running about and chasing insects, or picking up anything they could find to eat, with the old hen following them and clucking and calling to them from time to time. When the hawk saw the chickens, he made up his mind that he would take one, so he swooped down and caught the smallest in his strong claws. Immediately he had seized the chicken the cocks began to make a great noise, and the hen ran after him and tried to make him drop her child, calling loudly, with her feathers fluffed out and making dashes at him. But he carried it off, and all the fowls and chickens at once ran screaming into the houses, some taking shelter under bushes and others trying to hide themselves in the long grass. He then carried the chicken to the king, telling him that he had returned the owlet to his parents, as he did not want him for food; so the king told the hawk that for the future he could always feed on chickens.

The hawk then took the chicken home, and his friend who dropped in to see him, asked him what the parents of the chicken had done when they saw their child taken away; so the hawk said—

"They all made a lot of noise, and the old hen chased me, but although there was a great disturbance amongst the fowls, nothing happened."

His friend then said as the fowls had made much palaver, he was quite safe to kill and eat the chickens, as the people who made plenty of noise in the daytime would go to sleep at night and not disturb him, or do him any injury; the only people to be afraid of were those who when they were injured, kept quite silent; you might be certain then that they were plotting mischief, and would do harm in the night-time.

XXXVIII.

The Story of the Drummer and the Alligators

There was once a woman named Affiong Any who lived at 'Nsidung, a small town to the south of Calabar. She was married to a chief of Hensham Town called Etim Ekeng. They had lived together for several years, but had no children. The chief was very anxious to have a child during his lifetime, and made sacrifices to his Ju Ju, but they had no effect. So he went to a witch man, who told him that the reason he had no children was that he was too rich. The chief then asked the witch man how he should spend his money in order to get a child, and he was told to make friends with everybody, and give big feasts, so that he should get rid of some of his money and become poorer.

The chief then went home and told his wife. The next day his wife called all her company together and gave them a big dinner, which cost a lot of money; much food was consumed, and large quantities of tombo were drunk. Then the chief entertained his company, which cost a lot more money. He also wasted a lot of money in the Egbo house. When half of his property was wasted, his wife told him that she had conceived. The chief, being very glad, called a big play for the next day.

In those days all the rich chiefs of the country belonged to the Alligator Company, and used to meet in the water. The reason they belonged to the company was, first of all, to protect their canoes when they went trading, and secondly, to destroy the canoes and property of the people who did not belong to their company, and to take their money and kill their slaves.

Chief Etim Ekeng was a kind man, and would not join this society, although he was repeatedly urged to do so. After a time a son was born to the chief, and he called him Edet Etim. The chief then called the Egbo society together, and all the doors of the houses in the town were shut, the markets were stopped, and the women were not allowed to go outside their houses while the Egbo was playing. This was kept up for several days, and cost the chief a lot of money. Then he made up his mind that he would divide his property, and give his son half when he became old enough. Unfortunately after three months the chief died, leaving his sorrowing wife to look after their little child.

The wife then went into mourning for seven years for her husband, and after that time she became entitled to all his property, as the late chief had no brothers. She looked after the little boy very carefully until he grew up, when he became a very fine, healthy young man, and was much admired by all the pretty girls of the town; but his mother warned him strongly not to go with them, because they would make him become a bad man. Whenever the girls had a play they used to invite Edet Etim, and at last he went to the play, and they made him beat the drum for them to dance to. After much practice he became the best drummer in the town, and whenever the girls had a play they always called him to drum for them. Plenty of the young girls left their husbands, and went to Edet and asked him to marry them. This made all the young men of the town very jealous, and when they met together at night they considered what would be the best way to kill him. At last they decided that when Edet went to bathe they would induce the alligators to take him. So one night, when he was washing, one alligator seized him by the foot, and others came and seized him round the waist. He fought very hard, but at last they dragged him into the deep water, and took him to their home.

When his mother heard this, she determined to do her best to recover her son, so she kept quite quiet until the morning.

When the young men saw that Edet's mother remained quiet, and did not cry, they thought of the story of the hawk and the owl, and determined to keep Edet alive for a few months.

At cockcrow the mother raised a cry, and went to the grave of her dead husband in order to consult his spirit as to what she had better do to recover her lost son. After a time she went down to the beach with small young green branches in her hands, with which she beat the water, and called upon all the Ju Jus of the Calabar River to help her to recover her son. She then went home and got a load of rods, and took them to a Ju Ju man in the farm. His name was Ininen Okon; he was so called because he was very artful, and had plenty of strong Ju Jus.

When the young boys heard that Edet's mother had gone to Ininen Okon, they all trembled with fear, and wanted to return Edet, but they could not do so, as it was against the rules of their society. The Ju Ju man having discovered that Edet was still alive, and was being detained in the alligators' house, told the mother to be patient. After three days Ininen himself joined another alligators' society, and went to inspect the young alligators' house. He found a young man whom he knew, left on guard when all the alligators had gone to feed at the ebb of the tide, and came back and told the mother to wait, as he would make a Ju Ju which would cause them all to depart in seven days, and leave no one in the house. He made his Ju Ju, and the young alligators said that, as no one had come for Edet, they would all go at the ebb tide to feed, and leave no one in charge of the house. When they returned they found Edet still there, and everything as they had left it, as Ininen had not gone that day.

Three days afterwards they all went away again, and this time went a long way off, and did not return quickly. When Ininen saw that the tide was going down he changed himself into an alligator, and swam to the young alligators' home, where he found Edet chained to a post. He then found an axe and cut the post, releasing the boy. But Edet, having been in the water so long, was deaf and dumb. He then found several loin cloths which had been left behind by the young alligators, so he gathered them together and took them away to show to the king, and Ininen left the place, taking Edet with him. He then called the mother to see her son, but when she came the boy could only look at her, and could not speak. The mother embraced her boy, but he took no notice, as he did not seem capable of understanding anything, but sat down quietly. Then the Ju Ju man told Edet's mother that he would cure her son in a few days, so he made several Ju Jus, and gave her son medicine, and after a time the boy recovered his speech and became sensible again.

Then Edet's mother put on a mourning cloth, and pretended that her son was dead, and did not tell the people he had come back to her. When the young alligators returned, they found that Edet was gone, and that some one had taken their loin cloths. They were therefore much afraid, and made inquiries if Edet had been seen, but they could hear nothing about him, as he was hidden in a farm, and the mother continued to wear her mourning cloth in order to deceive them.

Nothing happened for six months, and they had quite forgotten all about the matter. Affiong, the mother, then went to the chiefs of the town, and asked them to hold a large meeting of all the people, both young and old, at the palaver house, so that her late husband's property might be divided up in accordance with the native custom, as her son had been killed by the alligators.

The next day the chiefs called all the people together, but the mother in the early morning took her son to a small room at the back of the palaver house, and left him there with the seven loin cloths which the Ju Ju man had taken from the alligators' home. When the chiefs and all the people were seated, Affiong stood up and addressed them, saying—

"Chiefs and young men of my town, eight years ago my husband was a fine young man. He married me, and we lived together for many years without having any children. At last I had a son, but my husband died a few months afterwards. I brought my boy up carefully, but as he was a good drummer and dancer the young men were jealous, and had him caught by the alligators. Is there any one present who can tell me what my son would have become if he had lived?" She then asked them what they thought of the alligator society, which had killed so many young men.

The chiefs, who had lost a lot of slaves, told her that if she could produce evidence against any members of the society they would destroy it at once. She then called upon Ininen to appear with her son Edet. He came out from the room leading Edet by the hand, and placed the bundle of loin cloths before the chiefs.

The young men were very much surprised when they saw Edet, and wanted to leave the palaver house; but when they stood up to go the chiefs told them to sit down at once, or they would receive three hundred lashes. They then sat down, and the Ju Ju man explained how he had gone to the alligators' home, and had brought Edet back to his mother. He also said that he had found the seven loin cloths in the house, but he did not wish to say anything about them, as the owners of some of the cloths were sons of the chiefs.

The chiefs, who were anxious to stop the bad society, told him, however, to speak at once and tell them everything. Then he undid the bundle and took the cloths out one by one, at the same time calling upon the owners to come and take them. When they came to take their cloths, they were told to remain where they were; and they were then told to name their company. The seven young men then gave the names of all the members of their society, thirty-two in all. These men were all placed in a line, and the chiefs then passed sentence, which was that they should all be killed the next morning on the beach. So they were then all tied together to posts, and seven men were placed as a guard over them. They made fires and beat drums all the night.

Early in the morning, at about 4 a.m., the big wooden drum was placed on the roof of the palaver house, and beaten to celebrate the death of the evildoers, which was the custom in those days.

The boys were then unfastened from the posts, and had their hands tied behind their backs, and were marched down to the beach. When they arrived there, the head chief stood up and addressed the people. "This is a small town of which I am chief, and I am determined to stop this bad custom, as so many men have been killed." He then told a man who had a sharp matchet to cut off one man's head. He then told another man who had a sharp knife to skin another young man alive. A third man who had a heavy stick was ordered to beat another to death, and so the chief went on and killed all the thirty-two young men in the most horrible ways he could think of. Some of them were tied to posts in the river, and left there until the tide came up and drowned them. Others were flogged to death.

After they had all been killed, for many years no one was killed by alligators, but some little time afterwards on the road between the beach and the town the land fell in, making a very large and deep hole, which was said to be the home of the alligators, and the people have ever since tried to fill it up, but have never yet been able to do so.

/ XXXIX.

The 'Nsasak Bird and the Odudu Bird

A long time ago, in the days of King Adam of Calabar, the king wanted to know if there was any animal or bird which was capable of enduring hunger for a long period. When he found one the king said he would make him a chief of his tribe.

The 'Nsasak bird is very small, having a shining breast of green and red; he also has blue and yellow feathers and red round the neck, and his chief food consists of ripe palm nuts. The Odudu bird, on the other hand, is much larger, about the size of a magpie, with plenty of feathers, but a very thin body; he has a long tail, and his colouring is black and brown with a cream-coloured breast. He lives chiefly on grasshoppers, and is also very fond of crickets, which make a noise at night.

Both the 'Nsasak bird and the Odudu were great friends, and used to live together. They both made up their minds that they would go before the king and try to be made chiefs, but the Odudu bird was quite confident that he would win, as he was so much bigger than the 'Nsasak bird. He therefore offered to starve for seven days.

The king then told them both to build houses which he would

inspect, and then he would have them fastened up, and the one who could remain the longest without eating would be made the chief.

They both then built their houses, but the 'Nsasak bird, who was very cunning, thought that he could not possibly live for seven days without eating anything. He therefore made a tiny hole in the wall (being very small himself), which he covered up so that the king would not notice it on his inspection. The king then came and looked carefully over both houses, but failed to detect the little hole in the 'Nsasak bird's house, as it had been hidden so carefully. He therefore declared that both houses were safe, and then ordered the two birds to go inside their respective houses, and the doors were carefully fastened on the outside.

Every morning at dawn the 'Nsasak bird used to escape through the small opening he had left high up in the wall, and fly away a long distance and enjoy himself all day, taking care, however, that none of the people on the farms should see him. Then when the sun went down he would fly back to his little house and creep through the hole in the wall, closing it carefully after him. When he was safely inside he would call out to his friend the Odudu and ask him if he felt hungry, and told him that he must bear it well if he wanted to win, as he, the 'Nsasak bird, was very fit, and could go on for a long time.

For several days this went on, the voice of the Odudu bird growing weaker and weaker every night, until at last he could no longer reply. Then the little bird knew that his friend must be dead. He was very sorry, but could not report the matter, as he was sup-posed to be confined inside his house.

When the seven days had expired the king came and had both the doors of the houses opened. The 'Nsasak bird at once flew out, and, perching on a branch of a tree which grew near, sang most merrily; but the Odudu bird was found to be quite dead, and there was very little left of him, as the ants had eaten most of his body, leaving only the feathers and bones on the floor.

The king therefore at once appointed the 'Nsasak bird to be the head chief of all the small birds, and in the Ibibio country even to the present time the small boys who have bows and arrows are presented with a prize, which sometimes takes the shape of a female goat, if they manage to shoot a 'Nsasak bird, as the 'Nsasak bird is the king of the small birds, and most difficult to shoot on account of his wiliness and his small size.

XL.

The Election of the King Bird
(the black-and-white Fishing Eagle)

Old Town, Calabar, once had a king called Essiya, who, like most of the Calabar kings in the olden days, was rich and powerful; but although he was so wealthy, he did not possess many slaves. He therefore used to call upon the animals and birds to help his people with their work. In order to get the work done quickly and well, he determined to appoint head chiefs of all the different species. The elephant he appointed king of the beasts of the forest, and the hippopotamus king of the water animals, until at last it came to the turn of the birds to have their king elected.

Essiya thought for some time which would be the best way to make a good choice, but could not make up his mind, as there were so many different birds who all considered they had claims. There was the hawk with his swift flight, and of hawks there were several species. There were the herons to be considered, and the big spur-winged geese, the hornbill or toucan tribe, and the game birds, such as guinea-fowl, the partridge, and the bustards. Then again, of course, there were all the big crane tribe, who walked about the sandbanks in the dry season, but who disappeared when the river rose, and the big black-and-white fishing eagles. When the king thought of the plover tribe, the sea-birds, including the pelicans, the doves, and the numerous shy birds who live in the forest, all of whom sent in claims, he got so confused, that he decided to have a trial by ordeal of combat, and sent word round the whole country for all the birds to meet the next day and fight it out between themselves, and that the winner should be known as the king bird ever afterwards.

The following morning many thousands of birds came, and there was much screeching and flapping of wings. The hawk tribe soon drove all the small birds away, and harassed the big waders so much, that they very shortly disappeared, followed by the geese, who made much noise, and winged away in a straight line, as if they were playing "Follow my leader." The big forest birds who liked to lead a secluded life very soon got tired of all the noise and bustle, and after a few croaks and other weird noises went home. The game birds had no chance and hid in the bush, so that very soon the only birds left were the hawks and the big black-and-white fishing eagle, who was perched on a tree calmly watching everything. The scavenger hawks were too gorged and lazy to take much interest in the proceedings, and were quietly ignored by the fighting tribe, who were very busy circling and swooping on one another, with much whistling going on. Higher and higher they went, until they disappeared out of sight. Then a few would return to earth, some of them badly torn and with many feathers missing.

At last the fishing eagle said—

"When you have quite finished with this foolishness please tell me, and if any of you fancy yourselves at all, come to me, and I will settle your chances of being elected head chief once and for all;" but when they saw his terrible beak and cruel claws, knowing his great strength and ferocity, they stopped fighting between themselves, and acknowledged the fishing eagle to be their master.

Essiya then declared that Ituen, which was the name of the fishing eagle, was the head chief of all the birds, and should thenceforward be known as the king bird. [13]

From that time to the present day, whenever the young men of the country go to fight they always wear three of the long black-and-white feathers of the king bird in their hair, one on each side and one in the middle, as they are believed to impart much courage and skill to the wearer; and if a young man is not possessed of any of these feathers when he goes out to fight, he is looked upon as a very small boy indeed.

THE END

---

13   As the king bird is always very difficult to shoot with a bow and arrow, owing to his sharp and keen sight, the young men, when they want his feathers, set traps for him baited with rats, which catch him by the foot in a noose when he seizes them. Except when they are nesting the king birds roost on very high trees, sometimes as many as twenty or thirty on neighbouring trees. They fly many miles from where they get their food, and arrive at their roosting-place just before the sun sets, leaving the next morning at dawn for their favourite haunts. They are very regular in their habits, and you can see them every night at the same time coming from the same direction and flying over the same trees, generally fairly high up in the air. There is a strong belief amongst many natives on the Cross River that the king bird has the power of influencing the luck or the reverse of a canoe. For example, when a trader, having bought a new canoe, is going to market and a king bird crosses the river from right to left, then if he is unlucky at the market that day, whenever the king bird again crosses that particular canoe from right to left he will be unlucky, and the bad luck will stick to the canoe. If, on the other hand, the bird for the first time crosses from left to right, and he is fortunate in his dealings that day at the market, then he will always be lucky in that canoe the day he sees a king bird flying across the river from the left to the right-hand side.

by Andrew Lang in 1910

MANY YEARS AGO a book on the Folk-Tales of the Eskimo was published, and the editor of *The Academy* (Dr. Appleton) told one of his minions to send it to me for revision. By mischance it was sent to an eminent expert in Political Economy, who, never suspecting any error, took the book for the text of an interesting essay on the economics of "the blameless Hyperboreans."

Mr. Dayrell's "Folk Stories from Southern Nigeria" appeal to the anthropologist within me, no less than to the lover of what children and older people call "Fairy Tales." The stories are full of mentions of strange institutions, as well as of rare adventures. I may be permitted to offer some running notes and comments on this mass of African curiosities from the crowded lumber-room of the native mind.

I. *The Tortoise with a Pretty Daughter.*—The story, like the tales of the dark native tribes of Australia, rises from that state of fancy by which man draws (at least for purposes of fiction) no line between himself and the lower animals. Why should not the fair heroine, Adet, daughter of the tortoise, be the daughter of human parents? The tale would be none the less interesting, and a good deal more credible to the mature intelligence. But the ancient fashion of animal parentage is presented. It may have originated, like the stories of the Australians, at a time when men were totemists, when every person had a bestial or vegetable "family-name," and when, to account for these hereditary names, stories of descent from a supernatural, bestial, primeval race were invented. In the fables of the world, speaking animals, human in all but outward aspect, are the characters. The fashion is universal among savages; it descends to the Buddha's *jataka*, or parables, to Æsop and La Fontaine. There could be no such fashion if fables had originated among civilised human beings.

The polity of the people who tell this story seems to be despotic. The king makes a law that any girl prettier than the prince's fifty wives shall be put to death, with her parents. Who is to be the Paris, and give the fatal apple to the most fair? Obviously the prince is the Paris. He falls in love with Miss Tortoise, guided to her as he is by the bird who is "entranced with her beauty." In this tribe, as in Homer's time, the lover offers a bride-price to the father of the girl. In Homer cattle are the current medium; in Nigeria pieces of cloth and brass rods are (or were) the currency. Observe the queen's interest in an affair of true love. Though she knows that her son's life is endangered by his honourable passion, she adds to the bride-price out of her privy purse. It is "a long courting"; four years pass, while pretty Adet is "ower young to marry yet." The king is very angry when the news of this breach of the royal marriage Act first comes to his ears. He summons the whole of his subjects, his throne, a stone, is set out in the market-place, and Adet is brought before him. He sees and is conquered.

> "It is no wonder," said the king,
> "This tortoise-girl might be a queen."

Though a despot, his Majesty, before cancelling his law, has to consult the eight Egbos, or heads of secret societies, whose magical powers give the sacred sanction to legislation. The Egbo (see p. 4, note) is a mumbo-jumbo man. He answers to the bogey who presides over the rites of initiation in the Australian tribes.

When the Egbo is about, women must hide and keep out of the way. The king proclaims the cancelling of the law. The Egbos might resist, for they have all the knives and poisons of the secret societies behind them. But the king, a master of the human heart, acts like Sir Robert Walpole. He buys the Egbo votes "with palm-wine and money," and gives a feast to the women at the marriage dances. But why does the king give half his kingdom to the tortoise? When an adventurer in fairy tales wins the hand of the king's heiress, he usually gets half the kingdom. The tortoise is said to have been "the wisest of all men and animals." Why? He merely did not kill his daughter. But there is no temptation to kill daughters in a country where they are valuable assets, and command high bride-prices. In the Australian tribes, the bride-price is simply another girl. A man swops his sister to another man for the other man's sister, or for any girl of whose hand the other man has the disposal.

II. The second story is a very ingenious commercial parable, "Never lend money, you only make a dangerous enemy." The story also explains why bush cats eat poultry.

III. *The Woman with Two Skins* is a peculiar version of the story of the courteous Sir Gawain with his bride, hideous by day, and a pearl of loveliness by night. The Ju Ju man answers to the witch in our fairy tales and to the mother-in-law of the prince, who, by a magical potion, makes him forget his own true love. She, however, is always victorious, and the prince

> "Prepares another marriage,
> Their hearts so full of love and glee,"

and ousts the false bride, like Lord Bateman in the ballad, when Sophia came home. In this case of Lord Bateman, the scholiast (Thackeray, probably) suggests that his Lordship secured the consent of the Church as the king in the tortoise story won that of the Egbos. Our tale then wanders into the fairy tale of the king who is deceived into drowning his children, in European folk-lore, because he is informed that they are puppies. The Water Ju Ju, however, saves these black princes, and brings forward the rightful heir very dramatically at a wrestling match, where the lad overthrows more than he thought, like Orlando in *As You Like It*, and conquers the heart of the jealous queen as well as his athletic opponents.

In the conclusion the jealous woman is handed over to the ecclesiastical arm of the Egbos; she is flogged, and, as in the case of Jeanne d'Arc, is burned alive, "and her ashes were thrown into the river." Human nature is much the same everywhere.

IV. *The King's Magic Drum.*—The drum is the mystic cauldron of ancient Welsh romance, which "always provides plenty of good food and drink." But the drum has its drawback, the food "goes bad" if its owner steps over a stick in the road or a fallen tree, a tabu like the *geisas* of ancient Irish legends. The tortoise, in this tale, has the *geisas* power; he can make the king give him anything he chooses to ask. This very queer constraint occurs constantly in the Cuchullain cycle of Irish romances, and in *The Black Thief*. (You can buy it for a penny in Dublin, or read it in Thackeray's *Little Tour in Ireland*.)

The King is constrained to part with the drum, but does not tell the tortoise about the tabu and the drawback. The tortoise, though disappointed, at least pays his score off in public, and then the tale wanders into the *Hop o' my Thumb* formula, and the trail of ashes. Finally the story, like most stories, explains the origin of an animal peculiarity, why tortoises live under prickly tie-tie palms. That explanation was clearly in the author's mind from the first, but to reach his point he adopted the formula of the mystic object, drum or cauldron, which provides endless supplies, and has a counteracting charm attached to it, a tabu.

V. *Ituen and the King's Wife.*—Some of these tales have this peculiarity, that the characters possess names, as Ituen, Offiong, and Attem. They are thus what people call *sagas*, not mere *Märchen*. All the pseudo-historic legends of the Greek states, of Thebes, Athens, Mycenæ, Pylos, and so on, are folk-tales converted into saga, and adapted and accepted as historical. Some of these Nigerian fairy-tales are in the same cast. The story of Athamas of Iolcos and the sacrifice of any of his descendants who went into the town hall, exactly corresponds to the fate of the family of Ituen (p. 32).[1] The whole Athamas story, in Greece, is a tissue of popular tales found in every part of the world. This Ituen story, as usual, explains the habits of animals, vultures, and dogs, and illustrates the awful cruelties of Egbo law.

VI. *The Pretty Stranger* is a native variant of *Judith and Holofernes*.

---

1   See the Platonic dialogue, Minos, 315-6, and Athamas in Roscher's *Lexikon*.

VII. A "Just So Story," a myth to explain the ways of animals. The cauldron of Medea, which destroyed the wrong old person, and did not rejuvenate him, is introduced. "All the stories have been told," all the world over.

VIII. *The Disobedient Daughter who Married a Skull.*—This is most original; though all our ballads and tales about the pretty girl who is carried to the land of the dead by her lover's ghost (Bürger's *Lenore*) have the same fundamental idea. Then comes in the common moral, the Reward of Courtesy, as in Perrault's *Les Fées*. But the machinery of the Nigerian romance leads up to the Return of Proserpine from the Dead in a truly fanciful way.

IX. *The King who Married the Cock's Daughter* is Æsop's man who married the woman that had been a cat. As Adia unen pecks at the corn, the other lady caught and ate a mouse.

X. *The Woman, the Ape, and the Child.*—This tale illustrates Egbo juridicature very powerfully, and is told to account for Nigerian marriage law.

XI. *The Fish and the Leopard's Wife.*—Another "Just So Story."

XII. *The Bat.*—Another explanation of the nocturnal habits of the bat. The tortoise appears as the wisest of things, like the hare in North America, Brer Rabbit, the Bushman Mantis insect, and so on.

XIII., XIV., XV. All of these are explanatory "Just So Stories."

XVI. *Why the Sun and Moon live in the Sky.*—Sun and Moon, in savage myth, lived on earth at first, but the Nigerian explanation of their retreat to the sky is, as far as I know, without parallel elsewhere.

XVII., XVIII. "Just So Stories."

XIX. Quite an original myth of Thunder and Lightning: much

below the divine dignity of such myths elsewhere. Thunder is not the Voice of Zeus or of Baiame the Father (Australian), but of an old sheep! The gods have not made the Nigerians poetical.

XX. Another "Just So Story."

XXI. *The Cock who caused a Fight* illustrates private war and justice among the natives, and shows the Egbos refusing to admit the principle of a fine in atonement for an offence.

XXII. *The Affair of the Hippopotamus and of the Tortoise.*—A very curious variant of the *Whuppitie Stoorie*, or Tom-Tit-Tot story, depending on the power conferred by learning the secret name of an opponent. These secret names are conferred at Australian ceremonies. Any amount of the learning about secret names is easily accessible.

XXIII. *Why Dead People are Buried.*—Here we meet the Creator so common in the religious beliefs of Africans as of most barbarous and savage peoples. "The Creator was a big chief." The Euahlayi Baiame is rendered "Big Man" by Mrs. Langloh Parker (see The *Euahlayi Tribe*). The myth is one of world-wide diffusion, explaining The Origin of Death, usually by the fable of a message, forgotten and misrendered, from the Creator.

XXIV. *The Fat Woman who Melted Away.*—The revival of this beautiful creature, from all that was left of her, the toe, is an incident very common in folk-tales, i.e. the Scottish *Rashin Coatie*. (The word "dowry" is used throughout where "bride-price" would better express the institution. The Homeric ἕνα is meant.)

XXV. *The Leopard, the Squirrel, and the Tortoise.*—A "Just So Story."

XXVI. *Why the Moon Waxes and Wanes.*—A lunar myth; not a poetical though a kindly explanation of the habits of the moon.

XXVII. *The Story of the Leopard, the Tortoise, and the Bush Rat.*—A "Just So Story."

XXVIII. *The King and the JuJu Tree.*—This is a fine example of Ju Ju beliefs, and of an extraordinary sacrifice to a Ju Ju power located in a tree. Goats, chickens, and white men are common offerings, but "seven baskets of flies" might propitiate Beelzebub. The "spirit-man" who can succeed when sacrifice fails, chooses the king's daughter as his reward, as is usual in *Märchen.* Compare Melampus and Pero in Greece. The skull in spirit-land here plays a friendly part, in advising the princess, like Proserpine, not to eat among the dead. This caution is found everywhere—in the Greek version of Orpheus and Eurydice, in the *Kalewala,* and in Scott's "Wandering Willie's Tale," in *Redgauntlet.* Like Orpheus, the girl is not to look back while leaving spirit-land. Her successful escape, by obeying the injunctions of the skull, is unusual.

XXIX. *How the Tortoise overcame the Elephant and the Hippopotamus.*—A "Just So Story," with the tortoise as cunning as Brer Rabbit.

XXX. *Of the Pretty Girl and the Seven Jealous Women.*—Here the good little bird plays the part of the popinjay who "up and spake" with good effect in the first ballads. The useful Ju Ju man divines by casting lots, a common method among the Zulus. The revenge of the pretty girl's father is certainly adequate.

XXXI. *How the Cannibals drove the People from Insofan Mountain to the Cross River (Ikom).*—This professes to be historical, and concerns human sacrifices, "to cool the new yams," and cannibalism.

XXXII. is unimportant.

In XXXIII. we find the ordeal poison, which destroys fifty witches.

XXXIV. *The Slave Girl who tried to Kill her Mistress* is a form of our common tale of the waiting-maid who usurps the place of her mistress, the Bride. The resurrection of the Bride from the water, at the cry of her little sister, occurs in a remote quarter, among the Samoyeds in Castren's *Samoyedische Märchen*, but there the opening is in the style of *Asterinos and Pulja (Phrixus and Helle)* in Van Hahn's *Griechische Märchen*. The False Bride story is, in an ancient French *chanson de geste*, part of the legend of the mother of Charlemagne. The story also occurs in Callaway's collection of Zulu fairy tales. In the Nigerian version the manners, customs, and cruelties are all thoroughly West African.

XXXV. *The King and the 'Nsiat Bird* accounts, as usual, for the habits of the bird; and also illustrates the widespread custom of killing twins.

XXXVI. reflects the well-known practices of poison and the ordeal by poison.

XXXVII. is another "Just So Story."

XXXVIII. *The Drummer and the Alligators.*—In this grim tale of one of the abominable secret societies the human alligators appear to be regarded as being capable of taking bestial form, like werewolves or the leopards of another African secret society.

XXXIX. and XL. are both picturesque "Just So Stories," so common in the folk-lore of all countries.

The most striking point in the tales is the combination of good humour and good feeling with horrible cruelties, and the reign of terror of the Egbos and lesser societies. European influences can scarcely do much harm, apart from whisky, in Nigeria. As to religion, we do not learn that the Creator receives any sacrifice: in savage and barbaric countries He usually gets none. Only Ju Jus, whether ghosts or fiends in general, are propitiated. The Other is "too high and too far."

I have briefly indicated the stories which have variants in ancient myth and European *Märchen* or fairy tales.

END OF VOLUME ONE

IKOM FOLK STORIES FROM
FROM
SOUTHERN NIGERIA

Preface

THESE FOLK STORIES have been told to me by natives of the various countries to which they relate in the Ikom district of Southern Nigeria. In all cases they have had to be translated by an interpreter, and frequently it has been found necessary to employ two. Some of the stories are very old and have been handed down from one generation to another, but it is most difficult, almost impossible, to judge with any degree of accuracy how old they really are. The word "dowry" comes frequently into these tales, and is used as meaning the amount paid to the parents of the girl by the husband. In the introduction to my *Folk Stories from Southern Nigeria,* published in 1910, Mr. Andrew Lang suggests that the term "bride-price" would better express the institution, and, no doubt, he is perfectly right. I have, however, adhered to the old expression of "dowry" as it is in general use, and is so well known on the "Coast." When a man is asked how much "dowry" he paid for his wife, he will frequently produce his "bush book", consisting of bundles of small sticks tied round with "tie-tie", one bundle for each year. He will then take one stick from a bundle, and holding it up will say: "That is two calabashes of tombo I gave to the father." He will then place the stick on the ground and take another, saying "This is one fathom of cloth I gave to the girl." The next stick may represent twenty yams given to the mother, and the following sticks may mean twenty-five rods, a silk handkerchief, a bar of soap and some bottles of gin. And so he goes on until the bundles are finished, the value of each article being noted in order to ascertain the total amount paid. The marriage customs vary considerably in different parts of the district. In most of the Cross River towns above Abaragba there is no restriction placed on young girls as to sexual intercourse, but when they are married twenty-five pieces of cloth (value 5s. per piece) would be paid as damages for adultery. There is, however, an old custom existing between several towns that no damages can be claimed for adultery. It may be of interest to the reader to state here briefly the usual form of marriage in vogue in this district as the point of several of the tales turns on the position of the woman with reference to her husband or lover. I do not, however, propose to enter into details, but merely to indicate what constitutes a binding form of marriage in this part of the country according to native custom. When a man takes a fancy to a young girl and wishes to marry her, he informs the parents of his intention, and gives them presents. For example, the mother would receive a piece of cloth, and the father a piece of cloth and two bottles of gin. The brothers and sisters of the girl would be given *tombo* to drink, and in addition the sisters would receive one fathom of cloth each. The man would work on the parents' farm for some months, and the girl would receive small presents from time to time. Later the mother would be given two bars of salt, one spoon, one bar of soap, and twenty yams, the balance of the dowry being paid on the completion of the marriage ceremony. The girl would go and live with the man. If she did not prove satisfactory, she would be returned to her parents, who would refund the amount of dowry received up to date, and the girl would be given a present of about 8s.; she could then marry another man. If, however, she satisfied the man, he would then have her circumcized by her parents, and the man would touch her with camwood. Having done this he would hand the girl over to his best friend to rub all over with camwood. The man would then build a house for the woman, being helped with the mudding of the walls by his sisters and the sisters of the girl. He would then buy two pieces of cloth and one blanket, and hang them round the walls of the house. While the girl was being rubbed with camwood the friends of the husband would give her presents of sometimes four or five rods each, and his best friend would fire off a gun in the compound where the girl was. When the parents heard the gun, they would go in and say: "There is your wife, we have handed her over to you." The man would then tell everybody that the girl was his wife. The girl would remain in one room for about two weeks after the above mentioned operation, until the wound was healed, and then the man would give a feast to all his friends, the cost of the food forming part of the dowry. The girl would then go to live with her husband, and the ceremony would be completed.

There appears to be a considerable divergence of opinion between the chiefs and the young men as to whom the children brought forth by a woman before her marriage should belong. Most of the old chiefs say that such children should go to the man who marries the mother and pays the dowry, as children are a valuable asset. On the other hand, the younger generation maintain that when the children are old enough to leave their mother they should be handed over to their proper fathers. This conflict of opinion is not difficult to follow, as the young men are generally the fathers of the children born before marriage, and the old chiefs who are wealthy are generally the husbands, and both the putative fathers and the lawful husbands are anxious to possess the children. It is a vexed question, and each case would be decided upon its own merits, the opinion of the parents of the woman weighing largely in the balance. This opinion is influenced to a great extent by the value of the presents received from the young man and how much he has helped the parents with their work on the farm. If the parents were satisfied, they would probably say that the child or children should belong to the father, but if, on the other hand, the presents were not large enough, they would most likely urge that the children of their daughter born before she was married should belong to her lawful husband. It should be remembered that the feelings of the girl are in no way considered, and she is handed to the man, as a wife, who is in a position to pay the largest amount of dowry. It is therefore often somewhat difficult to distinguish the difference between the dowry paid for a girl on her marriage and the price which was formerly paid for a slave, seeing that the inclinations of the girl are not consulted and she has absolutely no say in the matter of a choice of husband. When the dowry is paid she is taken away from her lover, together with any children she may have had by him, and handed over to the husband by her parents, the question of the rightful ownership of the children being settled usually when they are old enough to leave their mother. In the olden days when "might was right", these children were taken by the husband, who kept them by the "strong hand" if he were sufficiently powerful; but there is a growing feeling amongst the younger chiefs and the more intelligent trading classes that the children born before marriage should be given to the father when they are weaned.

It will be observed on perusing some of these stories that in several of them the greater part of the tale has nothing, apparently, to do with the main object, which frequently might be dismissed in a few sentences. But that will not surprise anyone who knows the native well, as he can never come to the point at once, but must always first beat about the bush. For example, a native will come to make a complaint that certain goods belonging to him have been stolen and he wants to have the thief punished. After the usual salutations have been exchanged, he will make his complaint, which when translated by the interpreter will be something like the following: "My father and father (grandfather) catch one man goat and one woman goat. They done born two piccane. One piccane done die and leff one piccane. Them piccane, them leff, born two piccane. My father and father done die and him brother take all them thing; but he be big hunter man and no care them goat too much, so he done dash my father. My father catch one slave man, they call 'im Okon and he good man, so my father clash him them two goat. Okon catch wife and two piccane. One he mammie piccane, they call 'im Awa, she fine too much, when she done grow I marry her proper and take her brother Abassi for make my head boy. Last moon I send him Calabar for my canoe with twenty bag kernel and one puncheon palm oil. I tell 'im for factory and bring tobacco and cloth and gin. He done catch them thing and one night he stop for one country, he no know how them call him. Them people come and thief them gin for night time but he no look them man cause he live for sleep, so I make them boy pay for them gin and now I want catch them thief man."

Anyone who takes the trouble to read these folk stories seriously will notice that a great deal has to be taken for granted or understood. Although I have made a special study of witchcraft, ju-ju, and poison, and the various societies in this district for over nine years, I must confess that I understand and *know* for certain very little about ju-ju. In fact, the more one learns about ju-ju the more hopeless it seems. It must seem incredible to people at home that a man can die because a ju-ju has been made against him – for example, two sticks crossed on the path with, say, a rotten egg and a fowl stuck on astick, the man's name having been "called".And yet one knows of numerous instances where men have died, and young, healthy men, too, against whom such a ju-ju has been made. The man whose name has been "called" and who has passed the ju-ju firmly believes in its power to kill him, and he will go home, refuse to eat, and in a short time will pine away and die. He will probably also just before he dies accuse the man whom he thinks made the ju-ju of having witched him. It is always possible, of course, in these cases, that poison may have been administered, but it is most difficult to get any proof. No amount of argument has any effect on the native mind, and you cannot convince the man that a ju-ju, such as the one mentioned above, is harmless. They generally reply: "Black man ju-ju no be strong enough to hurt white man, but black man he go die one time."

When I first came to this district, poisoning was rife, and human sacrifices were of frequent occurrence. Whenever a chief died several slaves were killed and buried with him, and it was no uncommon thing for a whole family to accuse another family of witchcraft.

They would then resort to the usual trial by ordeal of burning oil and *essure* (poison) bean, which would result in several deaths. These evil practices have been practically stopped now, but the native belief in witchcraft and ju-ju is just as strong as ever, although they know quite well that, to call a man a witch is an offence for which they will get into trouble. As an instance of the native belief in the witchbird (the owl), I would mention a case which came under my notice. Some few years ago I happened to be having some bush cleared and some large trees cut down on the station at Okuni. An owl was disturbed from one of the trees which was covered with creepers, and flew out hooting. One of the station labourers who knew a little English, said: "Poor Okuni!" I at once asked him why he said so, and he replied, "When them witch bird cry for daytime, some man go die." I said, "Nonsense," or something to that effect, and thought no more about it. Shortly afterwards the eleven o'clock bell rang, and the boys went home for food. When they returned at one o'clock to work, the boy who had spoken about the owl said, "Man done die for Okuni when them witch bird cry." I then sent to the town and found that a man had died in the morning. This was proof positive to the boy's mind that whenever the owl hooted in the daytime a man would die, and no amount of explanation would alter his belief. It was a case of "I told you so."

It is noteworthy that when you get over the watershed between the Cross River and the Katsena (Niger), and into the Munchi country, ju-ju does not seem to exist in the same way as it does further south. In the year 1909, while I was Political Officer on the Anglo-German Boundary Commission, I marched up through the

Munchi country into Northern Nigeria, and back again, being absent from my district altogether about six months. During the whole of that time there was not a single death in any of the Munchi or Domi towns where I stayed. It was so noticeable that even the soldiers and carriers remarked upon the absence of deaths, and could not understand the reason. It may have been that the country was more healthy, and we may have been very fortunate, but the fact remains that where there was no ju-ju there were no deaths, and when we returned to the country of ju-ju deaths were of frequent occurrence.

It has been suggested in one of the criticisms on my *Folk Stories from Southern Nigeria,* that the native words should be given on one side of the page, and a fairly literal translation on the other. This would, however, involve a larger expenditure of time than I have at my disposal. There are ten different languages spoken in this district, and it would be extremely difficult to give exact translations of the stories, particularly as some of them as told would be quite unfit for publication. The stories have, however, been set down as nearly as possible in the way they were related to me, the only alterations made being those necessary to render the tales into simple English, as bush English would not be understood, and certain passages containing objectionable matter have been omitted.

In some of the stories it may be noticed that articles such as plates, glasses, bottles of gin, brass pans, and pots have been mentioned, also the use of locks and keys has been introduced into at least one of the tales, although it is quite obvious that the above-mentioned articles could not have existed in this country when the majority of the stories were first related, I have written them down when they were so translated by the interpreter. It is not difficult to understand how some of the things crept into the stories. For example, demijons (which are brought up river from Calabar filled with rum) are used every day in most of the towns for tombo, and glass tumblers are also quite common, and it is easily conceivable that a native, who is accustomed to using these articles, in relating a story might say in his language the equivalent for "The pourer-out then took the demijon of tombo and poured some into a glass which he gave to the chief," instead of saying, "The pourer-out then poured some tombo from the calabash into the drinking-horn which he handed to the chief." The latter translation would probably be far nearer to the original version. It is also extremely doubtful whether brass rods, which are mentioned so frequently, existed at the date of many of the stories. The approximate date of the importation of rods into this country is probably known, and cannot be more than about sixty years ago, and most likely considerably less. The author is of the opinion that in the early days there was no form of native currency in the Ikom district. At the present time, rods are not used furthernorth-east from Ikom than Umbaji, and in 1909, whilst on the AngloGerman Boundary Commission, he found that there was no form of native currency at Bassankwala, and no substitute therefore, with the possible exception of a few native forged iron hoes which found their way down from the north-west, and had a fixed marketable value. But the use of these implements is doubtless of a comparatively recent date, as nearly all the natives in that part use wooden hoes lashed on to the bent handles with tie-tie. In the country mentioned, all trade was and is still done by a system of barter and exchange. The Umbaji people exchanging salt and *house rats* (which form an article of diet for the Bassankwala people, who are cannibals) for palm oil and yams. The Bassankwala people admitted to the author that they ate human beings, and had always done so, but they asserted vehemently that they did not eat their own dead – these they passed on to the next town, who sent them theirs in exchange. Prisoners taken in fighting or people killed were also eaten, and, from what the adjoining countries told the author, natives straying into their bush were similarly treated. These people, however, all promised, and were apparently perfectly sincere, at once to stop this abominable practice, at the same time saying that they were unaware they had been doing wrong, as they had never heard the white man's laws before.

It is perhaps noteworthy that these people, who are pure cannibals, all file their teeth to a sharp point.

With reference to the eating of rats, it may be remarked that all the natives in the Ikom district eat the bush rat, which is quite different from the house or domestic species, but the Bassankwala people are the only natives the author has met who eat the "common or garden" house rat. The large fruit-eating bats, about which so many native stories are told, are looked upon as a great delicacy, and at Insofan on the Cross River, there is quite a trade done in them, one bat selling for one rod or sixpence in English money. In the evening, just before it gets dark, you can frequently see thousands of these bats flying off, high up in theair, to their favourite feeding places. The way they are obtained for food is simple and may be worth mentioning. On the bank opposite to Insofan there are some very tall trees covered with creepers, in which many thousands of these bats sleep during the day. A few hunters go out with their long Dane guns and station themselves one under each tree. Then when one man has found a thick cluster of bats, he fires into them, and with luck brings down a few. (The author has killed seven at one shot, with number 6 from a full choke 12-bore, at the particular request of a chief who wanted them for food.)

Immediately the bats hear the gun fired, they desert the trees they are sheltering in, and commence circling around in the air, flying about in a most aimless and erratic sort of way, until, after about ten minutes, they settle on a different tree. Then another hunter fires, and so the game goes on. In connectionwith these creatures, it is curious to notice the agitation amongst the birds, should one happen to be disturbed in the day time. The same applies to the large eagleowls, who are invariably chased by the smaller birds, whenever they appear while the sun is up, but it is seldom the owl comes out in the day time, and then he takes shelter in some thick covert as soon as possible.

Elphinstone Dayrell

I.

How an Inkum Woman Abandoned
One of Her Twins in the Forest,
and How it was Saved by the Hawk

Awu was a native woman of Inkum, a town on the right bank of the Cross River, consisting of five compounds separate one from another by about half a mile of bush. Awu was a fine girl, but preferred to enjoy herself as she liked rather than to get married, which would mean too hard work. She used to walk from one town to another, and attend all the dances and plays, as she was a good singer and dancer. She always wore a cloth of the latest pattern, and a silk handkerchief round her head, with plenty of hairs from the elephant's tail round her neck, and strings of beads round her waist. She also wore a piece of black braid tied round each ankle, and some rings on her fingers. These are the signs of a girl who is popular with young men. Awu had men friends in every town she visited, but she never stayed long with any of them, being what is called a "walking woman".

At last she conceived, and when she was about eight months gone with child she happened one day to go into the forest to gather firewood to cook her morning food. While she was thus engaged a branch fell from a tree and hit her on the belly, this immediately brought on her confinement, and she gave birth to twins in the forest. The first born was a girl, to whom she gave the name of Aro, and the second was a boy, whom she named Agbor. When Awn found that she had given birth to twins she was very much ashamed of herself, and was afraid to take both the babies back to the town as they would be killed by the people, and she would be turned out of the town and left to starve in the bush. She therefore decided to take the first-born child Aro back with her, but Agbor she left on the ground underneath a tree.

Very soon after Awu had departed, the driver ants discovered Agbor and quickly covered him, commencing to eat him. The bites of the driver ants made the child cry. All this time a hawk had been circling around, high up in the air, searching for food, and when he saw Awu had deserted her baby he swooped down and carried the infant off with him to the top of a high tree. The hawk, seeing what a fine child Agbor was, thought he would try to save his life, and immediately set about removing the ants from Agbor's body. He lit a fire and boiled some water, with which he washed the child, and the ants very quickly disappeared.

The hawk looked after Agbor until he grew up. One day Awu sent her daughter Aro to get her some fire, and Aro, after wandering about, eventually found herself at the hawk's house, where she saw Agbor sitting down.

Aro was so taken with Agbor's good looks that she continued to stare at him without speaking, until at last Agbor said, "Why do you look at me like that?" but Aro did not reply, and picked up some fire, continuing to stare at Agbor. Then he repeated his question, and added, "Do I resemble either your father or your mother? If so, let the fire you are holding go out," and the fire went out at once. Aro then took up some more fire, and Agbor put the same question to her again, and the fire Aro was holding went out a second time. This was done three times, each time with the same result. Then Aro ran home to her mother and reported what she had seen, and said what a fine boy Agbor was.

When Awu, the mother, heard about the fire, she knew at once that Agbor must be her son whom she had deserted and left to die in the forest. She therefore made up her mind that she would go and see him. The following morning, therefore, she rose at first cock crow and went to the hawk's house, where she found Agbor and took a great fancy to him. Awu wanted to get Agbor away from the hawk and keep him for herself, but did not quite see how it could be done.

At last she thought of the porcupine, who was wellknown throughout the country as a clever and resourceful person, and went to him and told her story.

Now, the porcupine was a lot caster, and when he had cast lots he decided that the best thing that Awu could do was to go to a house and lie down, pretending to be dead. The porcupine told her that, if she did this, directly the hawk heard that she was dead he would send Agbor to his dead mother's side to mourn for her. Then Awu would be able to seize him. The mother having paid the porcupine for his advice went away, and did what she had been told to do. When the hawk heard that Awu was dead he told Agbor that the next day he should go and cry at his mother's side, so, when the morning came, the hawk dressed Agbor up and he started off to cry.

When he arrived at the house Agbor wanted to sit at the head of his mother, but the people who had assembled would not allow this, and told him to sit at Awu's feet, which Agbor did. Directly he sat down, his mother jumped up and seized him, and said she would not let him go again.

Very soon afterwards, the hawk arrived on the scene to take Agbor away, but his mother would not part with him. Then the hawk became angry, and addressed the people, as follows:–

"Here is a 'walking woman' who, several years ago, gave birth to twins in the forest, and, being naturally ashamed of herself, deserted her baby boy, and left him on the ground to be eaten by the driver ants. I saved the boy's life and have brought him up and fed him. I now demand that he shall be returned to me at once."

When the people heard this, they said to the hawk: "If you will let Awu have her son back we will give you a slave in his place", but the hawk refused this offer indignantly.

Then they offered him cows, sheep, goats, and pigs, all of which the hawk refused with scorn.

The people then suggested giving some cocks and hens to the hawk, to which he replied that, although he would not accept them for Agbor, they were getting nearer to what he possibly might accept.

At last the people offered him a large basket of eggs, whereupon the hawk immediately closed the bargain, handed over Agbor to his mother, and flew away with the basket of eggs in his claws.

The next morning early the hawk started off with his basket of eggs, and left one egg in every house all round the country, until all the eggs in the basket were exhausted. He then returned home in the evening with the empty basket.

After a few months had elapsed, the hawk said to himself: "The time has now come for me to take my revenge upon the people for taking my boy Agbor from me."

So he flew from town to town, taking chickens from every compound.

This is the reason why hawks always take chickens wherever they find them, and in those days the people never thought of making any trouble with the hawk, as he had a right to the chickens, but nowadays when a hawk swoops down and seizes a chicken, the people shout out and try to kill him, as they have forgotten the story of how the twin child Agbor was redeemed by a basket of eggs.

This story was related by a native of Inkum called Abassi. [E.D., 25.5.10.]

ll.

The Cunning Hare; or,
Why the Tortoise has a Patched Shell

The hare *(asima bieso,* native name) was known to everyone as a very cunning animal. He was very fond of meat, although he was unable to kill anything himself. He therefore thought out a scheme by which he would be able to obtain meat without any trouble.

The first thing the hare did was to call all the animals together, and when they arrived, be said: "We ought to have a king over us," to which the animals agreed, and, after some discussion, the elephant was chosen. A law was also passed, at the hare's suggestion, that a piece of ground at the roadside should be set aside for the king's own private use, and that if anyone was caught defiling this piece of ground in anyway he should be killed and eaten.

In the night time the hare went to the king's private piece of ground and made a mess there.

When the morning came he hid himself in the bush near the place, in order to see who might be the first animal to pass the piece of ground, so that he could give false information against him.

After he had been waiting for a short time, a bush cat passed on his way to the farm, whereupon the hare jumped up and said:

"Have you visited the king's piece of ground this morning?" Upon the bush cat saying "No," the hare ordered him to go there at once. He did so, and returned saying that the place was very dirty indeed. The hare then said: "How is that possible? I visited the place myself this morning, and it was quite clean then. You must have defiled it yourself, and I shall report you."

The hare then ran into the town and told the people what he had seen. The big wooden drum was then beaten, and when all the animals had come together the bush cat was put upon his defence.

The bush cat told the people what had happened, and that he had nothing to do with the matter. But the hare stood up as the accuser, and the people decided that the bush cat was guilty, and the king ordered him to be killed, and said that the meat was to be dried by Keroho and brought to him in the morning.

Now, Keroho is a fruit-eating animal, who is very lazy, and sleeps most of the day. He always seems tired, and after he has taken a few steps he lies down, and sleeps for a time.

The hare had suggested to the king that Keroho should be told to dry and guard the meat, and said to the king that, as Keroho only eat fruit, he would not be likely to steal any of the meat.

In reality the hare suggested Keroho for a very different reason, and that reason was that Keroho was a fat animal in good condition, and far too lazy and sleepy to guard the meat properly.

When the evening came, Keroho made a fire and cut up the body of the bush cat and set it out to dry. He then went to sleep.

The hare, being very greedy and fond of meat, wanted to have it all to himself, so, when all the people had gone to bed, he slipped out of his house by the backway, and very soon had taken the dried meat out of Keroho's yard and returned to his house, where he made a good meal, and buried what he could not eat.

Early in the morning the hare went and beat the big drum to call the animals together at the king's house.

Keroho, hearing the drum, got up and went to the fire in his back yard, where he had left the meat drying, and, to his intense astonishment, found that it had vanished. He was very frightened at this, and went to the meeting trembling in every limb. He tried to explain that he had left the meat before the fire when he went to bed, but the hare got up at once and said, "Do not believe him, most likely he has sold the meat to get some money. I propose that Keroho be killed so that we shall not lose our meat."

All the people agreed to this, so Keroho was killed and cutup, the meat being given to the bush cow to keep.

The hare, in order to make himself acquainted with the bush cow's house, waited until sundown, and then went to the bush cow's house with a large calabash of strong tombo. The hare was careful to drink only a little himself, and very soon the bush cow had finished the whole calabash.

That night the bush cow slept very soundly, and at midnight, when nothing could be heard but the occasional hoot of an owl or the croaking of the frogs in the marsh, the hare went very quietly and stole the meat from the bush cow's fire and took it home with him, as before.

The following morning he beat the drum as usual, and the people met together. The bush cow, failing to produce the meat, was killed by the king's order and his meat given to another animal to dry.

As usual, the hare stole the meat at night and the animal was killed the next day. This went on until there were only seven animals left.

The meat of the last animal that was killed was handed over to the tortoise. The tortoise at once placed his wife on guard over the meat, and went off into the bush to cut rubber.

Now, the tortoise was looked upon as one of the wisest of all animals. For some time it had seemed to him very curious that every night the meat should disappear and another animal should be killed. He therefore determined that, when it became his turn to dry and guard the meat, he would take every precaution possible, and would try to catch whoever it was who always removed the meat at night, as he had no intention that his body should supply food for the remaining six animals.

Before going into the bush, he gave his wife strict injunctions not to let the meat out of her sight.

When he returned in the evening, he cut up the meat, saying as he did so: "Ah, there goes another poor animal. I wonder whose turn it will be tomorrow, but it shall not be mine if I can help it."

So he made a big fire and put the meat on, and then covered it all over with the rubber he had brought back with him from the bush.

The tortoise then told his wife that he was tired, and went to bed pretending to be asleep, but he had one eye open all the time, and that eye he kept fixed upon the meat, as he was not going to take any risks, knowing full well that, if the meat disappeared, as it had a habit of doing, he himself would be the next victim.

When all was quiet, and the hare thought everybodyhad gone to sleep,he went round to the back of the tortoise's house and put his right hand out to take the meat, but when his hand closed on the rubber, he found that he could not remove it because the rubber was so sticky. He tried his hardest to get his hand away, but without success. He then called out softly, because he was afraid of waking the tortoise, "Let me go! Let me go!" but the rubber never answered, and held on tighter than ever. This made the hare angry, so he whispered to the rubber, "Look here, if you don't let my right hand go at once I will hit you very hard with my left hand, and then you will be sorry." He got no reply, but thought he heard a laugh somewhere. The hare then hit the rubber with his disengaged hand as hard as he was able, and that hand also stuck fast.

Then the hare heard the tortoise murmur, "Yes, tomorrow I will discover that rat who is always stealing the king's meat."

At length the hare became absolutely terrified, and kicked the rubber hard with one of his feet, which became as fast as his hands were, and very shortly the other foot also became caught up, so that he was held quite securely.

When the morning came, the tortoise called his wife to help him, and together they put, the meat and rubber into a basket with the hare on top, and carried them all to the king's house.

When the drum was beaten, the people assembled as usual, and discussed amongst themselves to whom the meat of the tortoise should be given when he was killed. In the middle of the discussion, the tortoise appeared carrying the meat with the hare on top.

The tortoise then charged the hare with attempting to steal

the king's meat,and told the people of the trap he had set. The hare was found guilty, and was ordered to pay a large number of brass rods, and he was told that if they were not forthcoming, he would be killed, and that his mother and sister would be killed with him, as he had been the cause of the death of so many animals.

The hare begged for a little time to enable him to get the rods, which was allowed to him.

He then ran home and got his mother and sister to come with him at once to the foot of a big cotton tree, and, having got a rope round the lowest branch, he very soon got to the top of the tree, where he built a small hut for himself and his people.

The hare then went down to the lowest branch where the rope was, and hauled his mother and sister up. He put them in the hut at the top of the tree, and sat down himself next to the rope with a sharp knife in his hand.

As the hare did not appear at the appointed time to pay the rods, the people went to his house, and found that they had all disappeared. It did not take long, however, to discover that he had taken refuge in the cotton tree, so they all went there and found the rope hanging down.

Then they all began to climb the rope together, leaving the tortoise on the ground, and just as he was about to commence to climb, the others having already reached halfway, the hare cut the rope with one cut of his sharp knife, and all the animals fell down upon the tortoise, smashing his smooth shell into small pieces, and hurting themselves very much. No one was killed, however, and they limped home one after the other.

On the way they passed the tortoise's house, so they told Mrs. Tortoise that they had fallen on her husband from a great height, and that his shell was broken into pieces.

On hearing this the mammie tortoise got her basket and went off to the cotton tree. Having picked up all the pieces of her husband's shell, and having placed them in the basket, she lifted the tortoise and carried them all home.

When she got inside she put all the little pieces of the shell together and placed them on her husband's back, where they grew quite strongly, but the marks showed where the pieces were joined together, and that is why you always find that the shell of a tortoise is covered in patches, and not smooth as it was formerly.

Told by Abassi, an Inkum boy. [E.D.,26.5.10.]

NOTE.
The Inkum people came from a country about five or six days' march north west of the site of their present town, where hares abound. There are no hares in the country now occupied by them on the Cross River. This is one of their old stories, which they brought with them when they were driven south by the Awala tribe, and is still handed on from one generation to another.

LLL.

The Story of Igiri and her husband Inkang, who brought up a Mushroom Baby Boy, and what became of Him

Chief Inkang of Inkum was married to a woman named Igiri. She was a fine well-made woman, and the chief was so fond of her that he would not have any other wives.

Igiri was quite faithful to her husband, and never went with other men. They lived together for several years without having any children, much to their mutual grief.

Inkang then told his wife to consult the ju-ju man, to see what should be done, in order that she might bear a son who would inherit his father's property and look after his mother in her old age. The ju-ju man was consulted by Igiri, and the usual sacrifices of fowls and eggs were made, but without any result.

When the time for collecting mushrooms arrived, which is the beginning of the rainy season, about the month of May, Igiri went out with her basket to collect mushrooms for their food, and her husband went with her.

When they arrived at the forest they separated, Igiri going in one direction and Inkang going off in another, but not so far away that they could not hear one another shout.

Igiri went on gathering the mushrooms and putting them in her basket, until at last she came across a very large mushroom which was fat and white. Then Igiri said, "How I do wish that this mushroom would turn into a boy baby, which we want so badly."

The mushroom, who was kind-hearted, then took pity on Igiri, and turned itself into a boy baby, much to the joy of the woman, who at once picked the baby up and placed him in her basket with the mushrooms.

Without troubling to look for any more mushrooms, she put the basket on her head and called out to her husband, saying she was going home at once, and that he was to follow.

When she reached the house, she was so pleased at having got the baby, that she asked Inkang to help her down with the basket. At this he was rather surprised, as, although it is the custom for anyone near to help the women to put down their heavy loads when they come in from the farm, this would not be done with a light load like mushrooms.

Inkang therefore said to his wife, "What have you put in the basket to make it so heavy that you want me to help you down with it? Is it not mushrooms you have there?"

His wife replied, "Only help me with the basket, and you shall then see what I have got."

Inkang's curiosity was immediately aroused, so he went to his wife and helped her to place the basket carefully on the ground. Then they opened the basket together, and, to the chief's intense surprise and joy, he saw a fat little baby boy lying smiling in the bottom of the basket, half covered with mushrooms. He then embraced his wife, who told him all that had happened in the forest.

Inkang then said, "We must hide the boy in the house until he grows up, so that the people will not know what we have got."

Igiri took great care of the child for the next six years, and he grew up a strong boy.

When the planting season came round, which is towards the end of the dry season, the chief and his wife used to go off every morning early to their farm, returning in the evening. The boy was always left at home, but the woman prepared food for him and placed it high up over the fireplace, and showed the boy how to get at it by standing on a native-made box.

The first day they went to the farm the little boy got his food down and eat it, but did not notice that a small boy from the neighbouring town was watching him. The next day the small boy from the town, who was hungry (yams being scarce at that time), waited until the mushroom boy had gone out, and then went softly in and stole all the food, filling the calabash with water, which he replaced where he had found the food. This happened for three days in succession, until the mushroom boy became so hungry that he determined to go back to the forest where he came from, and turn himself back into a mushroom again. He was anrgy with Inkang and Igiri because he thought they were fooling him, and, of course, he knew nothing about the thief boy who had stolen his food each day.

On his way to the forest he met his foster parents returning from the farm, and told them what his intention was. They did their best to persuade him to return home with them, but he was obstinate, and ran away to the place in the forest where he came from, and, having arrived there, turned himself into a mushroom and disappeared forever.

Since that time the mushroom has refused to take pity on women who have no children, and he has never changed himself into a baby again.

Told by Abassi of Inkum. [E.D., 27.5.10.]

IV.

How Elili of Inkum Died, and was Brought Back to Live Again

Elili and Aikor were both Inkum women, the wives of Chief Nyip. They each had a female child by him.

Elili was the head wife and looked after the house, and for several years everything went well, until at last Elili became sick, and, after a short illness, died, and was buried.

Her daughter Oga was quite young when her mother died; her breasts were only just beginning to get round, and she had not been circumcised.

On Elili's death Aikor took charge of the house, and cooked all the food.

When it was time to hand the food round, Aikor always gave her daughter Nagor the best food, and only gave a very small portion to Oga, as she was a very jealous woman, and disliked Elili and her daughter.

This went on for some time, until one day Oga took the food which was not sufficient for her to her mother's grave, and sat there crying and calling for her mother until the evening came, when she went home. The next day she went again and wept on the grave, until at last the grave opened, and she could see the top of her mother's head. Oga continued to cry until sunset, and then she had to go home.

The following day, as soon as it was light, Oga started off again for the grave, and cried more, and by sundown her mother's head and shoulders had appeared.

The day after, by constant crying, she induced her mother to come out as far as her waist, and, after a few more days of persistent weeping, she got her mother out altogether.

As it was dusk at the time, Oga led her mother to the back of the house, and hid her in a small room which was used only for storing yams and baskets. There she remained undiscovered for three days, and then Oga went to her father and said, "If you will give me a good present, I will show you my mother alive."

Her father then gave her a piece of cloth, and Oga took him to the room where Elili was hiding, and said, "Here is my mother, who I have got alive again out of the grave."

Chief Nyip was delighted to get his favourite wife back again, and they lived together as they had done before.

Very soon after the return of Elili from the grave, Aikor died, leaving herdaughter Nagor in the charge of Elili and Oga. Elili then began to revenge herself upon Nagor for the way Oga had been treated. Nagor was made to do all the hard work of the house, and was also half starved.

This caused Nagor to go and cry on her mother's grave. After crying bitterly for three days, her mother began to come out of the grave, and on the fourth day, when Aikor's head and shoulders were showing above the ground, Nagor was so anxious to get her mother out altogether that she caught hold of her head and pulled with all her might, with the result that she pulled her mother's head off her shoulders. Nagor then took the head and placed it in the same room where Oga had put her mother Elili.

She then called her father to come, but when he saw his dead wife's head, he was very angry with Nagor, and told her to go and bury it again in the grave. Instead of doing as she was told, Nagor threw her mother's head amongst the young palm oil trees. This caused them to bear fruit which resembled a woman's head in shape and size, and even at the present time the young palm trees have bunches of fruit which look like a woman's head with the plaits of hair allround.

Told by Abassi of Inkum. [E.D.,27.5.10.]

V.

Concerning the Human Sacrifices which took Place on the Death of Chief Indoma

Chief Indoma was a very powerful chief. It was he who led the Inkum people to the site of their present town when they were driven out of their own country by the Awalas. When he arrived at the Cross River, he established the five compounds which still exist, and ruled over all the people. They were very fond of Indoma, as he was a just man.

A few years after they had built their compound, the two adjoining countries, Inde and Akparabong, made war against the Inkum, but Chief Indoma, who was skilled in warfare, led his people so well and wisely that both countries were driven back, and they have occupied the land ever since.

Indoma had two sons by his wife Isibe, whose names were Agatin and Ogum. When they were grown up, Chief Indoma died. All the country people were very sorry, and a big play was held, and the mourning was kept up for a long time.

Then a large and deep grave was dug, and a number of slaves were killed by knocking them on the head with wooden clubs. Their bodies were placed in the bottom of the grave, and Chief Indoma's body was put on top. The head chief then ordered four young men to be caught alive and bound. One was placed under lndoma's head as a pillow, another under his feet to make him more comfortable and the other two were placed one on either side of the corpse, so that it was surrounded by living boys.

Then the head chief remembered that lndoma had been very fond of a boy named Edim, so they caught him, and, having tied him up, placed him in the grave near the dead chief's head, so that he and the other four young men should be able to work for their master in the spirit land.

As the grave was very big and deep they put sticks across it, wedged firmly into the sides, planks were then placed over the sticks, and the planks were covered with sand.

By this time the grave was about half full, and the people left it until the next day, when more slaves were being brought in from the farms to be killed and put in the grave to fill it up.

When night time came, Edim, who had not been very securely fastened, called to the other four boys, and, managing to get his teeth to the tie-tie which bound the boy nearest to him, he bit it through, and the boy who was then released undid Edim's thongs, and together they freed the other three boys. Edim then made a hole in the planks and sand, and got out of the grave.

When he had helped the others out, they all ran down to the beach, where they seized a canoe and paddled clown river as hard as they could go to Akuna Muna. When they got there they presented themselves to King Egugo, and told him their story.

The King then took Edim as one of his boys, and, finding him to be intelligent, made him his head canoe boy.

After five years had elapsed Edim had made a lot of money, so he returned to Inkum with the other four boys, knowing that, even if he were recognised, he would not be killed, as the people had filled the grave with bodies the day after he had escaped.

Edim very shortly afterwards became one of the head men of the town under Agatin and Ogum. He married some wives, and had many children, and lived to a good age.

Told by Abassi of Inkum. [E.D., 27.5.10.]

Chief Indoma of Inkum, son of the powerful Chief Indoma, about whom are several stories told.

VI.

The Story of the Witch who tried to Kill her Husband; or, why Native Dogs refuse to Obey their Masters

Chief Leku of Inkum married a woman called Achor, and lived with her for some years.

At that time there was a very fine woman walking about the towns named Akoba. She was a yellow (light skin) woman, and had many hairs from the elephant's tail, and beads round her neck. She did not wear any clothes, as she preferred to walk about naked, so that everyone could see her fine skin. Akoba had very large breasts, which hung down, but this did not in any way spoil her beauty in the young men's eyes.

Many of them, including chiefs, wanted to marry her, but Akoba refused them all, as she made a lot of money out of them, and would not bind herself down to one man.

When she saw that so many men were bidding for her, she got a calabash and painted it different colours. Having placed the calabash some little distance off, Akoba said that anyone who wanted to marry her must hit the calabash with a small stone.

Many young men and chiefs tried who were anxious to possess her, but did not succeed, as she had put a ju-ju on them.

At last, however, Chief Leku managed to hit the calabash with a stone, and at once took Akoba home as his wife. He then called all the women together and held a big play, fired guns off in the town, rubbed Akoba with camwood, and told all people that she was his wife.

Akoba lived with Chief Leku for a little time, but very soon got tired of him. So she made up her mind that she would kill him and resume her former life. She said to herself, "It is very dull living with Leku all the time. If I kill him, I can have any man I fancy and make plenty of money, as all the young men want me, and are willing to pay, whereas now I have to do all the housework, and work hard on the farm, and Leku does not 'dash' me anything."

Now, Chief Leku was a hunter, and made his living by killing animals (bush cows, buck, and kobs) and selling their meat. He had five dogs who were very clever, and had been taught to follow animals by scent . When they were young, a ju-ju was made for them, and certain leaves were mashed up and rubbed on their noses, which gave them very strong smelling powers, and they could follow wounded animals in the bush, which was most useful to Chief Leku.

The morning after Akoba had made up her mind to kill her husband, she said to him, "I want you to come into the forest with me to cut some palm nuts, but leave your hunting dogs behind as I do not like them." Chief Leku, suspecting nothing, agreed, and they started off together.

When they got to the palm tree, the chief put his climbing belt of tie-tie round the tree, and, having secured it round his back, walked up to the top and commenced to cut the leaves or branches off round the nuts.

Akoba then beat her breast, and produced a sharp axe with which she began to cut down the tree, at the same time calling out to her husband that she was going to kill him. Very soon, the tree began to fall, but was fortunately caught by another tree growing near. Then Leku climbed into the other tree. Akoba, who was a witch, then started to cut down the tree in which her husband had taken refuge.

So the chief called a bird to him and sent it off with a message to his hunting dogs to come and rescue him. Immediately the dogs got the message they started off to help their master, but the witch Akoba caused a flood to overflow the path, so that the dogs could not track her. At last one of the dogs jumped into the water and swam across, and was very soon followed oy the other four.

When they reached the foot of the tree the Chief told them to kill the woman so they all leaped on her, and bit her until she died.

Then the chief came down from the tree, and divided Akoba's body into five bundles, and told his dogs to carry them to his house, which they did.

When they reached the house it, was night time, so the chief went to bed and told Achor what had happened to his new wife.

In the morning Achor saw the five bundles outside, and asked her husband how he had managed to carry them all, but he refused to tell her. So when night came and the chief went to bed, Achor said to him, "I will not sleep with you unless you tell me how you managed to carry those five bundles." Now, Chief Leku was very fond of Achor, and wanted her badly, so he gave in, and told her that his hunting dogs had carried the bundles for him. Achor then went to bed, but the next morning she rose early, and calling the dogs to follow her, she went to the farm, where she collected five bundles of firewood and placed them in a row. Then Achor said to the dogs : "If you can carry bundles for your master, you can carry my firewood. Take those loads to my house at once."

The dogs did not answer, but picked up their loads and carried them to the house. As each dog placed its load of firewood on the ground, it dropped down dead. Then the chief came out and said to Achor, "Look what you have done. All my hunting dogs are dead. This is what comes of telling you that my dogs carried the bundles for me."

Ever since that day dogs never speak or do anything for their masters, although they can understand quite well. The reason the dogs will not obey now is because they say that the chief broke their dog law when he told his wife what they did for him.

Told by Abassi of Inkum. [E.D., 27.5.10.]

VII.

How Two Friends fell out:
the Spider and the Grasshopper

Long ago the spider and the grasshopper were good friends. Unfortunately the spider was intensely greedy, and this led to much unpleasantness.

Now the spider wanted to go some distance from his house to marry a wife in a strange country, so he called upon his friend the grasshopper to accompany him. They started off together in the morning before the sun was hot, and when they had gone some little way, the spider said to his friend, "While we are away together, I want you to call me 'Stranger,' and I will call you 'Dabi.' We must not call one another by our proper names, as I do not want the people to know who we really are." To this the grasshopper readily consented, little knowing what he was letting himself in for.

Shortly afterwards they arrived at the first town, and were welcomed by the chief. The grasshopper said he was called Dabi, and introduced his friend as "Stranger."

The chief then ordered food to be placed before them, but the spider, whilst thanking the chief for his kindness, said : "Surely the custom of the country is, when a stranger arrives in a town, to first of all offer him 'the peace dish,' consisting of dried meat and kola nuts, to show that he is welcome, and that there is peace between them."

The chief replied, "Yes, there is certainly that custom here, but as I thought you were hungry after your long walk, I ordered the food to be brought at once." He then told one of his slaves to bring the dried meat and kola, and when it was brought, the spider eat all the meat and kola except two nuts, one of which he returned to the chief, and the other he gave to the grasshopper, saying, "You must wait, my friend Dabi, for your food, as this meat and kola was brought for the stranger, and your name was not mentioned.

Later on the general supply of food was passed round, a certain amount being set on one side for the strangers. This the spider also eat, saying, "I am sorry, Dabi, but there is no food for you, as this was brought for the stranger, and that is my name."

The next day they resumed their journey, and when they arrived at the town where the girl lived whom the spider was about to marry, he went to his future father-in-law's house, whose name was Tawu, and said, "Tawu, I have come to marry your daughter."

Now Tawu had a wife called Osegi, who was a very good-natured woman, which was lucky for the grasshopper as things turned out.

When Tawu had embraced his future son-in-law, he ordered a cow to be killed to welcome him. And when the people brought the food, they said, "Here is the stranger's portion." Immediately the spider said to his friend, "Did you hear that, Dabi? Your name was not mentioned, so you have no right to this food, which is all for me, 'the stranger.'" But the grasshopper kept quiet and never said a word to anyone, although he was very hungry.

The marriage between the spider and Chief Tawu's daughter was celebrated the following day. All the people were called together to dance and play, guns were fired off in the town, and Chief Tawu killed four more cows for the strangers who had come from a distance.

The grasshopper longed to eat the food, but did not see how he could manage it, as he was known as Dabi, and his name was never called. The spider therefore eat his own share and the grasshopper's as well, while the poor grasshopper sat down by himself, feeling very sad, and not speaking to anyone.

When he had finished the food the spider went out to dance and play with his new wife, but the grasshopper did not go, as he was very hungry and weak, and not feeling at all up to singing and dancing.

After he had been alone for a little while, the Chief's wife Osegi came in, and seeing the grasshopper looking so miserable, went up to him and said, "Why are you so silent and sad at my daughter's wedding, when all the other people are feasting and dancing?"

At this the grasshopper could contain himself no longer, and burst into tears saying, "Three days ago, when we left our home, the spider asked me to call him 'Stranger' and said he would call me 'Dabi.' During all this time I have been starving, and I am very hungry indeed, as all the food has been brought for 'the· Stranger,' and the spider has eaten it because my name is Dabi, and I was never mentioned." Then Osegi said she would tell the people what their proper names were so that when the food was brought the grasshopper would have his share. Osegi then went out and gave the necessary orders, and told her slaves to be most particular to call the grasshopper's name the next time there was food so that he should be able to eat. In the afternoon this was done, but when the spider heard his friend's name called out, he was so angry that he would not eat.

The second day the servants did the same, and the spider again refused the food when it was brought. Early in the morning of the third day the spider told his father-in-law that he was going home, and that he would leave his wife for a time, and come back for her later.

Tawu then said he would make another feast to celebrate their departure, and that he should like to see his son-in-law dance once more before he returned home; so the people were called to another play, and the chief milked one more cow for their food. When the food was ready the spider said to his friend, "Come on, Dabi, let us go and dance." But the grasshopper refused and said," No, you go and dance, and I will join you later." So the spider went by himself, leaving the grasshopper in the room where the food was. Seeing there was no one about, he took his out side skin off very quickly and hung it up on a peg on the wall, making it look just like a living grasshopper; he then went out and joined the dancers.

When the spider saw the grasshopper had arrived and was busily engaged dancing, being very hungry he stole off by himself to the room where the food was and put his hand into the pot. But, just as he was going to take out a piece of meat, he happened to look up and saw the skin of the grasshopper, which was so lifelike that it deceived him into thinking that it really was his friend on the wall, so he pulled his hand out of the pot and said, trying to laugh, "It is all right, Dabi, my friend, I was not going to eat anything, I just came in to see what the food was like." He then went out again to where the people were dancing, and to his great surprise he saw the grasshopper, where he had left him, dancing and enjoying himself with some pretty young girls.

The spider could not understand how it was that the grasshopper had managecl to get back to the play so quickly, but, as he saw him there, he was too hungry to trouble much about that, and went back again to get the food he was so much in need of. Everything was quiet when he returned, so he lifted the lid again, and took out a large piece of yam, and had only taken one bite, when his eye was caught by the grasshopper's skin in the same place where he had seen it before. The spider was amazed at this, and thought there must be some ju-ju in it, so he put the yam down and ran out of the house, shouting as he went, "All right, Dabi, I only thought I would like to taste the food to see that it was good."

But when he got to the dance he again saw, to his intense astonishment, that the grasshopper was dancing away as merrily as before.

The spider then went up to his father-in-law and asked him to stop the dance, as he wished to go home at once. This was done, and they all went back to the chief's house together.

Chief Tawu then gave both the spider and the grasshopper a dog each as a present, and shortly afterwards they started off together on their return journey.

After walking a short distance outside the town, the spider was so hungry that he stopped and killed the dog his father-in-law had given, and very soon had eaten the whole of it .

He then tried to get the grasshopper to kill his dog, but he refused, saying, "The dog was given to me by the chief as a present and not for food. I shall take it home with me."

When the spider had finished eating his dog, he put the skull of the dog in his bag, and asked the grasshopper to go in front of him. Shortly after this, the dog, scenting some game, dived into the bush, and very soon returned to the path with a small bush buck in his mouth. As the grasshopper had gone on in front and had not waited for his dog, the spider took the buck, and, having cut its head off and put it in his bag next to the dog's skull, he sat down and eat the body.

When he rejoined the grasshopper later in the day, he produced his bag, and took out the buck's head, and told the grasshopper that his dog's skull was very clever, and had killed the buck. Although the grasshopper knew quite well what had happened, he did not say anything, but walked on again in front with his dog as he had done before.

That night they slept in the bush, and the next day, when they got near the first town they had passed through when leaving home, the dog again dashed off into the forest, and chased a bush cow which he bit very badly in the leg.

When they reached the town, the spider told the people that the grasshopper's dog had chased one of the chief's cows and bitten it very badly. This made the people angry, and they all turned out with sticks to beat the grasshopper, but when he saw them coming, he called out to them and soon convinced them that his dog had not bitten the chief's cow, but had chased a bush cow and had wounded it badly. He then offered to show the hunters where the place was, and they gladly accepted his offer. The hunters then got their bows and arrows, and having been shown the tracks of the bush cow by the grasshopper, they had little difficulty in tracking it by its blood, and eventually killed it.

The people then carried the meat back to the town and placed the horns in front of their ju-ju. Half the meat was given to the grasshopper, and the remainder divided amongst the people, the spider getting nothing.

When the spider saw this he was vexed, and told the grasshopper that he did not want him for his friend again. He then set himself to make a net of web in order to revenge himself on the grasshopper, and has ever since lived on insects.

This story was given to me at Akparabong by a native, but there would appear to be some doubt as to whether it is a local story or not. A native from Cavally on the Kroo Coast affirms that he first told this story which was afterwards related to me, and this boy certainly gave me afterwards the main features of the story, but with a different local colouring.

VIII

How Ewa Abagi, an Inkum Woman, was Drowned in the Cross River, and how She was Rescued by the Young Men of Insofan

In the olden days, Ewa Abagi lived at Inkum. She was very rich and was considered to be a most beautiful woman. She made most of her money by trading in palm kernels and camwood, but, as she was so popular wherever she went with the young men of the country, she also made a lot of money out of them, as, if they did not pay her well in advance, she would have nothing to do with them.

She received many offers of marriage, but refused them all, until one day a chief of Insofan named Awor sent a message to her that he wished to make her his wife, as he had heard what a fine woman she was.

Ewa Abagi then sent word back to the chief that she could not marry him just then as she was expecting to bear a son, but that, some time after the child was born, she would go up the river to Insofan and marry him as she had heard that he was rich and was a good man.

The child turned out to be a girl, and shortly after her birth, Ewa Abagi bought a young slave woman called Mossim to look after her baby, while she herself went to the different markets trading.

When the girl baby had become six years old, Ewa Abagi dressed herself and her daughter up in their best clothes, and crossed over the river to Okuni with the slave woman Mossim carrying her load. They then proceeded to walk overland to Insofan.

On reaching the Abum River which is quite close to Insofan, Ewa Abagi went to bathe, and took her little daughter with her, putting down her cloth and beads on the ground. As the river was very shallow, it being the dry season, they walked and waded down to the Cross River.

When she got there, she washed her daughter and then called upon Mossim to scrub her back. The slave woman then came up behind her mistress, and pushed her into the Cross River, where she at once disappeared.

When the little girl, whose name was Essere, saw that her mother had gone, she began to cry, but Mossim said, "Do not cry. You must call me your mother, and I will treat you well. When we get to the town, you must not tell anyone that I am not your mother, or I will punish you severely."

She then dressed the child and put on the cloth and beads of Ewa Abagi herself, having just tied up her own clothes into a bundle with some stones and thrown them into the Cross River.

Mossim and the child then walked on to Insofan, and, when they got there, the slave woman went to Chief Awor's house and said, "I am Ewa Abagi whom you wanted to marry, and this (turning to the little girl) is my daughter Essere." The chief welcomed her, but was not very pleased, as he had expected to see a much finer woman from all the reports he had heard of her beauty.

When the people of Insofan heard that the chief's new wife had arrived, many of them went to see her, as she was so well known by name. When they saw Mossim, they were not greatly impressed by her looks, and said so quite freely in very plain terms.

Now, one of the young men of the town, who had been down the river trading, knew Ewa Abagi very well indeed, and, when he saw the slave woman, he recognized her as the servant, so he told Chief Awor. The chief said, "Very well, I hear what you say, and will not marry the woman at present. We will wait for a time, and I will make enquiries."

In the morning Mossim told the girl to go and get water from the spring, and the little girl went off with the water pot on her head. Essere, however, did not go to the spring as she had been told, but went to the place where she had seen the slave woman push her mother into the water. She then sat down and began to cry for her mother.

When Ewa Abagi heard her daughter crying, she came out of the river and talked to her. She then painted her daughter with *okukum*,[1] and having helped the child with the water pot, she returned to the river, and Essere went home.

When she arrived at the house, Mossim asked her who had painted her with okokum and why she had been so long getting the

---

1   Okukum is the juice extracted from a fungus like a very small mushroom. It is painted on to the skin with a small stick, and is a light brown liquid paste. Curious designs are made all over the body, the lines running parallel. The paste is then allowed to dry for about a day, and eventually rubs off. By this time the acid has eaten into the skin, and the dark marks remain, showing the pattern for several months. They cannot be washed off by water. The Okuni and Infoit people call this fungus *oboma* and the Boki people *katium*. The indigo black markings last less than a week, and the Okuni people call it *ebim*.

water from the spring. The child did not answer, so the slave woman said to her, "Don't you be so long another time, or you will get into trouble."

The next day Essere went to get the water at the same place. She called for a long time, but her mother did not come out, as she saw a man making tombo in a tree near at hand. At last, however, as she did not like to hear her little daughter crying, Ewa Abagi came out very quickly, helped Essere with the water pot on to her head, and went back again into the river.

The man, who had been watching, saw Ewa Abagi and recognized her. He therefore came down from the tree and went at once to the chief and told him what he had seen.

The chief then told all the young men of the town to go early the next morning to the place where Ewa Abagi had been seen and to try and get her out of the river. He promised them that, if they succeeded in bringing the woman to him, he would hold a big play and "dash" them plenty of tombo and food.

The chief told Essere that, when she went in the morning to get the water, if she wanted to get her mother back, directly she had got the water out of the river she must take the pot back some little distance into the bush.

When the morning came, the little girl went off with her pot, as before, and having filled it with water, carried it back into the bush some little way from the river, and then sat down, and called for her mother to come and help her.

The young men, who had gone to the place before it was light, and who had lined both banks of the Abum river, by the chief's orders, were all hidden out of sight, and, when Ewa Abagi came out of the water, they immediately surrounded her and caught her before she could get back to the river. They then carried her back to the chief.

The slave woman was then seized, and tied up to a tree, and, when the morning came, the chief charged her with trying to kill her mistress. She was found guilty, and was ordered to be killed as a sacrifice to the water ju-ju.

Mossim was then handed over to the young men who had rescued Ewa Abagi, and they took her to the place where she had pushed her mistress into the river, and, having cut her head off, threw the head and body into the river. This is one of the reasons why slaves are always killed and put into the grave of their master or mistress when they die, as a warning to other slaves not to try to kill their owners.

Told by Abassi of Inkum. [E.D., 1.6.10.]

AUTHOR'S NOTE.

There is a firm belief amongst all the natives in the Ikom district that the slaves who are killed and buried with their master will meet him again in the Spirit Land, where the conditions of life will be the same as they were on earth. The master will recognise his slaves and they will work for him. They also believe that, when a chief arrives in the Spirit Land, accompanied by these slaves, carrying the gin cloth, rods, etc., which were placed in the grave, the people of the Spirit Land will say, "This is a chief coming. Look at his slaves, etc."

Some years ago a road was being made through an old compound which had tumbled down and disappeared, leaving no trace of any human habitation. The road passed through an old grave of a chief who had been buried in the house, and mauy things, including rods, bottles of gin and plates, had been put in the grave. The natives who were working on the road were afraid to touch anything in the grave, but a native foreman, who came from another country where they held different beliefs, opened a bottle of gin and drank some of it. When the natives saw that nothing happened to him, they all rushed in and there was a regular scramble for everything.

Thomas, District Clerk, Inkom, told me this grave incident, and said it happened in his presence some years ago at Calabar, when he was time-keeper in the P.W.D.

IX.

The Story of the War between
Inkum and Enfitop

When the Inkum people first came to the Cross River about one hundred years ago Chief Indoma established the five Inkum towns on the right bank of the river, and Chief Awum took his people over to the other side, and, having given the Enfitop people presents, asked them to allow him to build his town there, and also requested them to give him sufficient bush where he and his people could make their farms.

The Enfitop people eventually agreed to do this, and Chief Awum built his town, which he called Aliese, and appointed a man called Osode to be his second chief. Both these chiefs were under Chief Indoma of Inkum.

When the houses were finished and their farms made, Chief Awum called a society to play, the name of the society being Eber-ambi.

It was one of the rules of the society that anyone wishing to join must pay fifty rods, one goat, and five pots of tombo, which would be divided amongst the members.

Then Chief Osode sent invitations to the young men of Enfitop to come and join their societ,y, and altogether about fifty of them became members.

Now, when the young men of Enfitop joined and paid their goats, rods, and tombo, Chief Osode divided up all the things they brought amongst the Inkum members, and never gave the Enfitop boys their share.

This caused great dissatisfaction, and at last they became so vexed that the Chief of Enfitop gave orders that for the future no more of his boys were to join the Eberambi Society.

When Chief Awum heard this, it made him angry, so he made a scheme or plan to rid the society of the Enfitop boys, who were no longer of any use, as they had paid up their presents to the society.

The Chiefs Awum and Osode then went into the bush, and searched about until they found an open space, which could be cleared without much trouble. There was a big rock in the middle, and the members all began working on the ground, and after a few days had it quite clear.

Chief Awum then told his young men to dig a very deep pit on one side of the rock next to its deepest side, and, when it was finished, he placed sharp stakes firmly in the ground with the points upwards.

A meeting of the members was called for the next evening, and the chief told his young men to sit all round the rock.

When the Enfitop boys arrived, they all sat together a little distance off, and one of their head boys was told to sit on the rock with his back to the pit, which he could not see, as it was dark.

The singing and dancing then began, and the tombo was

passed round, but when it came to the turn of the man sitting on the rock, just at the moment when he began to drink, one of the Inkum boys, who had been instructed by the chief what to do, seized him by the ankles and pushed him over backwards, so that he fell into the pit on the sharp stakes and was killed at once. As it was quite dark and such a noise was going on, no one missed the boy or saw what had happened.

Then, in the early morning, before it was light, the Inkum boys went to the pit, and having taken out the body, covered the blood stains with sand and carried the body back to the town. The body was then cut up into small pieces and divided amongst the members of the society, who lit fires and cooked and eat their portions.

That night Chief Awum said to Osode: – "Well! that accounts for one of the members, and I hope soon that we shall have got rid of all of them."

Chief Osode said that he thought the plan a very good one, particularly as it brought them in a supply of food which was always welcome.

Then, for four nights running, the same thing was done, and the boy who had been killed the previous night was divided up and eaten by the Inkum members of the society on the following day.

On the sixth night, however, the Enfitop boys met together, and counted their numbers. Finding that there were five of their members missing, they could not understand what had happened, so they decided not to attend the play that night.

This enraged the Inkum people, and the next day Chief Osode went to Enfitop and told them that, as they had refused to attend the

Chief Indoma's compound.

play, they would not be members of the society any longer. So, after that, the Enfitop boys did not go to the play again, and the Inkum people lost their chance of getting any more of them for food.

After a short time had elapsed, Chief Awum consulted with Osode as to how they should get some more Enfitop boys to eat. After thinking some time, he said he thought the best way was to steal the children from the town.

So the following morning the Inkum young men surrounded Enfitop, but hid themselves in the bush, and waited there until all the men and women had gone to their farms to work, leaving only the old people and young children in the town.

When they had all gone, the Inkum men went very quietly into the town from house to house, and stole all the children they could find and carried them off. They did not take any of the old people as they were not much good for food.

That night they had a great feast in the town.

When the parents of the children who had been stolen returned from their farms they missed their little ones, and so they went and complained to the head chief.

The next day he called all his people together, and they held a big palaver to settle what should be done. At the meeting, one of the boys who had been a member of the Eberambi society got up and said that five of their members were missing, and he believed that it was the Inkum people who had killed them, and that they had stolen the children as well.

After a long discussion, it was decided to drive the Inkum people away, and to send them back across the river again, so a message was sent to Chief Indoma to tell his people to leave their town at Enfitop and go over to the Inkum side.

Chief Indoma could not understand the reason of this message being sent, so he replied that he certainly would not tell his people to move, and that he would see what they could do.

When the Enfitop people had completed their preparations for war, the head chief took one of his slaves to his ju-ju as a sacrifice, and the blood was sprinkled all round the ju-ju, the chiefs dancing in it. The body was then cut up and divided amongst the fighting men, who eat it. The chief then addressed the ju-ju as follows: – "You always help us in the time of trouble. Here are my fighting men. I want you to make them strong and so that they will not receive any wounds from their enemies. If you help me, when the war is over, I will bring all the heads of the men we kill to you as tribute. I will also bring the prisoners we capture and kill them before you as a sacrifice."

The chief then put his hand into the ju-ju pot containing water, rotten eggs, and mashed-up leaves and roots, and having stirred it well up, the fighting men all came up to him one after another, and he smeared them with the liquid on the forehead and breast.

After this ceremony was over, all the people went to the chief's compound, where he consulted his head ju-ju man as to what the result of the war with the Inkum people would be. The ju-ju man then cast lots, and told them that they would drive the Inkum people away, killing many men and taking many men, women and children prisoners, but he warned them that they must not commence the fight, as it was the Inkum people who were in the wrong and had killed the Enfitop people.

They then armed themselves with bows and arrows, stones, and short heavy throwing sticks sharp at both ends, so that one end or the other would stick into their enemies. The next morning they surrounded the town of Aliese, and very soon the Inkum men came out.

The first arrow was fired by an Inkum man named Osim, and at once the fight became general. They fought for the greater part of the day, until at last the Inkum men were beaten, many having been killed and wounded. The survivors, including Chief Indoma, who was present at the fighting, escaped into the bush, leaving the women and children and old men at the mercy of the Enfitop people.

Most of the old men were killed, and the women and children were made prisoners and taken to Enfitop.

That very night they held a big play, and the heads of all the men who had been killed were placed before the ju-ju. Six of the best of the prisoners were then killed in front of the ju-ju, and after their blood had been sprinkled on the ground, the bodies were cut up and given to the fighting men, who lit fires and boiled the flesh with yams, pepper and salt.

While the food was cooking, a big dance was being held, and one of the prisoners was placed on his back upon the ground in front of the ju-ju. He was then staked securely to the ground, and a heavy wooden drum was placed upon his stomach and was beaten with sticks while the fighters were dancing.

When the food was sufficiently cooked the fighting men eat it, and then, after drinking plenty of tombo, went to bed. The prisoner was left on the ground all night with the heavy drum on top of him.

The next morning the head fighting man released the prisoner, and having tied him up to a tree, cut his head off with his matchet. He then dressed himself up in the long hair (mane) of a ram, wrapped a leopard skin round his waist, painted his face, breast and right hand with white chalk, and placed four feathers from the black-and-white fishing eagle in his hair, one down the centre in front, one behind, and one on either side. He then took the head of the man he had just killed in his left hand, and holding his matchet in his right, he danced all round the town, shouting out that they were great fighters, and that the ju-ju had made them successful in the battle. When he had been all round, he went into the open space in the middle of the compound, and the women came up to him with presents; some would present him with a fathom of cloth, but the poorer people would offer a few rods, yams, or some salt. The body of the man was then divided up amongst the chiefs, the head chief getting the right arm, shoulder and breast for his share, and the head fighter was given the man's heart to eat.

All the heads were then collected and placed over a fire to singe the hair off. They were then given to the head chief, who boiled and eat the meat off them with his sons and people. The chief placed the skulls on the ground of the room where he slept, so that the room was quite paved with them. This was done so that the chief could put his feet on them, to show that he had trampled on the enemies whom he had conquered.

The head of the man who was first sacrificed before the war commenced was not eaten, but was left on the ground in front of the ju-ju as his share.

To return to the Inkum people, who had escaped into the bush on the night of the battle, as soon as it was dark, Chief Indoma called them all together and asked his ju-ju man what he had done to make him so unfortunate in the battle and to lose so many people. The ju-ju man told him that Chief Awum and Chief Osode had caused all the trouble by killing the Enfitop boys and stealing the children for food. He also said that the Inkum people had gone to fight like women; they had not consulted him (by which he lost a handsome present) neither had they killed a slave as a sacrifice to their ju-ju.

Chief Indoma agreed with the ju-ju man, and said he would not forget again, and that in the future when he went to war he would see that the proper precautions were taken and the usual sacrifices made as had always been done in the past.

He then spoke to Awum and Osode, saying "I am very angry with both of you. Up to the present I have been known to all people as a good fighter and leader, but I shall always be ashamed to meet the Enfitop people now. You have done wrong. You have killed and eaten many of the Enfitop people and told me nothing about it. When they sent a message to me, I told them that I would not move my people across the river, as I never thought they would fight against me, but now I am compelled to do so, as they have either killed or taken as prisoners nearly all the men, women and children of the town. I look to you to arrange how to get me and the remaining people over the river in safety.

Then Chief Osode stood up, and said that he could manage that quite easily, as he was a ju-ju man, and would make a bridge for them out of his body.

Skulls in head Chief's house at Abragha. The Chief always sat with his feet on the skulls. He was the head of the Infam ju-ju.

Now, in those days there was a big snake who used to live on the land, and when he grew to be as long as a palm oil tree is high, he forsook the land and lived in the small creeks and rivers, where he grew to a tremendous size. The name of the snake was Ku Ku Barakpa.

In the early morning, Osode turned himself into the snake, and placed himself across the river with his tail on the Enfitop side and his head on the lnkum side, his back being out of water, so that the people could cross over in safety. As soon as he had done this the survivors of the lnkums, headed by Chief lndoma, walked over the snake's body, but, when the Enfitop people tried to follow them, the snake waited until they were in the middle and then sank, leaving the Enfitop men to drown. After two days their bodies floated and were picked up by the lnkum people who carried them back to their town and eat them.

Chief lndoma blamed Chief Awum very much for what had happened, but he praised Chief Osode for getting them back in safety across the river, and also for his ingenious device in getting them some more human food without any risk or fighting.

Told by Abassi of lnkum, 7th June, 1910.

X.

How an Inkum Boy was Drowned by His Companions and How they were Punished

There was once an Inkum woman named Omegha, who was considered very good-looking, but, curiously enough, no man had ever wanted to marry her, although she was very popular and went about from one man to another. She also went from town to town, showing off her beauty, in the hopes that some man might fancy her and ask her to marry him.

At last she got tired of walking about, and returned home to live with her parents. Her father was very fond of her, but often said that he wished she had been a boy as she would then have been able to help him with his work on the farm.

After Omegha had been living at home for a little time, her father said to her, "I wish you would get a son who would help me on the farm when he grew up." Omegha replied that, although she slept with plenty of men, she had never conceived. Her father then warned her that she would never bear a child if she went on as she was doing, always changing and sleeping with so many different men.

He then advised her to live with the same man for a whole month, and then see what would happen. Omegha waited for a week, and then did as she had been advised to do by her father, and, after a month had elapsed, she found that she had conceived.

A few months after this, Omegha's father died, leaving her mother and herself in the house. Then her mother said to her "Now that your father is dead, you must not go about as you did before, as there are only two of us. You shall stay at home and I will look after you and the child who is soon to be born." They then wrapped the dead body up in mats, and made a hole in a room at the back of the house, where they buried the corpse.

Some time afterwards, Omegha gave birth to a son, whom she called Ogor.

The boy grew very fast, and after a time he was able to walk.

As Omegha was a poor woman, she used to take her little son with her to the farm every day. But when Ogor was six years old, she got tired of doing this, and used to leave him in the house with his grandmother, who was very fond of him. Then Omegha used to go off alone, and visit her numerous men friends.

Ogor had often been told by his mother not to go near the river, and he was frequently warned not to play about with the other boys of his age in the town, as they would surely lead him into mischief.

One day, while his grandmother was cooking, he heard the company of small boys to which he belonged playing outside, so he stole out of the house and joined them. When the boys saw who it was had come to play with them, they asked him why he did not always come out and join them, so he told them that his grandmother would not allow him to go out of the house.

The boys then said they were hot from playing and were going down to the river to bathe. They invited Ogor to go with them, but he refused and ran home.

Before he reached the house, his mother, who was returning from visiting one of her lovers, met him and gave him a sound flogging for being so disobedient.

That night, the boys belonging to Ogor's company, of whom there were eight, met together and decided that Ogor had been very rude to them. They therefore determined to punish him the next time they caught him.

A few days afterwards, Ogor again stole out of the house when his grandmother was busy, and joined his companions who were· playing in the town not far from the beach.

When the play was finished, they all went down to the river to bathe, and swam out to a sand bank in the middle of the river, it being the dry season.

One of the boys had brought some strong tie-tie with him, and two others went off and soon came back again with a heavy stone. Ogor was then put on his back and securely fastened to the stone with the tie-tie. He did not struggle or cry out, as he thought it was all done in play.

When the boys had finished tying up their companion, they looked round very carefully to see whether anyone was watching them, but, finding there was no one about, they carried Ogor out into the river, and threw him into the water where it was deep, and he sank at once. The boys then swam back to the beach, and went off to their various homes.

Just about this time, Omegha returned home, and, missing Ogor, asked her mother what had become of the boy. The old woman told her daughter that Ogor had stolen out of the house as he had done on the previous day, and she thought he had most likely gone to join the small boys' company as she had heard them playing in the town.

Both the women then went out to look for the boy, but could not find him or any of his companions, as they had all returned to their parents' houses. They searched everywhere for Ogor, but could not find him, so at last Omegha thought of the porcupine, and made up her mind to ask his advice as to what had happened to Ogor, and what was the best thing to do to get him back again. She then walked to the porcupine's house and told him that she was in great grief as she had lost her only son Ogor, and could not find out what had become of him. Omegha then asked the porcupine to help her, which he promised to do. He then went into his back room to consult his ju-ju, and, being very clever, it did not take him long to find out what had happened to the boy, so he soon returned to Omegha, and told her that her son had been thrown into the river by his companions, and that the water ju-ju had taken him to his house at the bottom of the deep pool in the river.

Omegha then went down to the beach with the porcupine, and, when they arrived at, the water's edge, the porcupine, who was a very good swimmer, at once dived into the river and swam to the water ju-ju's house. The porcupine then told the water ju-ju that he had promised to help Omegha, and asked if the boy was there. The water ju-ju replied that he had saved Ogor's life as he was sorry for

Omegha and her mother, who were poor people, and only had this one boy.

He then said that he had no objection to returning Ogor to his mother, and that the porcupine might take him away when he departed, but he insisted that the boys who had thrown Ogor into the river should be punished, and told the porcupine to tell the chiefs of the town that, if they did not punish the boys very severely, he would seize everyone who came into the river and keep them in his house for all time.

The water ju-ju also told the porcupine that he must take Ogor to his mother when it was dark, and hide him in the house until the palaver was heard, so that no one should know that Ogor was alive.

The porcupine waited until the evening came, and then, having thanked the water ju-ju for his kindness, swam off with Ogor, and took him to his mother's house, taking care to go by the back way so that no one should see them, Omegha was delighted to get her son back again, and hid him away. She then thanked the porcupine, who went off to the chiefs of the town and delivered to them the message from the water ju-ju.

The chiefs at once sent the drummer round the town to tell all the people to attend at the palaver house the next clay, that no one was to go to their farms, and that all the small boys of the town were to attend,

In the morning, the chiefs took their seats, and the people sat down all round, them. The porcupine was then called upon to tell all the people what had happened. So he stood up and said that Ogor, the son of Omegha, had been thrown into the river by his companions, they having first tied him up and fastened a heavy stone to him to make him sink. They had then left him to drown, but the water ju-ju, being kind-hearted, had saved him.

Ogor was next called, to the great astonishment of the eight boys who thought he was dead. He pointed them all out, and told the chiefs which of the boys had tied him up and those who had carried him and thrown him into the river,

The head chief then said that all the eight boys were guilty of trying to drown their companion, and that they should all be taken to the beach and killed as a warning to other boys not to kill one another. He also pointed out that the water ju-ju had threatened to seize all the people who went into the river if the boys were not properly punished.

All the people agreed that it was a just sentence, but one chief, called Eka, refused to allow his son, who was one of the eight boys, to be killed, and said he would see what the water ju-ju could do.

All that night, the mothers of the seven boys cried bitterly; and begged the chief not to kill their sons, but he told them that the sentence must be carried out, as otherwise the water ju-ju would be angry and kill many people.

The next clay, the seven boys, were taken down to the beach and killed, and their fathers took their bodies home and buried them. The town then mourned for three days.

The head chief then called the porcupine to him, and told him to go to the water ju-ju and tell him that the seven boys had been killed, but that Chief Eka had refused to allow his son to be killed, and had defied the water ju-ju to do his worst.

So the porcupine set off and dived into the river and reported to the water ju-ju all that had happened. The water ju-ju said the head chief had done quite right to kill the seven boys, as had he not done so, he would have made the people suffer very much. He also said that he would deal with Chief Eka's son later on. Then the porcupine returned to the land and reported to the head chief all that the water ju-ju had said.

When Chief Eka heard the threat of the water ju-ju he at once gave orders to all his people that none of them were to go into the river, but that, if they wanted to wash, they must carry the water to their houses for the purpose.

This was done for two years and nothing happened, but, in the commencement of the third year, Chief Eka's son, thinking he was quite safe, thought he would like to bathe, so he went down to the river and went into the water as far as his knees; he then washed himself and returned home. As nothing had happened to him the first day, he went down again in the afternoon when the sun was not quite so hot, and jumped into the deep water, but the water ju-ju, who was waiting for him, at once seized him and dragged him out of sight under the water.

The people who were bathing at the time, when they saw the boy disappear at once, guessed that it must be the water ju-ju who had taken him, so they went and told Chief Eka what they had seen. When he heard what had happened, he went to the porcupine and asked him to go to the water ju-ju, and offer him two slaves if he would return his son. The porcupine agreed to go, providing Chief Eka gave him one slave and 500 rods for his trouble. The chief willingly agreed to this, and the slave and rods were brought to the porcupine's house that very night.

In the morning the porcupine went down to the river, and dived in as he had done before, and swam to the water ju-ju's house and told him that Chief Eka offered to give him two slaves if he would release his son. But the water ju-ju refused them, and said, "Tell Chief Eka, if he wants to see his son, let him look in the river in two days' time." So the porcupine went back and delivered the message to Chief Eka, who was very sorry as he was so fond of his son.

Two days afterwards, Chief Eka went down to the beach, where he saw the dead body of his son floating down the river, so he sent some men out in a canoe and they brought back the dead body and it was buried.

Ever since that time, the people of Inkum believe, when anyone is drowned and his body floats after three days without being eaten by the fish or crocodiles, that the water ju-ju has killed the dead man because he had done some evil thing.

Told by Abassi of Inkum. [E.D., 9.6.10.]

XI.

How a Father Tried to Kill
One of his Sons but Failed

Osewo of Inkum was a rich chief and had many slaves. He also had five wives, four of whom had two children each, but the fifth wife whose name was Agbor had no children. As a child did not come quickly to Agbor the chief used to beat her and use her very badly as he thought she might never have a child and then he would have paid all the dowry and marriage expenses for nothing. Agbor bore all the ill-treatment she received without complaining, and although her husband gave her no money (rods) or food, she remained faithful to him. A year later, however, she gave birth to a male child whom she called Agberamfe. This did not alter the chief's feeling in any way towards her, and he took a violent dislike to the little boy. Up to the time the infant was one year old he never gave the mother or child a present, and when, as he grew up, the father saw his little son playing about the house he never called him to come to him or dashed him anything as he did to his other children. Up to the time when the baby boy could walk about, Chief Osewo never told Agbor to come and sleep with him but she never complained to anyone. This caused the Chief to dislike her more than he had done before, and he told some of his other wives that he believed that Agbor was going about with other men. His servants, however, told him that Agbor was quite faithful to him, but he would not be convinced. After another year had passed, Osewo, having drunk a lot of tombo one evening, sent for Agbor to sleep with him, and in due course she conceived and gave birth to a little girl baby whose name was 'Nse. Even this did not change the chief's dislike to his son Agberamfe, and by degrees he got to hate the boy, until at last, when the planting season came round, he made up his mind to kill him, but he did not want to do this in such a way that any one could blame him.

Osewo then called all his sons together and gave each of them a sharp matchet, but to Agberamfe he gave a piece of iron. He then told the boys that he would take them into the bush the next day, to the place where he intended to make a farm, and that they should clear some ground for him. The boys then went back to their different houses and told their mothers what the chief had said. When Agberamfe saw his mother he told her that his father had given each of his brothers a matchet but that he had received only a piece of iron to work with although he was the youngest of them all. Agbor at once thought that her husband must have some evil design upon her son; so that night she went to the place where her husband was going to make his farm and saw the Queen of the White Ants. She told the Queen the whole of her sad story, and said that she feared that her husband would try to injure her son. Then the Queen of the White Ants asked her what she could do to help her. So Agbor asked the Queen to send all her people to the place where her son was going to work, and tell them to bite through the roots of the grass and bush so that her son could make a big clearing with his piece of iron without any trouble. This the Queen promised to do, and Agbor thanked her.

Agbor then went to the rabbit [2] who was a great friend of hers, and having told him her story, asked him to dig a hole underneath the bed of her husband so that he could hide there and hear what the chief said at night to his other wives in case he should be planning evil against her son, and Agbor also asked him to tell her every morning what he had heard. The rabbit then went off and dug a hole under the chief's bed so that he could hear all that passed in the room above him, and when it was dark he went into the hole to listen. In the evening when the chief's favourite wife came to join him, the rabbit heard him tell her that the next day he was going to take all his sons into the bush to clear his farm, and that the one who was last in doing his share of work would be killed, and that all the boys would be placed in a line and he would tell them to clear the bush to where he would be standing and that as he had given Agberamfe a piece of iron instead of a matchet, he was certain to be last and would be killed. When the rabbit heard this he went off and told Agbor, who was very glad th at she had arranged matters with the Queen of the White Ants. When morning came Chief Osewo went into the bush calling upon his sons to follow him, but Agbor went with her son. The chief then placed the boys in a row and told them to clear the bush to the place where he would be standing, and told

---

2   A sort of burrowing bush rat.

them that the boy who finished last would be killed as a warning to the others what would happen to them if they did not work hard. He then went off 50 paces into the bush and gave the signal to start. Agbor, however, had taken care to place her son in the place where the white ants were, and he started off cutting right and left with his piece of iron and everything fell before him so that he very soon reached his father before the other boys had got so far as half way. This made the chief very angry. So he called out that he had changed his mind, and told his sons to stop working and go home without finishing the work. Then for some time he did not try to injure Ag-beramfe. But when the rainy season came he made another plan to kill him, which he told his wife at night, fortunately in the hearing of the rabbit, who told Agbor. The plan worked out as follows:–

Chief Osewo sent all his slaves to the other side of the river to cut the leaves of the tombo palm to make roof mats with; they were also to take some rats with them and catch a crocodile. When they returned they were to place eight bundles of the leaves in a row along the road, and they were then to put the crocodile on the ground and cover him up with leaves for the ninth bundle. The slaves did as as they were ordered, and after three days returned and reported to the chief that everything had been done as he had directed. Then the chief called his nine sons together and told them to go down to the beach one after the other and bring up a bundle of the leaves, and they were then to start making mats to repair the houses, but he told Agheramfe to go last because he was the youngest. Agbor, who was waiting outside, then gave her son some strong tie-tie which had been made into a running noose. She also gave him a sharp spear and told him that he was to spear the bundle before he went near it as there was a crocodile hidden beneath the leaves. She also told him that if the crocodile showed his head he was to cast the noose round him and tie him up securely. Agberamfe then went down to the beach and threw the spear as hard as he could at the bundle. He was fortunate in pinning the crocodile to the ground and very soon it showed its head through the leaves, where upon the boy threw the noose round its jaws and made it fast to a tree. He then withdrew tile spear and stabbed the crocodile until it was dead. Agberamfe then placed his bundle of leaves under the crocodile, and having got it on to his head carried it up to the house and placed it in front of his father. The chief was more angry than ever at this, and determined to make another plan that would not fail.

So when the dry season came round he told his favourite wife at night time that he had arranged with a blacksmith to kill the boy. That the next day he would send Agbor's son to blow the bellows, and that when the iron was red hot the blacksmith would plunge it into the boy's inside, and that he would die in great pain. The rabbit, who was listening all the time, told Agbor of the plan he had heard, and she warned her son not to blow the bellows, but to watch the blacksmith carefully. In the morning Chief Osewo told his son to go to the blacksmith and blow the bellows for him as he was making something for him. Agberamfe went as he was told but he stood outside the shelter and watched the blacksmith very carefully until he saw him pull the red hot iron out of the fire and make a dart for him. He was quite prepared, fortunately, and ran off home at once and told his father what had happened. His father pretended to pity the boy, and told him that he would send him the next day to his friend the leopard to look after him, and that he should stay there for ten nights. In the evening Chief Osewo sent for the leopard and told him that he was going to send his son Agberamfe to him for ten days, and that during that time he must contrive to kill him by stealth and send the boy's skin to him so that he might be quite sure that his son was dead at last. This time Aghor had no plan, but she told Agberamfe to be very careful all the time he remained in the leopard's house. The boy started off the next day, and when he arrived at the house he was much surprised to find that the leopard was as rich as his father. After they had finished their evening meal the leopard told Agberamfe to sleep with his sons, but the boy suspecting that the leopard had designs upon his life, waited until the leopard's sons had gone to sleep and then having placed a log in his bed went outside to sleep. The leopard came in the middle of the night, when it was so dark that he could not see very distinctly, and killed the boy he thought was Agberamfe, but he was mistaken and killed one of his own sons instead. The leopard was very angry when he found what he had done, so that the next evening he shut the boy up in the goat house. But Agberamfe very soon undid the fastening and got out, closing the door behind him. He then went to sleep in the same place where he had slept the previous night. About midnight the leopard brought fire and burnt the house down, thinking that he had made certain of the boy this time. But when the morning came Agberamfe greeted the leopard as usual, much to his surprise. The leopard then went to the house he had burnt, and found that he had destroyed all his own goats, leaving the boy still uninjured. This annoyed the leopard so much that he determined to take the boy back to his father and not to try and kill him any more as each time he tried he did something to damage himself. The leopard then returned the boy to his father, and said he could not kill him as he was too cunning.

By this time, Agberamfe had grown into a fine good-looking young man. Some little time after the leopard had tried so unsuccessfully to kill the boy, the Chief thought he would make a trial to see which of his sons liked him best. So the next day he told his wives not to wake him as he was not feeling well. He woke up in the middle of the day and refused to eat until the evening. He then told his wives to sleep in their own houses as he was ill. In the morning he pretended to be very weak. He shut his eyes and held his breath from time to time. The boys, thinking their father was about to die, began to dispute amongst themselves as to what share of their father's property each should take. But Agbor's son sat beside his father's bed the whole day.

When the night came the Chief saw that Agberamfe was looking sad, and told him to go home to his mother, but the boy would not go, and told his father that he was too fond of him to leave him and let him die alone. So he stayed all that night with his father while his brothers were laughing and playing outside, and the Chief clearly saw that they did not care in the least that he was ill.

The following morning, the Chief got up from his bed, and having called all his people round him, explained the trial he had made, to see which of his sons loved him the most. Osewo also told him of the behaviour of his sons when they thought that their father was dying, and that Agberamfe had stayed by his side and looked after him all the time, although he had so often tried to kill him. The people then advised the Chief to divide his property into two shares, so that when he died, one share should belong to Agbor's son, who would be able to look after his sister; and the other share would be divided amongst the other eight boys. This the Chief did.

Moral. It is not the one who makes the fire to boil the koko yams [3] who is most likely to eat them. And it is not always the ones you love most who will care most for you.

Told by Abassi of Inkum. [E.D., 10.6.10.]

---

3   Koko yams are cooked for several hours. They are boiled in three different waters, and so that each water is steamed away before the fresh water is added. The yams are then left in the pot until the following morning. The ordinary yam is cooked and eaten at once.

XII.

Concerning the Okuni Witches
and Cannibalism

In Okuni, a long time ago, there dwelt a chief called 'Ndabu. He was considered to be a rich man in that part of the country, and was the owner of numerous slaves. He also had a large farm and many canoes. Chief 'Ndabu was, however, not a happy man, as all the time he was young he never had a son who should inherit his property when he died. On this account, he married thirty wives, but none of them had a child. At last, the Chief consulted a ju-ju man, and gave him a big "dash." The ju-ju man then made ju-ju, and finally told the Chief that the only wife he had, by whom he could get a child was a woman called Iya Agagim. He advised the chief to pull down all the houses where his other wives lived and to send them away. He should then build an entirely new house for Iya Agagim, and make a sacrifice of a white goat and a white fowl, to which he should add a white piece of cloth which should be tied up inside the door of the new house. The ju-ju man told the chief not to sleep with anyone until the house was built, and that then Iya Agagim was to go into the river and wash herself all over, and having thrown away all her old clothes, she was to put on a new cloth before she joined her husband so that she would be an entirely fresh woman. When the chief heard this, he was very pleased, and went home.

Having called all his wives together, he told them what the ju-ju man had advised him to do, and although he was very sorry to part with them, still they would all have to go as he was determined to get a son if possible. That night all the wives cried bitterly. The following day the chief sent to his farm for yams which he gave to his wives, and many rods as a dash; he then sent them back to their respective parents. Iya Agagim was also sorry to lose her old companions. When they had all departed the chief pulled down all the houses where they had been living, and then built a new house on a different piece of ground. When this was completed he made the sacrifices as he had been directed to do by the ju-ju man. Iya Agagim then went down to the town beach on the Cross River and washed herself very carefully. She then threw all her old clothes away and walked back to the house where she put on a new cloth and joined her husband. After a month had elapsed she found that she had conceived and told her husband, who was delighted at the good news.

The chief then called a play for all the young men and young women of the town, and told them what had happened. He also gave them plenty to eat and drink so that they might rejoice with him in his good fortune. Chief 'Ndabu then went to the ju-ju man, taking many presents with him, and having thanked him for his good advice which had turned out so well, he then asked how many children he would have by his wife; and when the ju-ju man said he would have twenty-one children, he was very glad and went home, but he did not tell his wife. The chief then sent his slaves off to the farm to make it larger, as in the future he would have to make provision for a larger household. From the time Iya Agagim conceived, the chief kept her in the house, as he was afraid that if she met any of his former wives they might be jealous, and try to do her some injury.

In due course, the woman gave birth to a boy baby, and the chief held another big play which lasted for three days and nights, and much tombo was drunk. Then the chief went again to the ju-ju man, and having given him a big "dash," asked whether the boy would live. The ju-ju man said that he would live, and that some day one of his sons would discover something which the Okuni people had ne-ver heard of or known before. Then the chief went home. Altogether Iya Agagim gave birth to twenty-one children, and the last boy who was born was called Amoru. The chief then knew that his wife would not bear any more children.

As they grew up, whenever he went to his farm, Chief 'Ndabu used to take all his children with him, and there were many people in the town who were very jealous of him on account of his large family. At last, some of the towns people met together and decided to get rid of the chief and all his family. One of the Okuni chiefs, called Elullo, who was a witch, said that he was willing to go to Chief 'Ndabu's house at night and see what he could do, but he was afraid of the ju-ju which the chief kept in a corner of the house, as it was very powerful against witches and might kill him. At last, he thought of a plan, so he went to one of Chief 'Ndabu's former wives, who was called Elilli, and asked her what sort of ju-ju her former husband had to protect him against witches. Elilli then asked him why he wanted to know, so the chief told her that they were tired of Chief 'Ndabu and all his family, and wanted to kill them, but that they were afraid of his ju-ju. Elilli said that she was also very jealous of Iya Agagim having so many children, and that as she was a witch herself she would like to join with Chief Elullo and kill the whole family. Elilli said that the safest way to dispose of them all was to put a witch into Amoru the last born, and that he would take them to his father's house so that they would not then do anything contrary to the chief's protecting ju-ju. Chief Elullo then invited Chief 'Ndabu to dine with him, and asked him to bring his wife and all his children. The chief gladly accepted the invitation and Elullo prepared large quantities of palm oil chop and tombo for his guests. One portion of the food he set aside for the boy Amoru, and this portion was bewitched.

In the evening Chief 'Ndabu came with his family, and they all enjoyed their dinner. But the prepared food had been given to Amoru who eat it. After they had dined, they all went home and, shortly afterwards, went to bed. During the night, Chief Elullo turned himself into a witch-bird (the owl) and went to 'Ndabu's house, where he called the boy whom he had witched. By this time a lot of witches had arrived, and when Amoru came out he was surprised to see so many people. Chief Elullo then cautioned the boy never to tell anyone what he saw, and then took him to the place where they cooked human food, and gave him a piece of flesh and some yam to eat. Amoru eat the yam, but took the flesh home and hid it. He hid the meat inside his mother's fire-place, and covered it over with pots. Although he never spoke about what he had seen, he could not help wondering how it was that he could go in and out of the house when all the doors were fastened. The next night when he heard the witches play in the town, he was compelled by the witch inside him to go and join them, and found when he got to the cooking place that a man had been killed and hung up to the branch of a tree by his neck. Chief Elullo told the boy that they were going to eat the dead man as they had eaten the man the previous night, and that he should have his share as before. Amoru was very frightened when he saw what was done, but dared not say anything. The dead man was then cut up and cooked with yams. When the food was sufficiently cooked it was divided amongst the witches who sat down and eat it, but Amoru only eat the yam and took the meat home and hid it in the same place. Every night for a month and a half the boy attended the feast of the witches, and either a man or a woman was always killed and eaten; but Amoru always took his piece of flesh home and placed it with the other meat. All this time Chief 'Ndabu had been making sacrifices to his ju-ju to protect him against witchcraft, and he used to call all his sons together to sit round the ju-ju while the sacrifices were being made, but Amoru sat outside as he was afraid to go near his father's ju-ju on account of the witch in him.

One night when the boy went to the feast the witches told him that it was his turn to provide a body for food, but Amoru said he was too young and had no one to give. Then Chief Elullo said, you have a father and mother and plenty of brothers and sisters, we shall be pleased to eat any of them. But still the boy refused, saying that he was much too fond of his people to have them killed for the witches' food. Chief Elullo replied that he could not help his feelings, and that, Amoru had seen a man or woman killed every night for a month and a half and that he had received his share although the people who had been killed and eaten were the dear relations of some of the witches. Amoru then begged the witches to have another round and that when it came to his turn again he would give either his father or mother up to be eaten. To this they all agreed, and they went on in their usual way killing and eating a man or a woman every night: but Amoru never eat his share. The witch people used to play every night from the time other people went to bed until cock crow when they were obliged to go home. When the time came for Amoru to supply a man to be eaten, he began to get frightened. So at last he made up his mind to tell his eldest brother, whose name was Nkan-yan, all about the witches and the difficulty he was in. Amoru then got his big brother to go into the bush with him so that no one could hear what he said, and then told him how he had been made a witch in secret and was compelled to attend the meetings where the dead bodies were eaten, but he explained that he had not eaten any of the human flesh, having hidden it in the fireplace. Amoru then said, "the time has now arrived when I have to produce a man or a woman for the witches to eat, and they want my father or mother or one of us children, but as I do not want to give them anyone I thought I would get you to help me as you are big and strong." At first Nkanyan could not believe his young brother's story, so Amoru brought him to the place where he had hidden the meat, and showed it to him asking him not to tell anyone as he had thought of a plan. Amoru then told his brother to lie down in a bed opposite the door, but that he was not to go to sleep. He was to arm himself with a matchet, and when he heard the witches coming he was to stand at the head of his bed with the matchet in his hand and his arm raised ready to strike. Amoru also said, "one of the witches will present the calabash holding 'the night' three times, and on the third time you must smash the 'night' calabash [4] with your matchet, and it will at once become light." He told his brother to be brave and not to make a noise or tell anyone until the calabash was broken. He must then call out to the people who must catch the witches and tie them up.

Amoru told Nkanyan that when the time came he would hide under one of the beds, but the witches would run outside, and could be easily distinguished from the other people, as they would be all naked.

That evening, after all the people had gone to bed, the witches met as usual for their feast and play, and Amoru went and joined them. Chief Elullo said it was Amoru's turn to provide a body for food and asked him who he was going to give. Amoru replied that he would give them his eldest brother Nkanyan. The chief then told the people to take the night calabash with them, and to bring Nkanyan out of his father's honse, but Amoru asked Elullo to lead the people, as he was the chief of the witches. To this the chief agreed, and Amoru showed the way to his father's house, and having opened the door showed them the bed where Nkanyan was supposed to be sleeping.

Then the man presented the "night" calabash towards Nkan-yan three times, but as he held it out for the third time, Nkanyan hit it with his matchet and smashed it to pieces with one blow. Directly this had been done, it became light at once, and all the witches were

---

4   The "night" calabash was used by the witches when they were going to kill anyone for their feast, as it prolonged the night and the Okuni people still believe when the nights are unusually long that the witches are out with the "night" calabash and are killing people.

discovered naked, and at once started screaming and running away, trying to hide.

But Nkanyan called out in a loud voice for everyone to come out and seize the witches, and very soon they were all caught and securely fastened up. The people then took the witches to the palaver house, and Chief 'Ndabu sent word to the other chiefs that they would be tried at once.

The big wooden drum was then beaten to call the people together. The people of the town were much surprised that the night had been so short, but when they heard that the night calabash had been broken and the witches captured, they were very glad, and went to have a look at them.

Chief 'Ndabu told the chiefs what had happened in his house the previous night.

When all the people had assembled, it was noticed that there were very few chiefs present as most of them and the head men had joined the witches' society.

Amoru was then called upon to give evidence. He told the people all that had happened and the number of people he had seen killed and eaten. He also produced the basket of human flesh which had been given him as his share.

Nkanyan also told the chiefs and people how the witches had come to kill him, but be had broken their ju-ju calabash and turned the night into day, when all the naked witches were caught.

The chiefs then went outside to consult as they were afraid to talk in front of the witches. When they returned they ordered the witches to be tied up to trees and burnt alive, but Chief Elullo, being the leader was tortured and kept alive for some time. They cut small bits of flesh from him, and cooked it before his eyes. They then made him eat his own meat. After a time he died in great agony. His body was then burnt all except the skull which would not burn, so the people cut it into pieces with an axe and threw the broken pieces on the fire. The basket of meat which Amoru brought was also burnt.

The sons and daughters of the witches were sorry to lose their parents, but they were glad that all the witches in the town had been caught and disposed of.

The chiefs then consulted together as to how they should get the witch out of Amoru. They decided that he should be sent to a ju-ju man named Ewa who could take witches out of people, and they agreed to pay his charges, which amounted to one slave between them.

So Amorn went to Ewo, the ju-ju mau, and he took the witch out of his heart and put it under a rock.

When the boy returned to Okuni, he told the people that he was quite cured and was no longer a witch man.

The chiefs were very glad to hear of this, and sent Amoru round the towns, when he received many presents of cloth, rods, and tombo.

The people then collected all the ashes of the witches who had been burnt and threw them into the river, saying they had got rid of all the witches in their town. The chiefs then ordered two cows to be killed to make a feast, and a big play was held.

A month later Chief 'Ndabu died and his funeral was at tended by all the chiefs and people of the town. His body was dressed up in his best clothes and it was made to sit up in a chair, some of his wives fanning it to keep the flies off. It was kept there for three days, and the chiefs sat round the dead body and eat their food, but each mouthful was first offered to the dead man to eat. Those people who were very fond of 'Ndabu went so far as to touch his mouth with the food before they eat it.

The body was then wrapped up in sleeping mats and buried, and many rods and pieces of cloth were placed in the grave.

Nkanyan then took the place of his father and looked after his mother and brothers and sisters, who lived in peace and died natural deaths without being troubled by witches.

Told by Ennenni, an Okuni woman. [E.D., 16.6.10.]

XIII.

Of Chief Amaza, his wife Achi
and the Tortoise

Achi was a fine-looking Okuni woman, the wife of Chief Amaza. He was very fond of her and would not have any other wives.

She lived with her husband for some time, and eventually conceived. The chief then told his wife that she was not to go out of the house as she might give birth to the child when there was no one about to help her.

About this time a ju-ju man called Nkendeng was driven out of the Okuni towns into the bush near Insofan because he used to kill people with a poison called Ekpinon.

When the dry season came, it was the custom of the Okuni women to go into the bush to the small rivers, and having dammed them up with sticks and clay, they would bale the water out and catch the fish. As a rule they stayed out in he bush for several days, and on these occasions the married women were accompanied by their husbands, and the young women would have their men friends.

As Achi was skilful at catching fish, she begged her husband to allow her to go, but he refused on account of her condition. Achi was, however, determined to go and bothered her husband so much that at last he consented and they started off together.

Chief Amaza did not take any of his slaves with him as he did not wish to stay more than two days in the bush on account of his wife's condition.

When they arrived at the river, which was close to where the ju-ju man lived, they found that most of the people had already dried their fish and were returning home. The chief then begged his wife to go back with the other people to the town as he was afraid of the ju-ju man. But Achi refused, and said she had taken a lot of trouble to come all the way from Okuni and she would not go back without some fish. When the chief saw that his wife was determined to stay, he made a bush shelter for them both to sleep in.[5]

Amongst the people who came to the fishing was the tortoise, who had made his shelter near the source of the stream. He did not fish himself, but he brought his drum with him and a large bag. In the evenings the tortoise used to play his drum very skilfully for the people to dance, and as a reward they used to give him dried fish, which he put in the bag.

The next day the few remaining people packed up their fish and returned to Okuni, but the tortoise remained behind, as he hoped to get some fish out of Achi and her husband.

Achi and her husband went fishing that day, and caught a lot of fish between them, which they dried on sticks in the smoke of the fire at night.

The next morning Achi was not feeling well, so she told her

---

5   These shelters are made out of palm leaves and are quickly put together, but they do not keep out the rain. They are, however, sufficient for the wants of the natives in the dry season.

   VOLUME TWO: Ikom Folk Stories from Southern Nigeria

husband to go and fish by himself. Achi was quite alone, when suddenly she felt pains, and shortly afterwards the child she was expecting was born. She then called for her husband to come and help her, but he could not hear.

The ju-ju man, however, had heard the child cry, and came to Achi at once and assisted her by boiling water for her to wash with. He then took the child up and washed it, and placed it on some soft dry leaves on the ground.

He then asked Achi what she would give him as a reward for the trouble he had taken. But Achi said "I have nothing to give you. Wait until my husband returns." But the ju-ju man said, "I know what you are thinking of, you want to put me off with a present of some fish, but I do not intend to accept anything of the sort. Nothing will content me but the head of your baby, which I intend to give to my Ekpinon ju-ju." When Achi heard this she began to cry, and while she was crying her husband came in, but no sooner did he see the ju-ju man than he threw his load of fish on the ground and ran off to the nearest farm as fast as he could go.

Shortly after this the tortoise came down to see what was the matter and he found the ju-ju man preparing to cut the baby's head off, and Achi weeping and imploring him to spare her new-born baby. The tortoise then asked the ju-ju man some questions, and at last agreed that he should take the baby's head, but that he should leave the body. He then reminded the ju-ju man that, when anyone was going to be killed, it was the custom to beat the drum and march the victim to the slaughter place. The ju-ju man agreed that there was such a custom, so the tortoise went off and fetched his drum.

Very soon afterwards he returned, and commenced to play and sing, and he played so well that the ju-ju man felt compelled to dance. The tortoise then beat his drum louder and louder, and faster and faster, telling the ju-ju man to dance further off, as he would hear the drum better. He did so, but very soon returned to see that Achi and her child was safe. He continued to dance a little way off, and then returned two or three times, until the tortoise told him that he could dance as far off as he liked, as he was there to look after Achi. He then went further away each time until the sixth time, coming back always to look at the child.

The tortoise told Achi that, the next time the ju-ju man danced away, she was to pick up her baby and cover it with her cloth, and then run by the nearest path, which he pointed out to her, to a farm which was not far off, and where he thought her husband had gone to.

When the ju-ju man had gone some little distance, Achi picked up her baby, and ran off as fast as she could go. The ju-ju man then returned, and the tortoise drew in his head and legs into his shell, but the ju-ju man was so angry at losing the baby that he picked up the tortoise and carried it home. He then placed the tortoise on the ground in front of his ju-ju, and drove a stake through his body, and said to the ju-ju, "This is the man who stole Achi's baby from me, and prevented me from making a human sacrifice for you, so you must take him instead."

Achi reached the farm safely, and found her husband, who took her away at once to Abijon, a town about five miles inland from Okuni. He then consulted a lot-caster called Aja as to the baby's future, and asked him whether the child would live or die as the ju-ju man had seen him.

Aja placed his mats on the ground, and having sat down with his legs crossed, he cast lots. He soon discovered that the tortoise had sacrificed himself for the child, and that the child would therefore live, but he warned the chief that the Ekpinon ju-ju walked about when the sun was high up in the sky, and that he must never allow the child to go out in the middle of the day, as the ju-ju would kill him. The chief, with his wife and child, stayed three mouths at Abijon, and then returned to Okuni.

Since that time tortoises have always been sacrificed to the Ekpinon ju-ju, and the Okuni people always warn their children never to go out in the middle of the day, when the sun is high up, as they might meet the Ekpinon ju-ju without knowing it, and when they returned home they would get sick and die.

Told by Ennenni, an Oknni woman dancer. [E.D., 17.6.10.]

XIV.

The Fate of Agbor the Hunter, who killed his Wife and Children

Agbor was an Okuni man, and was married to a woman named Awo, by whom he had two children, but they were both girls, much to his annoyance, as he wanted a boy who would be able to help him with his work when he grew up.

Agbor was a hunter and a trapper, and it was his custom to set traps all along the road to the boundary where the Okuni farms joined up with Insofan. Every morning he would start off with his bow and arrows to inspect his traps and take out anything he found in them, and sometimes, if he were lucky, he would shoot a buck or bush pig.

When he returned in the evening, Agbor used to worry his wife and tell her that he wanted a son, until at last Awo told her husband that, as she did not appear to be lucky with her children, he had better save up and buy a slave who could help him. This Agbor did, and after a time he managed to buy a slave called Edim. The slave always went with his master into the bush, and helped him with his trap-setting and carried the heavy loads.

One day Agbor caught a small bird in one of his traps, so he took it out very carefully and carried it home. He then made a cage for it, and fed it with seeds. Agbor warned his wife and two children that they were on no account to touch the bird, as he was very fond of it, and did not want any harm to happen to it. Then, for some time, Agbor took much trouble in taming the bird, and taught it to sing. In the evenings, when he returned from hunting, he used to take the bird round to some of the chiefs and head men of the town, and the bird used to sing to them. This pleased the chiefs so much that they used to give Agbor presents of tombo and yams.

One day, while Agbor and his slave Edim were absent in the bush hunting, one of Awo's daughters opened the cage and let the bird fly away.

When the hunter returned, he found that his pet bird had gone, and he was very angry indeed, so he asked his wife who had let the bird go, and Awo told him. Agbor then got a cutting whip, and flogged his daughter very severely until the blood ran. Awo was much annoyed with her husband for beating the child, so she packed up all her things, and said she was going to return to her parents and would take her children with her. But Agbor would not let her go, and told her to go to bed and take her children with her.

Agbor then got his matchet, and having sharpened it on a stone, went into the house and cut his wife's head off, and then killed his two children. When he had done this he was frightened, and ran away into the bush and hid himself.

The next morning at daylight Edim the slave went to wake his master as usual to go out and visit the traps, but he found that the hunter was absent. Edim then opened the door of Awo's room, and looked in. There he saw the floor was covered with blood, and the three dead bodies were lying together on the bed.

Edim then ran out of the house shouting, and told the people of the town what he had seen, and that Agbor was not in the house. The people then went to the house to look at Awo and her children, and the father and brothers of Awo at once armed themselves and set off into the bush to find Agbor.

After searching for some time they found him setting one of his traps, so they surrounded and caught him; then, having tied him up securely with his hands behind his back, they brought him into the town and handed him over to the head chief.

The chief asked Agbor who had killed Awo and the two children, and he replied that he had done so as they had made him angry. He told the chief that one daughter had let his pet bird fly away, and when he flogged her the mother had threatened to leave him and to take the children with her. The chief told Agbor that be had no right to kill his wife and children, and sentenced Agbor to be killed by degrees.

He was then led away and tied up to a post in the middle of the town. A man with a sharp knife then cut off Agbor's left hand. But Agbor said nothing, much to the disappointment of the people, who wished to hear him shout. So the torturer said, "Do you feel any pain, Agbor?" and he replied "No." Af ter a short time the man cut off Agbor's right hand, and as he still remained quiet, the man asked him, "How do you feel now, Agbor?" He replied as before, that he did not feel any pain. Then they cut off his left foot, and still Agbor remained quiet.

The people were not at all satisfied with this, so they lit a fire and put Agbor's right leg into it. The pain of the burning was so great that Agbor screamed with agony, but the people laughed and told him that he was now feeling what death was like, and to remember how he had killed his wife and children. Agbor implored the people to kill him at once, but they refused, and left him tied up to the post, where he died during the night from loss of blood.

When Agbor was dead, the father of Awo claimed his head, so it was cut off and given to him, and the body was buried. He then buried the head for two weeks, until the ants and maggots had removed the flesh. He then dug the skull up again, and placed it on the ground outside the door of his house. Then, every morning when he went out, he would hit the skull with his chewing-stick which he cleaned his teeth with, and say, "Ah, you killed my daughter, but I conquered you."

From that time, whenever the Okuni people go to war, they put the skulls of their enemies whom they have killed on the ground, so that they can show them to all people as the heads of their enemies whom they have slain, and they always hit them with their chewing-sticks when they go out in the morning, saying, "I conquered you; I conquered you."

Told by Ennenni of Okuni. [E.D., 19.6.10.]

XV.

What happened at Okuni when anyone was killed by Accident

Many years ago there were two small boys living at Okuni, named Ori Namfup and Ori, they were great friends and always used to play together. One day in the rainy season when the native pear trees were covered with fruit, Ori said to his friend let us climb up to the top of two of these pear trees, and when we are high up we can play at stoning one another. They very soon climbed up to the highest branches of the trees, collecting the fruit as they went, and started throwing them at one another, when suddenly Ori lost his bold and fell to the ground, breaking his neck. Ori Namfup was very frightened, and ran into the town and told the people that Ori had fallen from a tree, and was dead. His friends then came and carried the body of Ori to the head chief. When the father of Ori heard that his son was dead, he went to the chief and demanded that Ori Namfup's father should give him two slaves to replace the son he had lost. But the chief refused, and said that as Ori had been killed accidentally it was not right that two slaves should be given as compensation. But Ori's father being obstinate and very headstrong, insisted upon his claim so fiercely that the chief gave in and ordered the slaves to be paid. Ori Namfup's father then bought two slaves and handed them over to Ori's father, in order to settle the matter and so that there should be no bad feeling between them.

The chiefs then made a law that, for the future, whenever a man killed another by accident, he should pay two slaves to the father of the dead man, but he should not be killed as he would have been if he had killed the man on purpose.

Told by Ennenni of Okuni. [E.D., 19.6.10.]

XVI.

How Oghabi poisened his friend Okpa and family, or why a Host should Always eat First from the Food which he gives to his Guests

Oghabi and Okpa both lived at Inkum. They had always been great friends since they were boys, and when they grew up they made farms in the same place and used to feed together. As they became richer they bought slaves and canoes and lived in separate houses, each man having one wife. At last Oghabi became tired of the farming work and told his friend that he was going to be a hunter. He said that by his hunting he hoped to grow richer, as he intended to go from town to town and sell the meat of the animals he killed while Okpa could be looking after the farm.

For some time all went well with Oghabi, and he made a lot of money by selling his dried meat, but one day he went into the forest with two of his slaves and met with misfortune. He had hunted all day, and killed several buck, and when the evening came he skinned the animals, and having cut them in half placed the meat over the fire to dry in the smoke. He then went to sleep with the two slaves.

During the night a large python came and took one of Oghabi's legs in his mouth and swallowed it up to the thigh. Okhabi woke up in great fear and yelled for help, he tried to stand up but could not do so, as his leg was down the snake's throat.

He then called for his hunting knife which one of the slaves gave him, the other slave called Odo snatched a burning stick from the fire and ran off to call Okpa to come and help. But before Okpa arrived Oghabi had cut the snake's mouth and body right down with his hunting knife and released his leg. The leg was so swollen and inflamed that he could not walk.

Okpa arrived shortly afterwards with his wife and together with the help of the slaves they carried Oghabi and the meat he had killed back to his house. Okpa then went home with his wife, but the next morning he went to enquire after his friend, and having stayed a short time he went home again.

Later in the day Okpa's wife came to see Oghabi and had a conversation with his wife. She said she thought there must be something wrong about what had happened the night before as it was not usual for a snake to try and swallow a man, she therefore advised Oghabi's wife to consult a ju-ju man upon the matter. After she had gone home Oghabi's wife told her husband what Okpa's wife had said, and Oghabi agreed and sent off for the ju-ju man at once.

When the man came he consulted his skull and then said: "It was your best friend who sent the snake to kill you but I will not mention his name unless you promise to revenge yourself upon him." As Oghabi only had one good friend he did not want to promise what the ju-ju man asked, but his wife, who had great faith in the ju-ju man, at last persuaded him to pass his word. The ju-ju man then said, "It was your friend Okpa who sent the big snake to swallow you as he is envious of your being a hunter and making more money than him."

Oghabi would not believe this at first, but his wife convinced him after much argument that what the ju-ju man had said was true. From that day Oghabi grew to hate his friend, and when he recovered from the injuries he had received from the snake he began to plot as to how he should revenge himself upon Okp a and his wife.

At last he decided to poison them as he did not wish to kill them openly with a matchet. Having got some strong poison from the ju-ju man he told his wife to prepare palm oil chop for Okpa and his family. While she was getting the food ready Oghabi went out and made some tombo, and when he returned he divided the tombo into two calabashes, one large and one small. Into the large calabash he placed some of the poison, and the remainder be put in the palm oil chop. He then got ready and went with his wife to Okpa's house taking the two calabashes of tombo and the palm oil chop with him.

When they arrived Okpa received them gladly and ordered food to be prepared at once. When the food was ready Okpa and his wife sat down and eat it and drank the tombo from the small calabash. Oghabi then told Okpa and his wife that they could eat the food which they had brought for them, and when they had finished they could drink the tombo in the big calabash. Okpa and his wife then called their children together and sat down and eat the poisoned food and drank the tombo, but Okpa's youngest son would not eat or drink anything.

When they had finished Oghabi said he should go home but Okpa begged him to stay. Oghabi, however, refused and started off home with his wife. When they had reached half way and were sitting down to rest, Okpa's youngest son came running up to them and

Carved wooden table used in ju-ju dances from Inkum.

implored them to return with him and help his father as they were all very ill and in great pain. Oghabi said, "run back home at once and tell your father that I will come directly I have been home, and will bring some medicine which will make them vomit and they will then get well."

But Oghabi never went back to Okpa's house until the next morning, when he found they were all dead except Okpa's youngest son who was crying. Oghabi was very glad at what he saw, and the boy noticed that Oghabi did not cry, so he went and reported everything to the chief.

The chief sent for Oghabi and his wife and called the chiefs of the town together to hold palaver. The boy told them how Oghabi had brought food for his people the previous night and that he was the only one who had not eaten any, and all the others had died soon after Oghabi left the house. He also told the chief that Oghabi and his wife had not eaten any of the food, and that when he saw his friend and all his family were dead that he had not cried. The chief then asked Oghabi whether he had tasted the food he brought for Okpa, and Oghabi replied that he had done so and that his wife had cooked and eaten some of the food. As there was no one besides the boy to give evidence the chief said he could not treat Oghabi as a poisoner. He therefore took him to his ju-ju and made him swear that he had not killed Okpa, and that if he had the ju-ju should kill him. Oghabi's wife swore also.

The chief then sent word all round the towns that as Okpa and his family had been poisoned, for the future whenever anyone gave another person tombo, foo-foo, palm oil chop, or anything else to

VOLUME TWO: Ikom Folk Stories from Southern Nigeria

eat or drink, they must first partake of it themselves, to show that it was not poisoned.

Told by Abassi of Inkum. [20.6.10.]

AUTHOR'S NOTE.
It is a universal custom throughout the district that when food or drink is brought for strangers the provider of the food should first taste it, to show that it is not poisoned.
In connection with the above it may be of interest to note the formalities which are invariably observed whenever tombo is brought for people to drink, even when there are only a few present.
The "pourer out" (Ka-ammum (Ingor) pour drink) takes the demijon or calabash of tombo in his right hand and places it on his knee, then he takes a glass or small calabash in his left hand and having poured a little tombo into the glass he presents it to the chief or the head man present, who makes a little speech asking God (Ossor wor) to be good to them to prevent their children from dying, and to give them good yam crops, etc. He then throws the tombo on the ground. Having handed the glass back, it is filled and given to the chief's small boy, who stands behind him, to drink. The "pourer out" then pours out a glass and drinks it himself. After that the next glass is given to the chief who throws it on the ground as a libation to the dead ancestors, then the glass will be filled again, and the chief drinks it. The tombo is then poured out glass after glass and handed round until there is only one glass left in the calabash and that is drunk by the chief's small boy who drank the first glass, he leaves a little in the bottom of the glass and gives it to the chief who throws the contents on the ground to propitiate the evil spirits.
The reason that the glass is presented with the left hand of the " pourer out" is, that formerly the natives were afraid of being seized by the hand, when they held out the tombo, by some man who would seize them on behalf of a third person who owed him a debt, and if they held the glass out in their right hand and were caught by it they could not get at their knives which are worn on their right side, to protect themselves. On all other occasions things are given and taken with the right hand as the left hand is looked upon as "unclean" for certain reasons, and it is considered in consequence an insult to offer or take anything with the left hand. Natives eat their food with their right hands only. [E.D., 20.6.10.]

XVII.

How Chief Alankor and all his Family were Killed by a Big Frog, or why the Cock Crows at Dawn

A long time ago, Chief Alankor was one of the head chiefs of Ikom, he was rich and powerful. This chief had five wives and several children by each, but he disliked them all with the exception of the last born whose name was Eba. Wherever he went, whether it was into the forest to fell timber for making canvas, or to visit neighbouring towns, he used to take his little son with him and spoil him in many ways.

When all the people were working, including the women and children on the farm, Eba always stood with his father in the shade of a tree throughout the heat of the day, and when it was time to go home in the evening, and all the others were carrying heavy loads, some of firewood, and others of food, Eba only carried his father's bag, containing his snuff and horn. After the bush had been cut and burnt, and the ground prepared for the farm the Chief waited until some heavy rains had fallen, and then proceeded to distribute the yarns for planting. Eba carried the yams round for the others to plant. As he was putting the yams into the basket, he took a great fancy to one particular yam-tail which he thought he would like to take home and eat, so he placed the yam-tail behind the tree where his father was standing, and then took the remaining yams out to the people on the farm to plant. When the work for the day was finished, and it was time to go home, Chief Alankor called his people together and started off, Eba carrying his father's bag as usual. But he entirely forgot his yam-tail which he had left behind the tree until they got half way home. Eba then told his father, that he wished to return to the farm as he had left something behind which he wanted to get.

His father told him that it was most unusual for anyone to return to the farm after the work was over as it was well known that anyone going back might meet some evil thing. But Eba said he was not afraid, and as his father did not like to refuse his favourite son anything he allowed him to go, and told his people to sit down and wait until Eba came back. Eba then hurried back to the place where he had left his yam-tail, but when he got there he found the yam-tail was turning itself into a frog, which grew larger and larger every moment. Eba was very frightened, but continued to look at the frog until suddenly he caught its eye, when he dropped down dead.

Chief Alankor waited for some time for Eba, and as he did not come, sent two of his slaves back to fetch him, and then went on with the rest of his people.

Soon after they reached the house, food was brought for the chief, but he could not eat anything as he was anxious about his favourite son, and was expecting him to return with the two slaves every minute. When it became dark, as they did not return, Alankor sent four more slaves after the other two, and told them to search the farm all over for his son, but they did not return either.

The chief became more anxious as it got later, and there were no signs of any of the people he had sent out, so just before midnight he sent eight more slaves with fire-brands, to help in the search.

When the day was about to break, and there was no message from any of his people, Chief Alankor became thoroughly frightened, and called the rest of his slaves together, and having armed them with bows and arrows to protect themselves, he sent them off after the others and warned them to be very careful how they went. As nothing was heard from the last lot, the chief armed himself and his sons, and told his wives that he was going himself to look for Eba and the slaves who were lost.

He then started off. As the chief did not return, the wives and daughters went out to the farm to look for him and try to find out what had happened to everybody, thus leaving the house deserted except for the cattle and the fowls. When the morning came, the cock went to the cow, the sheep and goats, and said, "As our master is missing we should all go and look for him." So they started off, the cow leading the way, followed by the goats and sheep, and then came the hens and chickens, but the cock stayed some distance behind them all.

When they reached the farm, the cock flew up to the top of a high tree to watch and see what happened to everybody. On looking round the farm he saw the bodies of Chief Alankor and all his family, including the slaves lying on the ground apparently dead. Some little distance off he saw a creature like a gigantic frog covered with hair, sitting down with its head bent down, as he watched the cow and other animals walked past the monster, and as they looked in its eyes they fell down dead, one after the other.

The cock was very frightened, and flew down from the top of his tree and ran off as fast as he could to his friend the rabbit, and told him what had happened to his master and all his household, including the animals and hens.

The rabbit said that he thought he could bring the Chief and all his people back to life again, but they must be very careful not to let the frog look at them as if he did they would surely die. They then set off together for the farm, but they went by a different path so as to come in at the back of the frog. The rabbit then began burrowing, and the cock went into the bush and cut some strong tie-tie one end of which he made fast to a tree. He then sat down to wait for the rabbit.

After a time, the rabbit came out and said that he had burrowed away until he had come just under where the frog was sitting, and that he had made holes so that they could get at both his hind legs without being seen. The rabbit then led the way into the hole, and the cock followed dragging the tie-tie with him. When they got to the place where the evil monster was, they tied both of his legs very securely with the tie-tie, and then went back by the way they had come. When they got to the mouth of the hole, the cock cut a small piece of tie-tie and flew to the top of a tree, taking great care not to look in the direction of the frog.

He then tied his head in such a way that he could not catch the frog's eye. The rabbit remained in the hole so that he could not see or be seen. The cock then called out to the frog to make all the people come to life again at once or else he and the rabbit would kill him.

The frog tried to jump away, but found that be was helpless

as both of his hind legs were fast. Then the frog promised to cure the people, but begged the cock and the rabbit not to kill him but to throw him into the water to drown, this they agreed to do. The frog then pointed to some leaves growing near and told the cock to gather them, and to squeeze the juice into the eyes of the people and animals, and they would all wake up. The cock and the rabbit then untied the frog and threw him into the river; they then returned and squeezed the juice of the leaves into the eyes of all the people and animals, and they woke up immediately, none the worse for their experience but very frightened.

They all went home and were shortly afterwards joined by the cock and the rabbit. The chief then asked who it was that had redeemed him from death with all his household? When he heard it was the cock and the rabbit, he appointed the cock to be the head man of the house, and gave him power to wake everybody at daylight and tell them it was time to go and work. As a reward to the rabbit, the chief pointed to his farm and said, "you can eat as much as you like of the yams, cassava, and of the palm-nuts which fall to the ground, and take them home and nobody will take them from you.

From that day, the frog lived in the water, and seldom came to land except for food, and ever since, the young of the frog have had tails which show that they come from the frog which was made from the tail of a yam.

Told by Ewonkom, an Ikom woman. [E.D., 22.6.10.]

XVIII

How the River came into Existence; or, Why a Crab has no Head

When the Creator made the earth he appointed the elephant ruler of the world. In those days there were no rivers but the Creator made a pond for the elephant to drink out of. One day the elephant told his friends, the hawk and the crab, that he was going to hunt in the forest on a certain day. When the appointed day arrived the elephant and the hawk went off with their bows and arrows, and having surrounded a part of the forest, commenced to hunt.

Now the crab was a poor thing and could not walk fast, neither could he use a bow and arrow, so he took a long net with him into the forest and waited for the animals to run into it. When an animal which had been wounded by the elephant or the hawk ran into the net it very soon became entangled in the meshes of the net. The crab then went up to the animal and killed it with a stick; having thrown the arrow away he would put the animal on one side as his own.

At the end of the day the elephant had killed five buck and the hawk three, but the crab had secured ten animals all much bigger than himself. When the hunt was over the elephant told the hawk and the crab to bring to him all the animals they had killed, but when he saw that the crab had killed ten animals to his five he was very angry and told the hawk to put him down on the ground and cut his head off.

But the crab begged the elephant so hard to forgive him, and offered to give up the animals he had killed, that at last the elephant trumpeted: "Go!" in a very loud voice, and the crab went, leaving the ten animals behind him.

The crab was very angry at losing all the meat, so he thought he would revenge himself upon the elephant. He therefore crawled along sideways to the elephant's house, and told the elephant's wife that the place where they had been hunting was very cold and that her husband wished her to make him some good soup and that she was not to forget to put plenty of peppers in it.

The mammie elephant did as she was told, and the crab went down to the elephant's pond and filled it up with earth, so that there would be no place where the elephant could drink. When he had finished he dug a small hole where the pond had been and buried himself in it.

Shortly after this the elephant returned home, carrying the meat, and bringing his friend the hawk with him. The elephant's wife then brought the soup she had made, and the elephant and the hawk sat down together and finished it.

When the meal was over, the elephant told his wife to bring some water for them to drink, as the soup was so hot from the peppers that he had become quite thirsty, but his wife said that she had not got any water that morning, so they had better go to the pond, as it was not so far. The elephant went down to the pond but found to his intense surprise and disgust that there was no water, and that the pond was full of mud. At this he was very angry and went home and told the hawk.

Then the hawk, who was also very thirsty, went down to the pond with the elephant, and together they dug the mud out until at last they came across the crab. The elephant at once guessed that it was the crab who had filled up his drinking pond, and being in a furious rage, he cut the crab's head off and threw him into the pond.

The water came back into the pond at once and both the elephant and the hawk had a good drink and wash. After a time he thought that if he left the crab in the water that he would fill the pond up again, so he told the hawk to dig away at the lower end, so that the water could flow out of the pond. The hawk did as he was told and made a running stream. This stream became larger and larger until it grew into a big river. The crab then went into the river, but having no head he could not see, so he went to the fish and asked him to cure his wounds and give him a pair of eyes to see with. The fish cured his wounds after a time, but, having no eyes to spare, he sent the crab on to his friend the prawn.

The prawn got some eyes, which he placed on the shoulders of the crab, and they grew there, so that he could see quite well, but the crab has never had a head since that time.

Told by Ewonkom, an Ikom woman. [E.D., 22.6.10.]

XIX.

Why the Mist rises from the Water

Ogbaja of Ikom was the son of Chief 'Njum, and his mother was called Nara. Chief 'Njum was a poor man, but he had a farm and a few slaves to work for him. When Ogbaja grew up, he became a hunter, and being a good shot with his bow and arrows he nearly always succeeded in bringing back some meat, which he took to his father.

One year the season was so dry and the sun so hot that Chief 'Njum could not plant his yams in time, and when he did plant them it was too late, and there was a very bad crop in consequence.

When the food began to get scarce, Chief 'Njum told his son to go hunting every day to supply meat for everybody.

Ogbaja went out every morning with his bow and arrows, and generally returned in the evening just before it was dark, carrying the animals he had killed. He also used to bring some bush mangoes with him as well, as they were useful for making soup.

His father always sent Ogbaja to the chiefs every day with a small piece of meat and one mango for each, and after a time they got to know him quite well.

Just at that time there were eight wicked people who had been driven out of the town. Some of them were witches and others were poisoners, but one of them was a cripple, and could only scramble along on his hands and knees. These people were not allowed to make farms, so they were forced to live on the fruits and seeds which they found in the forest. Ogbaja knew all about these men, and was afraid to meet them, so he always gathered mangoes at a time when he knew they would not be near the tree.

One day Ogbaja's mother Nara said she wished to go with him to gather some fruit, but he told her that she could not go, as the witches were dangerous men and might kill her. Nara, however, made up her mind to go, so she put ashes in Ogbaja's bag which he always carried, and made holes in the bottom, so that she could follow him.

Ogbaja got up early in the morning, and took his bow and arrows with him to hunt; then as he went along he left a trail of ashes behind him, which Nara followed, and at last came to the mango tree, where she found Ogbaja picking up the fruit.

Her son said "Why do you come here? If you had waited at home, I would have brought you some fruit." But his mother told him that she wanted to get the fruit herself, and commenced gathering the mangoes and eating some of the ripe ones.

Ogbaja said, "I cannot take you home, as I must go out hunting to get food. I will therefore leave you at the top of the tree, where you will be safe from the wicked men, but you must be careful to keep very quiet and not move when they come." He then helped his mother up the tree, and left her sitting on a branch, telling her that he would return the same way after he had finished hunting, late in the afternoon, and take her home. He then went away.

At midday when the sun was high up, the witches came and started to pick up the mangoes, but they left the cripple underneath the tree. When they had finished, they told him they were going to the stream to get water and would return to him later.

Nara was very frightened when she saw the witches, and kept quite quiet, but when she saw them go down to the stream she thought they had all gone, so she moved about in the branches and looked all round. This movement soon attracted the attention of the cripple, who was lying on his back, and he looked up and saw Nara sitting on the branch.

Shortly afterwards the seven bad men returned with the water, and after he had taken a drink he told the others what he had seen in the tree. They looked up and saw Nara, so one of the witches climbed up the tree and threw her down. She was killed at once, and they cut the body up and divided it and took it home to eat. The cripple claimed the head for his share. As he was unable to walk, he crawled along the path on his hands and knees, rolling the head in front of him.

When Ogbaja returned to the mango tree after his hunting to take his mother home, he could not find her, but on looking about on the ground he saw the bloodstains where his mother's body had been cut up, and at once knew that she must have been killed by the witch-es. He never gathered any fruit, but returned home empty-handed.

Ogbaja was far too frightened to go to the place where the bad men lived to look for his mother, so he went home, feeling very sad.

When he returned, Chief 'Njum asked him what had become

of his mother, but Ogbaja's heart was so full of grief that he could not answer. Then his friends Bojor and Osobia came and asked him why he grieved so much. So he told them what had happened, sobbing all the time.

His father, in the meantime, had sent to call another chief called Agborleku, who was a very wise man, to consult with him as to what was the best thing to be done.

When Agborleku arrived, Chief 'Njum told him what had happened to his wife. Then Chief Agborleku sat for a long time without speaking, considering what was the best way to get rid of these wicked men.

At last he told Chief 'Njum not to do anything for two months, as, by that time, the witches would think they were quite safe.

He was then to prepare a big feast and make plenty of strong tombo, half of which was to be made from the tombo drawn from the top of the tree and the other half from a tree which had been cut down. He was then to mix the two lots of tombo together. Cows would then be killed and goats, and all the people of the country, including the witches, would be invited to attend the feast which would be given in honour of the chief's dead wife.

A certain house would be set aside for the witches to sleep in, and they were to be given plenty of tombo to drink, so that they would sleep well. When they were fast asleep, they would be covered up with dry palm leaves and then burnt to death.

Chief 'Njnm agreed that this was a good plan, and commenced making preparations for the feast. When they were completed, a man was sent to the eight witches with a message from Chief 'Njum, that he would like the people who had been turned out of the town to take part in the big feast he was giving in honour of his dead wife.

When the man had gone, the cripple tried to persuade the other witches not to go to the feast, as he said that the people of the town would be certain to revenge themselves upon them for the death of Nara, but the witches did not agree with him, and said that it was impossible for Chief 'Njum to know that they had killed his wife, as no one had seen them do it, and they did not think he would ask them to a feast, if he wished to harm them. They also said that they had not had a good feed for a long time, so, in spite of the entreaties of the cripple, they decided to go.

When the day of the feast arrived, the seven evil men carried the cripple to the town, and at once began to eat as much as they could, and drank large quantities of the strong tombo. But the cripple eat very little, and did not drink any of the tombo, as he was suspicious of the people.

Very soon, the seven witches were quite drunk, and lay down in the house which had been set-apart for them, and went fast asleep. The cripple also lay down and closed his eyes, pretending to be asleep, but in reality he was wide-awake and very watchful.

When Ogbaja saw that all the witches had gone to sleep, he covered them all over, very softly, with dry palm leaves, and, having set fire to them, went out and fastened the door.

The seven men were burnt to death, as they were too drunk to escape, but the cripple managed to crawl into a large water-pot which was kept in the room for drinking-water, and the fire did not hurt him, as he only kept his mouth just out of the water.

When the house was burnt down, Ogbaja went inside to see that all the witches were dead, and counted the bodies, but could only find seven. He thought he must have made a mistake, so he counted them again out loud, one, two, three, up to seven, and the cripple called from his pot after him the numbers up to seven. Ogbaja could not understand this, so he counted the bodies again aloud, and again the cripple copied him. Ogbaja then called the people in with hoes, and they dug up the ground, but could not find the eighth body. Ogbaja then counted the bodies again, and the people listened carefully; the cripple answered as before, and they guessed from the direction the voice came from that the last of the witch-men must be in the water-pot, so they looked in and found the cripple. They dragged him out of the pot at once, and said, "As you do not seem to like to be killed with fire, we will kill you with the water-pot you took refuge in." They then dragged the cripple down to the waterside, where they made a large fire, and put the water-pot into it. The cripple begged them not to put him in the fire, but no one answered him When the pot was red-hot, it was taken out of the fire and placed over the cripple's shoulders. He was then pushed into the river. The red-hot pot caused steam and mist to rise from the water, and it is still to be seen when the mornings are cold that mist rises from the river, and people say that this is caused by the red-hot pot which was placed over the shoulders of the wicked cripple when he was thrown into the water and the steam still continues to rise.

Told by Ewonkom, an Ikom women. [E.D., 23.6.10.]

XX.

How Ibanang Okpong and her Mother were Swallowed by a Man-eating Drum, and how they Escaped from its Inside

Years and years ago the Ikom people had never seen the large wooden drum called 'Ndofu. This drum was made out of the trunk of a hard-wood tree and hollowed out with a long slit at the top. When this drum was beaten with two soft pieces of wood, the sound carried for a great distance. This drum was used for dances and for calling the people in from the farms when there was any big palaver on, or if the town were going to be attacked. Messages could also be sent to anyone who understood the beat of the drum.

About this time, many people from the surrounding towns and countries disappeared and were never seen or heard of again, until at last it became known that one of these wooden drums lived in a town in the bush not far from Ikom, and if anyone strayed into the wooden drum's town by accident he was swallowed alive and was never seen again. The people of Ikom therefore warned their children never to go by themselves to the farms unless they knew the road very well indeed, as if they took the wrong path and went to the town where the wooden drum lived, they would be swallowed up and would disappear for ever.

In those days a man called Okongo Osim lived at Ikom. He had a very beautiful wife whose nam was Inkang Ezen. They only had one child, Ibanang Okpong by name, and both the father and mother were very fond of her. They took great care of the little girl, never allowing her to go about by herself, and frequently warned her about the bad ju-ju who lived in the bush and eat people. Ibanang, however, did not pay much attention to what her parents said, and, as she was never allowed to go out to the farm, she grew to be very discoutented.

The parents arranged that they would never go to their farm together, so one day Okongo Osim would go to the farm and leave his wife to look after their daughter, as she could help in the cooking and get water from the river. The next day the father would stay at home to look after the girl and his wife would go to the farm.

This went on for some time, until at last Ibanang became very dissatisfied, as she had never been to their farm and wanted to see what it was like very much. So she waited until the day when her mother had gone to the farm and she was left in charge of her father.

Ibanang then said she was going down to the river to get water to boil the yams in, but, instead of doing as she proposed, she left her water-pot on the ground outside the house, and ran off along the path which she knew her mother always took to go to the farm.

After she had gone for a little distance outside the town, Ib-anang came to a place where the path divided and, not knowing which way to go, she took the path which led to the right, and ran on until she came to a cripple sitting on the side of the path beneath a tree. He greeted her and offered her some kola. But Ibanang was in a hurry to find her mother, and would not stop. She ran on and paid no attention to the cripple, who shouted after her that she ought to go back, as the path did not lead to her farm.

After she had gone a little distance she was out of breath, so she stopped to rest for a time. While she was resting, a small wooden drum came up and spoke to her. He offered a kola nut, which she refused, and he then told her to go back, but Ibanang would not listen to him and said she was looking for her mother. She then ran on and passed several more wooden drums, each one bigger than the last; they all told her to return, but she was obstinate, and still ran on until at last she came to a clearing in the bush where there was an enormous wooden drum held up by forked sticks and resting on the ground.

As the girl had never seen anything like this drum before she went up quite close to it. The drum then said to her: "What are you doing in my town? No one is allowed to come here, and if anyone does come, they never go back again."

The girl then began to be afraid and looked round to see how she could escape, but the path she had come by had closed up and there was no way out, as she was entirely surrounded by thick bush. She then listened and could hear singing and dancing going on, but the sounds seemed to come from the inside of the drum, and, although she looked round everywhere, she could not see anybody.

While she was wondering where the sounds came from, the big drum opened his lips wide and swallowed her up. She slid down his throat and fell into a big compound where there were many people singing and dancing. Ibanang did not know any of the people, but they were those who had disappeared from the surrounding towns for some years. She then asked some of the people why they did not go back home; so they told her that the only way was to climb up and cut the heart and liver out of the drum, but they could not do that as they had no matchets or knives. This made the girl very sad, but, as she could not see any other way out of the place, she made up her mind to enjoy herself, and sang and danced with the rest of the people.

When Ibanang's mother returned from the farm her husband told her that Ibanang had escaped from the house and had gone to the farm. But her mother knew that she must have lost her way, as she had not been to the farm and guessed at once that she had gone to the town of the wooden drum, where she wonld be killed. She then abused her husband as much as she dared for not looking after their child properly, and pulled her hair down and cried all the night.

Inkang Ezen told her husband that in three days' time she would set out to find Ibanang, and that if she did not find her she would never return. The next two days Inkang Ezen spent in borrowing native razors from her friends and sharpening them. Then on the third day she started off, when there was no one about, with the razors in her cloth, and went by the road leading to the town of the wooden drum.

She had not gone far when she met the cripple, who was always in the same place from morning until sunset. He offered Inkang Ezen some kola, as he had done to her daughter, but she refused to take it. Then the cripple called her back and said she was on the wrong road and that if she went further she would never return; but the woman told him she did not care, as she was looking for her daughter, who had disappeared.

She went on, and met the small drum, who also offered her kola, and tried to persuade her to go back, but she would not listen to him. After that, she passed drum after drum, until at length she arrived at the big drum, who asked her why she had come, so Inkang Ezen said she was looking for her daughter Ibanang, and would like to go to the same place where she had gone. Then the big drum took her up, and, having opened his big lips wide, he swallowed Inkang Ezen in the same way as he had swallowed her daughter.

When she went down the drum's throat and reached the compound, she came across several people she did not know, but, on looking round, she saw her daughter, and ran to her and embraced her. She talked to Ibanang for some time, until the people came up and spoke to them. Inkang Ezen told them that Ibanang was her daughter, who had lost her way in trying to find their farm. She also told them that she had found out how to escape from the drum before she came, and had brought some sharp razors to help them to cut their way out. When the people heard this, they were so glad that they danced and sang all the night through.

In the morning Inkang Ezen gave her razors to the men, and they at once climbed up into the drum, and commenced cutting the drum's heart out, bit by bit. When they began to cut, the drum felt a great pain in his inside, and made such a noise that all the small drums and the cripple came to enquire what the matter was. When they came, the big drum told them that he had a bad pain in his heart, and thought that the people he had swallowed must be trying to cut their way out. He then asked them if they could do anything to help him, but the small drums said they could do nothing. All this time

Carved wooden drum at Inkum. (The man-eating drum.)

the men inside the drum were cutting away at his heart and liver with their razors, until at last the drum got up from his seat, and fell over dead.

When the drum fell down, Inkang Ezen told the men to work hard and cut their way out. They cut their way through the drum's heart and liver, and then made an opening in his lips big enough for a man to crawl through. One man got out, and told the people inside that it was quite light. Then all the people came out of the inside of the drum one after another, including the goats and other animals that the drum had swallowed.

Everyone praised Inkang Ezen very much for the way she had delivered them, and asked her to show them her house, so that they would know where to find her in the future. She was very glad to do this, and took all the people to her husband's house.

When they arrived, a report was sent round the whole country that the big wooden drum, the destroyer of men, was dead. Then the men went to the home of the big drum with axes, and cut the drum into pieces and carried them to Inkang Ezen's house.

After the body of the drum had been eaten up, the bones were preserved. They bored holes in the leg bones, and took the marrow out. The bones were then used to beat the drums with at dances and in times of danger.

The people who had escaped from the drum's inside each took one of his bones and departed to their different towns, where they all made big wooden drums like the one which had swallowed them.

Told by Ewonkom, an Ikom woman.-[E.D., 23.6.10.]

XXI.

Why the Head of the Male Goat Smells so Strong

There was once a male goat who cut a large cotton-tree down and then burnt it. When it was quite dead, mushrooms began to grow on the trunk. Now these mushrooms are very good in palm-oil chop, and the goat thought he would like to eat them. Unfortunately, just before he gathered them, the elephant went to the tree and rooted them all up. When the goat saw what the elephant had done, he was vexed, so he went and told the elephant that he had cut down the tree and burnt it in order to grow the mushrooms for his food, and as the elephant had spoilt them all, he demanded fish or meat to make soup, as compensation. The elephant said he did not care much for either fish or meat, and had none to give, so he gave the goat some beans instead. The goat was satisfied at receiving this present from the elephant, and took the beans home to his house and left them in a calabash on the floor. During the night, while the goat was asleep, a rat came into the house and eat all the beans up.

When the morning came, the goat, missing his beans, guessed that the rat had eaten them, and told him that he must pay for the beans he had stolen. The rat said he was willing to do so, and gave the goat one of his small children. The goat took the young rat home and put it on the ground just outside the house. He then sat down to watch, and very soon a hen came along who, being very hungry, swallowed the young rat. The goat at once told her that she must pay, so the hen gave him one of her chickens. The goat allowed the little chicken to run about, and went out himself to get some food. While he was gone, the hawk, who was hovering round, soon caught sight of the chicken, and swooped down and carried it off and eat it.

A sheep, who had been watching, told the goat, when he returned, what had happened to the chicken, so the next morning the goat went to the hawk and demanded payment. But the hawk, having nothing to pay with, gave the goat one of his feathers out of his wing to settle the matter, and said that those particular feathers were much liked by the young men, who were fond of dancing, and also by the fighting-men, as they put them in their hair for decoration and then danced round the town. The goat was not very satisfied with this, but as he did not see any way to get anything else out of the hawk, he had to pretend that he was contented, and took the feather home.

Next day, hearing there was a big play being held at Inde, and that all the young men who had returned from fighting, were gathered there, he went over, taking his feather with him. When he got to the town he put the hawk's feather on the ground in a place where everyone could see it, and then went for a walk round the town, eating a few freshly fallen leaves from the ju-ju tree as he went.

After a time he returned to where the people were dancing, and found, as he had expected, that his feather had been taken. It did not take him long to discover his hawk's feather, which was in the hair of one of the fighting-men. The goat went up to the man and told him that the feather was his, and asked for payment, so the man took the goat to his house find gave him one yam in satisfaction of his claim.

The next day the goat went one day's march inland from the river, where yams were unknown, and found that all the people were planting koko yams, which are very inferior in every way. The goat then asked the people why they grew koko yams, which were poor things to eat and showed them the big yam he had received from the fighting man from Incle. The goat told the people that in the country he came from they always planted the proper yams, and the koko yams were only used in the hungry season when food was scarce. The goat then put his yam on the ground and pretended to go away as if he had forgotten all about the yam, but he did not go far, and watched to see what might happen.

Very soon the owner of the farm, thinking he would like to grow some of these big Inde yams, took the yam up and, having cut it, planted it in the ground. When he had finished, the goat went up to him and said, "Where is my yam?" The farmer said be thought the goat had forgotten all about the yam, so he had planted it, but he was willing to pay, so he told one of his wives to bring a ball of cam wood, which he gave to the goat.

The next day the goat went on into a country where the people did not use cam wood as a part of the marriage ceremony, and went from house to house looking for a girl who had just been circumcised and was about to be married. At last he found one, so he went into the house and asked the woman if she were going to be married, and she said, "Yes." So the goat said, "How is it you are not rubbed with camwood?" and showed her his ball, saying, "In my country no woman can be properly married unless she is rubbed all over with cam wood." The girl replied, "In our country we have no such custom." So the goat left the ball of cam wood in the house and went out for a little while. On his return he found that the parents of the girl had taken his cam wood and rubbed their daughter all over with it. As usual, the goat demanded payment, and the mother of the girl gave him a sleeping-mat.

In the morning the goat went on to the next town, taking the sleeping-mat with him. He went to the chief's house, and, having had some food, placed his mat on the ground and went to sleep on it.

The next day one of the chief's slaves died, and when the people were going to bury the body, the goat, observing that they wrapped it up in plaintain leaves, at once said, "In my country, when anyone dies, they are wrapped up in sleeping mats." He then went out for a walk. When he returned he found that, as he expected, his sleeping-mat had been taken; so he went to the chief and asked for payment. But the chief replied, "You said that it was the proper custom to bury dead bodies in sleeping-mats, so we took yours to bury the dead slave in. If you have any complaint to make or wish to be paid, you had better settle with the dead body."

So the goat went to the corpse and asked it to give back his mat or else to pay him for it, but he received no reply.

The next day the goat went again, but again got no answer. On the third day, when the dead body did not reply, the goat became so angry that he charged the dead body as hard as he could, and butted it with his horns again and again. By this time the corpse had become quite putrid, and as the goat's horns tore the body his head was covered with bad-smelling blood.

When he had revenged himself sufficiently he returned to the town, and the people told him that he smelt very badly of dead bodies. The goat replied that in every town he had visited he had always been paid for anything belonging to him which had been taken, but that in this town the chief had referred him to the dead body of the slave, and as the corpse refused to pay he 'had butted it with his horn s, and the smell seemed to stick to him. Ever since that time the man-goat' s head has had a strong smell.

Told by an Okuni woman. [28.6.10.]

XXII.

A Story of the Great Famine

In the days of the great famine, when all men and animals on the land were starving, the alligators and the fish in the river had plenty to eat, and the parrots and bats were also well off for food. The parrot used to fly off very early every morning with his family to an island in the river where there were plenty of palm-trees, and return in the evening carrying his bag of palm nuts with him. All the people were very jealous of the parrot in consequence, and wanted to kill him and all his family. The hare (Nchigga) was very curious to know how it was that the parrot always managed to get food, so he went to him pretending to be a great friend of his, but could never find him at home in the daytime, so he went in the evening and met the parrot returning home carrying his bag, full of palm nuts as usual. The hare asked the parrot where he got all the palm nuts from, and said he would like to go with him. But the parrot said that the hare could not go, and that he was only able to take his own family to the place where the palm nuts grew.

The hare then went home, but made up his mind to go with the parrot, so that very night he hid himself in the parrot's bag.

At daylight the parrot put his bag round his neck and flew off with his family to the island. He then began to gather the palm nuts, and to fill up his bag. Now the palm-tree where the parrot was overhung the river, and the hare, thinking he would pay the parrot out for refusing to bring him, made a hole in the bottom of the bag so that the nuts dropped through into the water as fast as the parrot put them into the bag. When the parrot began to eat some of the nuts, the hare eat some also, and when the parrot dropped the kernel the hare dropped his at the same time through the hole in the bag. The parrot did not notice this, as he thought that some of his family were also eating close at hand, so he continued to put nuts into the bag, but could not understand why it was that the bag did not get full. At last the parrot thought there must be a hole in the bag, so he looked inside and found the hare there.

Then the parrot said, "My friend, what are you doing in my bag? Did I not tell you that I would not take you to the place where I got my food from? You must have hidden yourself in my bag without my knowledge." He then pulled the hare out of the bag, and having placed him on the top of the palm-tree, flew off to the next tree, where he was joined by the rest of his family, to whom he related the way in which he had punished the hare, and shortly afterwards they all flew home, leaving the hare on the island.

The hare managed with some difficulty to climb down the tree, but when he reached the ground he was afraid to cross over to the land from the island, as he thought the alligators or big fish might catch him. He looked all round the island for a place to make his house in, but it was all wet, as the river was high; so the next day he determined to swim across the river, and risk being eaten. But before the hare started he threw some small bits of dried stick into the river and watched the fish come up and look at them. When he saw that he was bigger than the fish, he said, "They cannot eat me," and without much fear jumped into the water and began to swim across.

The fish came round the hare and saluted him, saying, "Go on your way in peace." Just as he got near the land, however, he came across a large female alligator, who asked him where he came from and where he was going. When he said that he was swimming from the island towards the land the alligator caught him, saying, "I want you to do me a service first, and then I will let you go."

She then took the hare to her house at the bottom of the river, where she introduced him to her husband, and said, "This man can paint our children, and make them look nice to all people." At this time the alligators were grey-coloured without any markings, and had for some time been wanting to change their colouring.

Then the hare said, "I see you have many young alligators here, and I will paint them all for you, but you must not look at me while I am doing it. I will paint one of your children every day and show it to you, but you must first of all build me a house, into which you must put all your children, with plenty of food and firewood."

The next day the alligators built the house, and did everything the hare told them, a small hole being left in the wall of the house so that the hare could show the alligators each child as he painted it. The hare then went into the house and shut the door carefully. That day he painted the alligators' eldest son with long dark stripes across his body, and when he had finished he held the young alligator up to the hole for his parents to see, and asked them if they were satisfied. The old alligators told the hare that he had painted their son very well, and they were pleased. So the hare put the young alligator on the ground and closed the hole.

That evening the hare killed one of the young alligators and eat it. The next day he held up the alligator he had already painted to the hole for the old ones to see, and then put it down again, closing the hole as before. When night came he again killed another young alligator and eat it. The same thing happened every night until the hare had eaten all the young alligators except the one he had painted and showed to the parents each morning.

The hare then told the alligators that he had finished painting all their children, and wanted to go home, but he told them that they must not go into the house until after he had gone, as if they did his ju-ju would be broken and all the painting would be spoiled. He also asked them to allow him to be rowed across the river by an iguana, who is deaf and cannot hear anyone shouting.[6]

The alligators agreed to this, and told the iguana to bring his canoe and paddle the hare across the river. They then gave the hare presents of fish and yarns, and said good-bye to him. The hare then got into the canoe and pushed off, and the iguana commenced to paddle him over.

---

6   The native hunters say that if you shout at an iguana he does not move or take any notice, but if you point at him and whisper, "Look, there is an iguana," he will run away at once. An iguana never runs more than about fifty yards at a time; he then stops to get his breath. If you find him again he will be killed easily, as he cannot run so far a second time; there is, therefore, a second saying amongst the hunters that "A first run is a run for life, and when you are in danger you should run as far as you can before you stop to rest, as when you run the second time you will not be able to go so far."

When they had gone a little distance the father alligator went to the house where the hare had been, and when he looked in he found only his eldest son who had been painted, so he asked him where the other children were, and his son replied that the hare had eaten one of his brothers or sisters every night until he was the only one left. When the alligator heard this he was wild with rage, and went up the bank and called to the iguana to bring the hare back; but as he was deaf, the iguana took no notice. When the hare heard the alligator shouting and waving from the bank, he attracted the iguana's attention and made him understand that the alligator was so pleased at the good work he had done that he wished the iguana to row faster, so he paddled harder than before.

Seeing that the canoe did not return, the alligator dived into the river and swam after the canoe, but before he could catch it the hare had jumped to the land and ran up the bank. The alligator then scrambled up the bank to where the hare was sitting, and asked him why he had killed and eaten his children and told the hare he should kill him. The hare acknowledged that he had done wrong, but asked the alligator not to kill him at once, as his body was so small it would not be worth eating. He then advised the alligator to dig a pit and put sharp stakes, with their points upwards, in the bottom. The hare said, "If you do this, and then throw me up in the air as high as you can, so that my body will fall into the pit on the sharp stakes, then I shall die in great pain, and in three days' time my body will be much swollen and will then be better worth eating." The alligator thought this a good plan, and agreed to what the hare said, so he dug a pit and put the sharp sticks in the bottom. The alligator then threw the hare

     VOLUME TWO: Ikom Folk Stories from Southern Nigeria

into the air as high as he could, and he fell into the pit, but was careful not to be caught on the sharp sticks. The hare then commenced to scream with pain, pretending to be in great agony. So the alligator said, "Now I have got you, you cunning hare!" and walked away to the river. The alligator then swam home and told his wife, who was mourning her children, of the revenge he had taken upon the hare.

The next morning he went to the pit to see if the hare had grown any larger, but when he looked in he found that the hare had disappeared. He then made enquiries from some other animals about the hare, and they told him that he was alive and they had seen him running home.

When the hare got home, he went to the parrot and told him what had happened to him, and warned the parrot that he should do his best to kill him for leaving him on the palm-tree to the danger of his life, unless for the future the parrot lived by the waterside, as that was where he got his food from. Then the parrot was frightened, and moved his house to the top of a high tree on the island. Ever since that time the parrots have made their nests on high trees on islands, and when they are flying high up in the air you can hear them laughing at the hare, saying, "We are out of your reach, you cannot harm us now." And even at the present time you can see that the young alligators have stripes across their bodies, but the skin of the old ones, which is very rough, does not show the marks made by the hare, except on the tail part.

Told by Ennenni, an Okuni woman. [28.6.10.]

XXIII.

Why Edidor Killed Her Husband
and Her Lover

Edidor was a very pretty Okuni girl. She was a good dancer and singer, and won the love of plenty of young men, but although she liked to enjoy herself with them, she would not marry any of them. At last, however, she met a man called Ode, to whom she took a great fancy, and married him. Ode was a fine young man, and many women wanted him, but he would have nothing to do with them, and did not marry any other wives, as Edidor asked him to look upon her alone. Ode had three children by Edidor, the first-born being a boy, and the other two girls.

After a time Edidor got tired of Ode and ran away to one of the Inde towns, leaving her children with her husband. She went about from one man to another as she had done before she was married, and attended all the dances and plays until at last Ode heard where she was. He then took his three little children to his father-in-law, asking him to look after them for him, as he was going to Inde to try and get Edidor to return to him. The old man did not want Ode to get his daughter back, as he preferred her to walk about and go with different young men, as in that case he would receive numerous presents from them, whereas Ode, having paid his dowry, never gave him anything. He therefore sent a message secretly to Edidor informing her that her husband was going to look for her, and advising her to try and kill him, so that the children would become his property, as he knew his daughter would not want to look after them.

When Ode was ready he got into a small canoe and started down river for Inkum, but he had only gone a little distance when the canoe sank, and Ode swam to the shore. He looked upon the sinking of the canoe as a bad omen and a warning to him not to go that day.

When he returned home his friends encouraged him to make another attempt to get his wife back, and advised him to take a larger canoe, which would not be so likely to upset. Ode started off in a big canoe the following morning; but when be got to the other side of the river be beard a kingfisher making a noise on his right-hand side, in a bush overhanging the river. Not knowing what this omen might mean, he stopped at Okanja, which is only a little way lower down the river on the same side as Okuni, and went to see a friend of his who was known to be clever at reading signs, and told him that the kingfisher had made a noise on his right-hand as he was going down the river. The man then said to Ode, "What kind of a child did you first get when you were married?" And Ode told him that his first-born child was a boy. Ode's friend then said, "Your good fortune depends on your left.[7] You will meet with much opposition where you are going, and you will not bring back what you are going to seek." So

---

7   The natives believe that when a man whose first-born child is a boy happens to hit a toe on his right foot against a stone on his way to a town, that he will be badly received at that town, but if the toe which is hit by the stone is on his left foot, then the people will welcome him and treat him kindly.

Ode returned to his canoe and paddled on with much suspicion in his heart. He landed at Inkum, and went to see a friendly chief called Aigonga, to whom he told his story and asked him for help. The chief gave Ode one of his boys to show him the way overland to Inde, and they started off together.

Unfortunately for Ode, his wife Edidor had consulted a ju-ju man called Ekum at Inde, who had a very powerful medicine which enabled him to see what was going to happen, and this man told Edidor that her husband was on his way to catch her and take her home, and that if she wanted to stay at Inde she should hide herself at once.

When Ode arrived at Inde he searched all over the towns, but could not find his wife. He then asked some of the people what had become of her, and they told him that the previous day she had been seen talking to a very powerful ju-ju man, and that if he were wise he would leave his wife alone and go home at once, as his life was probably in danger. But Ode would not go home, and got an Inde boy to show him the place where the ju-ju man lived. Ode then asked Ekum what had become of his wife Edidor. Ekum did not at first reply, but gave Ode one sharp stick and one blunt stick, and after a time said, "Touch your body with the sharp stick and also with the blunted one; if you feel any pain with the sharp stick, go home at once and do not bother me any more; if you do not feel any pain, come to me to-morrow morning and ask me any questions you like concerning your wife."

The Inde boy who had gone with Ode, directly they had gone a little distance from the house, strongly urged Ode to go home, as the sticks the ju-ju man had given to him were known to be very dangerous, and if he went there again Ekum would probably either poison him or call upon the lightning to kill him, which he was quite capable of doing. The boy also said that by far the best thing Ode could do was to ask his father-in-law to help him to recover his wife, and not to come to Inde himself again.

Ode thought the advice good, and returned to Okuni with the two sticks Ekum had given him; these he gave to his father-in-law, telling him what had happened, and at the same time asking him to try to get Edidor back for him. When he saw that Ode's life had been in danger and that he had escaped the old man repented, and told Ode to stay at Okuni and he would try to make Edidor return to him. He therefore sent a messenger to Inde to tell Edidor to return at once to Okuni. But Edidor was enjoying her self too much, and had no desire to return to her husband.

The ju-ju man also had taken a fancy to her, and when he found that Edidor's father had been trying to persuade his daughter to return to her husband, he put some ju-ju into her food which made her take an intense dislike to her husband. When Edidor's heart had turned and she found that she hated Ode, Ekum made some strong poison, which he gave to Edidor and told her to put it in her husband's food, and that when he was dead she should return and marry him.

The next day Edidor started off for Okuni, taking the poison with her, and intending to kill her husband on the first opportunity, but when she reached the house Ode produced their three children and talked to her very kindly until her heart was cold. Edidor then lived with Ode for a month, until the ju-ju man, finding she did not return to him, made another strong ju-ju, which at once made Edidor want to go back to him at Inde. She therefore packed up her things, and was starting off for Inde when Ode seized her and said she was not to go. That very night Edidor put half the poison Ekum had given her into Ode's food. He then became very ill, and died after two days.

Ode was buried by his relations, but Edidor only mourned a very short time and then ran off to Inde, where she joined her lover. Ekum was very glad to get her back again, and called all his friends together. He then killed a goat, and they had a big feast, and he told all the people that Edidor was going to be his wife.

During the night Ekum asked Edidor to marry him properly, but she asked him to wait for a time until she knew all his ways and habits, and she promised she would then marry him. For some little time after this Edidor went about with different men, but Ekum always found her out, and when she returned to him he would tell her what she had been doing and the name of the man she had been with. This made Edidor afraid, but she dare not leave Ekum altogether, as he might get the lightning to kill her or cause his ju-ju to catch her .

Then Ekum again asked Edidor to marry him, and she agreed to do so, but said that before the ceremony took place she wanted to join his ju-ju, so that she might know everything and not be afraid. Ekum was pleased at this, and showed Edidor all the ju-ju he had, and explained them to her. When he had finished, Edidor was so frightened that she ran away and left Ekum. Ekum, however, looked into his ju-ju pot and saw at once where she was, so he sent a messenger, who seized her and brought her back.

Then Edidor made up her mind to kill Ekum, so she went to his ju-ju pot which he always looked into when he wanted to know where she had gone or what she was doing, and broke it. She then cooked the food and put the half of the poison Ekum had given her for Ode into the food and gave it to Ekum to eat; he died the next day. Before Ekum was dead, Edidor ran back to her father's house at Okuni.

When the Inde people found that Ekum was dead, they at once knew that Edidor must have killed him, as she had run away. They therefore went to Okuni to have the palaver judged. When all the chiefs and people had met together, Edidor was accused of having poisoned Ekum, her lover. Edidor then stood up and told the chiefs that Ekum had made her poison her husband, and that when she found his ju-jus were so powerful she broke them, and gave half the poison Ekum had given her for her husband to him in his food, and that he had then died at once.

After considering some time, the chiefs decided that they would not punish Edidor, and said that "The stone Ekum had thrown had returned and hit him."[8]

The chiefs then said that for the future, whenever a man had a poison ju-ju or other powerful medicine, he should not tell any of his wives or any other women, because if they wished to run away from their husbands they would first of all break their ju-jus and then poison them.

Told by Ennanni, an Okuni woman. [1.7.10.]

---

8   The origin of this saying is, that a man seeing a fine bird sitting on the branch of a tree threw a stone at it, but the stone hit the branch, and as the man was standing underneath the stone came back and hit him.

XXIV.

How 'Nyambi punished Chief Oga for trying to Commit Adultery with His Wife Obim

There was once a fine strong man living at Okuni, whose name was 'Nyambi. He was a good dancer, drum-beater and singer, and these qualities, combined with his good looks and fine manly beauty, won him the admiration of many of the young Okuni girls. He knew many of them, but never asked them to marry him.

At last, when 'Nyambi was about twenty-five years of age, he met a girl at a big dance, to whom he took a great fancy, and whom he wished to marry. So he went to her parents, and, having given them the usual presents, told them that he wished to marry their daughter Obim. The parents, however, were unwilling, and told 'Nyambi that they had already promised Obim as a wife to Chief Oga.

When Obim heard this, she told her parents that she would never marry Chief Oga, as he was too old, and she intended to marry 'Nyambi, who was such a fine young man, and she was very fond of him. The parents did their best to persuade Obim to marry Chief Oga, as they would receive far more presents and a bigger dowry from him than if they allowed her to marry 'Nyambi, who was not a rich man. Obim, however, was obstinate, and absolutely declined to have anything to do with the chief, so at last her parents consented to her marriage with 'Nyambi.

Then Obim and 'Nyambi took an oath that, when they were married, they would never part from one another, and they would both try to help each other and upset any ju-ju that Chief Oga might make against them, as they knew him to be a most revengeful man.

'Nyambi then bought the usual presents for the parents and collected the dowry, which he handed to Obim's father and mother, and rubbed the girl with camwood. She was then circumcised and kept in one room until the wound had healed.

When the gun was fired off and Obim was declared to be 'Nyambi's wife, Chief Oga was very vexed, and, although he wanted to speak to Obim, he dared not do so openly, as he thought the people might laugh at him if they saw him going after a woman who had only just been married, seeing that he had so many wives already himself. So, when it was dark, he went to Obim and told her that if she came to him he would make her very happy, as he had plenty of slaves who would do all the hard work and she would not have to toil in the sun. Obim, however, would not listen to him, so in the end the chief went away more vexed than before and more determined than ever to get hold of Obim, somehow or other.

That night Obim told her husband of the advances made to her by the chief, and they agreed not to take any notice, but to be very careful for the future.

The next day Chief Oga consulted a ju-ju man as to the best way to turn Obim's heart, so that she would hate 'Nyambi and come to him. The ju-ju man, after casting lots, told the chief that it would be quite easy to make Obim leave 'Nyambi and go to him, and that all the chief would have to do would be to give Obim some tombo to drink, which he would prepare with a strong medicine in it. The ju-ju man then made the tombo and put a ju-ju into it, and the chief, having given him a big present, took the tombo to his house, and sent word to Obim that he wished to speak to her.

When Obim arrived, the chief offered her some of the tombo to drink, but she refused to touch it. Chief Oga tried his best to make her drink, but Obim would not do so, and said she had merely come to hear what he might have to say. Oga then tried again to persuade Obim to leave her husband and go to him, but Obim refused as before.

Finding this plot had failed, the chief went again to the ju-ju man and told him that Obim had refused to drink the tombo. He then asked the ju-ju man to poison 'Nyambi so that he might get hold of his wife, and when he had given him another big present, he went home.

The next day, the ju-ju man joined the society to which 'Nyambi belonged, and went to all the dances, looking for an opportunity to put the poison he had prepared into 'Nyambi's drink, but he could never suceeed in making 'Nyambi drink anything, as, whenever he went to a dance or a play, Obim made him promise not to drink anything at the dancing place and she would have drink ready for him when he returned home. This probably saved his life, as the ju-ju man was unable to poison him, so after a time he went to Chief Oga, and told him that the year of 'Nyambi's death had not yet arrived, and he could do nothing with the young man.

Chief Oga then for twelve months did not try to do anything more to kill 'Nyambi, but sat down and waited until the proper time should arrive when he would be able to revenge himself upon 'Nyambi and take Obim away.

However, he frequently sent messengers to Obim, asking her to sleep with him, but she always refused. At last Obim became so annoyed at these repeated messages, that she told her husband what was going on between herself and Chief Oga, and advised him to revenge himself in his turn. She advised 'Nyambi to pretend to go down river to sell some camwood and she would then allow the chief to come to her at night when 'Nyambi should come in and surprise them together. Obim also told her husband that she hoped he would cut a certain part off the chief's body, which would punish him properly and prevent his troubling her for the future.

'Nyambi thought the plan a good one, so he put some camwood into his canoe and told the people that he was going down river to trade, and did not expect to return for some few days. He then started off but did not go very far.

Directly the chief heard that 'Nyambi had gone, he sent a messenger to Obim, asking her to sleep with him that night. But Obim told the messenger to tell his master that she could not come to him, but that he might come to her alone at night, and he was to be careful not to let anyone know what was going on between them.

Chief Oga was so glad when he got Obim's message that he at once went down to the river and washed himself. He then went home and put on a fine cloth and had food before it was dark. After that he sat down and waited as patiently as he could until all the people in the town had gone to sleep.

When he thought it was quite safe and no one would see him,

he went very quietly to Obim's house and knocked softly on the door. Obim let the chief in, and then fastened the door, telling him to lie down and that she would join him later on. Oga asked Obim to come to him at once, but she told him to wait a little, as all the people had not then gone to bed. Very soon Chief Oga dropped off to sleep, so Obim went to the door very quietly and undid the fastening.

Not long afterwards, 'Nyambi opened the door and found Chief Oga asleep in his wife's bed; so he fastened the door securely, and, having got his knife ready, made the fire blaze and woke the chief up.

When Oga awoke he saw 'Nyambi standing over him with his knife pointing at his breast. 'Nyambi told him to be quiet and not to make a noise or he would kill him at once.

He then said, "I find you as a thief and one who would commit adultery with my wife. I will not receive any present from you; I do not want to kill you, but I intend to take one of two things from your body, and, if you refuse, I shall kill you at once." On hearing this, Chief Oga was very much frightened, as he was no match for 'Nyambi in strength; so he lay there for some time, thinking of his life, his wealth, and his wives, until at last he asked 'Nyambi what it was he wished to take from his body so that he might go.

'Nyambi said, "I intend either to take your eyes out, which will prevent your looking at pretty girls any more, or else I will cut a certain part of your body off, which will stop your doing them any harm in the future."

Oga said he could not part with his eyes, so at last he consented to 'Nyambi's cutting the part off his body, provided he promised not to kill him and to let him go.

'Nyambi promised, and having told Oga not to make a noise, he cut the thing off, and turned the chief out of his house. Chief Oga then went home, but did not tell anyone what had happened to him. He was in such pain all the night that he was unable to sleep, and when the morning came, he asked one of his wives to boil some water and bring it to him. She did as she was told, and the chief went into the back-yard and bathed and dressed the wound.

He then sent one of his boys to call 'Nyambi to him. When 'Nyambi arrived he did not go inside the house, but stood a few paces from the door, as he thought that Oga might try to do him some injury; but the chief said he did not intend to hurt him and that he might safely come inside. Chief Oga then implored 'Nyambi not to tell any of the young men of the town what he had done to him, and begged him to keep it secret until the day of his death. 'Nyambi promised, and went home and told his wife.

The chief's wound took many days to heal, and at night, when his wives came to him, he had to send them away, saying he was not well. This went on for some time, until at last his wives got tired of being alone and began to desert him and go to other men, and very soon he was left with only boys in the house.

The chief then sent for all his wives to hear his last words. When they arrived, he said, "My dear wives, I am not angry with you for leaving me, for love of women has caused me to lose the dearest part of my body. But I will ask one favour of you, and that is, when I die you will all come and cry and mourn for me, as is usual. Then you will know why I did not sleep with you."

The women then asked the chief what was the matter with

him, so he pointed to his waist, and said he had great pain there, and was unable to move that part of his body. He then told them all to go away.

Chief Oga lived for a few more years and then died. His wives, who had by that time all married other men, got permission from their husbands to go and mourn for Chief Oga.

When the people took the chiefs body into the back-yard to wash it, they found that a certain part of his body had been cut off. His wives were very much surprised when they saw what had been done to their late husband, as during his lifetime, he had been quite all right. They therefore went and told the chiefs of the town. The chiefs then came and inspected the body, and afterwards met in the palaver house to try and find out who had mutilated Chief Oga. The drum was beaten and the young men of the town were told to attend the meeting.

Directly 'Nyambi heard the drum, he called all his company to his house, and told them what he had done to Chief Oga. He also told them that what he had done was for the good of all people, and asked them to support him at the meeting, and if it came to a fight, that they should all be on the same side.

When they had heard the whole story, the members of 'Nyambi's company agreed to back him up, and as they were the principal fighting-men of the town they went to the palaver house without much fear.

When all the people had arrived, the oldest chief of the town stood up, and said, "I have seen to-day what I have never seen before since I was born. Chief Oga, whom you all know, died this morning, and I went to look at his body. I then saw that a certain part of his body was missing. Now I want to know who did this thing, and what became of the missing part of the late chief. I shall be glad if any young man of the town who knows anything about this palaver will inform me."

Then 'Nyambi stood up and questioned the chief, as follows: "What will be done to the man who did this? Will he be killed or will he be allowed to go free? "The chief replied that the man would certainly be killed, if he had mutilated Chief Oga by force without a very good reason, but that if they considered he was justified in his action, he would be allowed to go free."

Then 'Nyambi told the people that he had done this thing, and addressed them as follows: "When I married my wife Obim, while she was still in the circumcision house, Chief Oga went to her and tried to persuade her to-go to him. After that he frequently sent messages to her, asking her to sleep with him, but she always refused. Again, when I was absent, Chief Oga went to my house to sleep with my wife, but I returned and caught him lying asleep on her bed.

'Nyambi then asked the question, "What do you do when you catch a thief in your stack of yams?" And the head chief replied," He is tied up to a tree, and left there to die." 'Nyambi then said that he treated Chief Oga as a thief, but he took pity on him, and instead of killing him, he gave him his choice whether he would have his eyes put out or have a certain part of his body cut off. The late chief chose the latter alternative, so he performed the operation. He then called his wife Obim, who brought on a calabash the part of the dead chief's body, which had been cut off and dried in the· sun, as proof of what he had said.

'Nyambi then asked the chiefs whether he was justified in the course he had taken or not; and the chiefs, after consultation, agreed that he had done right.

A law was then passed that, if a husband caught another man in his house having connection with his wife, he could do whatever he liked with him in the house, but once the man was outside the house, he should not be molested, and the case should be decided before the chiefs.

But the chiefs also added, that the man who was caught committing adultery might defend himself as well as he could, and would not be punished for so doing.

Told by Ennenni, an Okuni woman. [22.7.10.]

XXV.

How Two Bendega Young Men changed their Skins

Bendega is a town on the right bank of the Afi River, which runs into the Cross River opposite to Abaragha. In this town many years ago there lived two young men called Abang and Oga 'Ngigor.

Abang was famous for his personal beauty, and was recognized as the best wrestler, dancer, singer, and drum-beater in the country. Abang was never allowed to leave the town by his parents, as they thought he might be killed or get into trouble with other young men of his company, but in spite of this his fame as a singer and dancer, and stories of his manly beauty had spread through all the neighbouring towns, and many people wanted to see him. But as he was a dutiful son he stayed at home and did not accept any of the numerous invitations he received from the various countries to attend their plays and dances, although he was frequently offered quite large numbers of rods and other presents to go. Needless to say, all the young girls of the country wanted to marry him, but he looked after himself very well and kept away from the women in general, having his own particular friend to whom he was on the whole fairly faithful.

Oga 'Ngigor had also been a good wrestler, singer and dancer, until he caught a bad sickness which covered his whole body with sores. These sores were so bad that Oga could not walk about, and his body smelt so disgustingly that the people would not let him come near them. He was very poor, and consequently was often starving, as he was unable to go about and beg for food. While Oga was sitting down in his house feeling sad and miserable, he sometimes thought of Abang, who belonged to his company, and envied him his good looks and his popularity. So one day Oga went to Abang and asked him to change skins with him for a short while, as he would like to know what it felt like to be as strong and handsome as Abang was. He did this as he had made up his mind to run away in Abang's skin and go round the country, where he knew the people would be certain to give him many presents. After he had flattered Abang for some time, he took off his skin and placed it on the ground and asked Abang to do the same so that they could change skins for a short time.

At first Abang refused, as he did not like the idea of putting on the dirty skin, so he asked Oga if the sores hurt. Oga at once replied that the sores never hurt him, and he only sat down so that the people should not look at him. Then Abang took his skin off and put on Oga's, and Oga got into Abang's skin as soon as he was able.

Now when Abang got into Oga's skin he was unable to walk, and was obliged to sit down. Ogo knowing this, directly he had got into Abang's skin, ran down to the beach, and, jumping into a canoe, paddled himself across the Afi River, and ran off along the road to Akparahong as fast as he could go, leaving Abang sitting on the floor of the house calling to him to return at once and change skins. But

Oga ran on without hearing his cries, until at last he arrived at the Akparabong farms. When he got near the town one of the natives of the country, through whose farm the path passed, told him that Chief Ojong Egussa was dead, and that his funeral was being kept at 'Nkanassa compound, where a big play was going on and much drinking and feasting.

This was good news for Oga, as he felt certain of a good reception, so when he came to the small stream just outside the town, where the people always wash on their return from their farms in the evening, he took off his cloth and had a good wash. He then washed the cloth he had been wearing, and put on his best one, which belonged to Abang, so as to make a good impression on the people. As soon as he was ready he went to the house where the funeral was going on, and told the people that he was the celebrated Abang from Bendega, whom they had wanted to see for such a long time. The people and chiefs were very glad to see him, and asked him to play and sing for them, which he did. The people were so pleased at having Abang to play for them, and admired him so much that when the funeral was over the chief presented him with some cases of gin, cloth and rods, and gave him some boys to carry his loads on the road to Ikom.

Oga then started off, and arrived at Adaginkpor early in the afternoon. He went to the head chief, who was an old man, and told him that he was Abang from Bendega, and that he was going round the country to visit the people. The chief welcomed him, and said he had often wished to see him, as many people spoke of his personal appearance and his good qualities. Oga stayed at Adaginkpor for a few days, during which time dances were held every night, as the moon was full, and all the people came in from their farms to see Abang and hear him play and sing.

When Oga left the town he received many more presents from the people, and the young men's company carried his loads into Ikom, which is not far from Adaginkpor, and is a large town on the right-hand of the Cross River. The people of Ikom had heard from Adaginkpor that Abang was going to visit them, so they were ready for him, and gave him a big feast, and held a play which lasted several days, Oga taking his part in the playing, dancing and singing, as before. When he left Ikom, Oga was given more presents, and the chief lent him a large canoe and some paddles to take him to Okuni, a town a little lower down the river on the other side. Oga did the same at this town, and then went on to Okanga, and after a few days walked along the river bank to Enfitop. At each of these towns he received presents, and when he got to the next town, which is called 'Nporo Osilla, he crossed the big river again, and went through the Inde country, where all the people turned out to meet him, and when he left they gave Oga many yams and other presents, so that when he started off for the next town, which is called Inkum, he had a large number of carriers carrying his loads, which by this time had become very numerous.

Unfortunately for Oga, the chief of Inkum had heard from Abang's parents that Oga had changed skins with their son and that he was travelling about the country collecting dashes in Abang's name. When the chief heard that Oga had come, he at once sent a message to Abang's parents requesting them to come to Inkum as soon as possible and to bring their son with them. The chief then greeted Oga and persuaded him to stay on from day to day, and told him that a play was being brought from Bendega.

When the people from Bendega came near the town of Inkum, Abang, who was disguised in the dress of an Egbo and covered from head to foot in a very fantastic costume, sent some boys to Oga with a message telling him to come out and meet them. Oga was so proud at hearing that a play had come all the way from Bendega to escort him to the town that he willingly went out to meet them, not knowing that the real Abang had come with them.

When Oga arrived at the place where the people who had brought the play were resting in the shade of some large trees which grew by the side of the path, Abang stood up, and having thrown the Egbo dress on one side, he took off Oga's skin and placed it on the ground, at the same time telling Oga to do the like. At first Oga refused, and begged Abang not to shame him before all the people, but Abang insisted upon having his own skin back again, so Oga was forced to exchange. The people then knew that they had been deceived by Oga and that he had taken their presents wrongly. They told the real Abang that they were sorry they could not give him any more presents, and that the best thing he could do was to help himself from the things which had been given to Oga in his name. Abang however, was kind-hearted, and allowed Oga to keep all the presents he had received, as he was very poor and he was sorry for him having such a wretched body and being all covered with sores. And now whenever people are asked to change their skins they always refuse, but sometimes they will lend their best cloth to a friend.

Told by Abbassi of Inkum. [22.7.10.]

XXVI.

Concerning the Ju-Ju against Elephantiasis, or How The Hares lost their Long Tails

Okpa was a ju-ju man living at Okuni many years ago, and the name of his ju-ju was 'Nda.[9] The old man continually made sacrifices to his ju-ju of goats and fowls and all the young men of the town brought him presents as sacrifices so that they should not get the disease, which is very common throughout the country. Whenever a sacrifice was about to be made, all the people who belonged to the society used to meet together and sit down all round the ju-ju, but as the law of the ju-ju was that no man should open his legs, the people always tied their knees and ankles together with tie-tie, because if anyone opened his legs he would at once get elephantiasis.

Once while the people were feasting and playing round the ju-ju, the hare came along with his fine tail, and seeing them all eating goat's-flesh, fowls, foo-foo and yams, he asked Okpa if be might join in the feast, as the hare was very greedy and could never resist eating anything he saw. Okpa told the hare that he might join in the feast, but that when he had finished eating he must make the

---

9   "'Nda" in the Infor and Inde languages means "elephantiasis."

usual present to the ju-ju, and that if he went way without paying, something very bad would happen to him. The hare agreed to this, and sat duwn amongst the people and took his share of all the food; but as he was enjoying himself so much he did not notice that the people were sitting in rather a peculiar fashion, so he sat down in the ordinary way with his legs open.

When the food was finished the ju-ju man tied one of the young green shoots from the palm-tree round each of the members of the society. He then dipped his hand into the ju-ju pot, and having touched them one after the other on the forehead and breast, he told them to depart. But he did nothing to the hare, and when he came to where he was sitting he called upon the newcomer to go and bring the usual present of a goat or a fowl to sacrifice to the 'Nda ju-ju. The hare said he had nothing to give just then, and got up to go away, but found that a certain portion of his body had swollen to such a size that it touched the ground when he stood up. He then saw that he had caught the Elephantiasis, and asked Okpa to cure him of the disease, but the ju-ju man said he could not help him until he had made his proper sacrifice to the 'Nda ju-ju.

As the hare was very poor he was in a great state of mind as to how he should pay, and although he begged hard Okpa would not listen to him; so at last he made up his mind to consult his wife, and started off, dragging the Elephantiasis with him. On the road he planned how he should get rid of the disease and at last asked the Elephantiasis to leave him for a little time, as he wanted to relieve himself. The Elephantiasis replied that the hare could relieve himself quite well without his going away, so the hare was compelled to do so; he then returned to the path again.

After he had gone a short distance further the hare thought he would try another trick to get rid of the disease, so, seeing some rubber vines growing near with ripe fruit, he said to the Elephantiasis, "I am still very hungry, are you not hungry also? I want to climb up and get that ripe rubber fruit, but cannot do so as you are so heavy. If you will stop on the ground I will climb the vine and throw the rubber fruit down to you, and you can gather it and put; it in the bag, and then we shall have plenty to eat on the road."

So the Elephantiasis, who really was hungry, agreed to stop on the ground, and the hare, relieved of the great weight, at once climbed the rubber vine and commenced to throw down the fruit, which the Elephantiasis gathered and put in the bag. As the hare gathered the fruit he threw it further and further away from the vine, and the Elephantiasis rolled himself away after it until at last he had gone some distance from the tree, so the hare slid down to the ground; and ran towards his home as fast as he could go.

When the Elephantiasis got back to the vine he called out to the hare, but as he did not receive any answer he guessed the hare had run home, so he rolled himself along the path after the hare, but although he was neatly round he could not travel nearly as fast as the hare, who was a very swift runner indeed. The hare therefore reached his house some time before the Elephantiasis, and at once called out to his wife and told her to go and stay with a neighbour of his for a few days as he was running away from a man, and his enemies were following him to kill him or take him prisoner, and he feared that they might catch her. His wife then picked up her things and went off to their friend's house, and the hare having said that he would probably be absent for some days, ran off in another direction, leaving his home deserted, so that when the Elephantiasis arrived he found no one about the place.

The hare took a path which led through some farm and after a time came across some people who were clearing the ground for their new farm. He went up to them, and having told them a long story about the cruel enemy he was running away from, begged them to hide him and cover him up with leaves and branches so that he should not be discovered. As the people were sorry for the hare, they agreed to do what he asked, and put him in a heap of rubbish where he could not be seen; they then went on with their work.

Shortly afterwards the Elephantiasis rolled himself up to where the people were working and asked them whether they had seen the hare pass that way, but the people told him that the hare had not called at their farm. Then the Elephantiasis said, "Oh, I see you want to deceive me, for I tracked him as I came along the path; but let me tell you the hare is a great friend of mine; unfortunately he has long legs and can run fast, whereas I have no legs and can only roll along slowly, and thus got left behind." But the people still maintained that they had seen nothing of the hare. Then the Elephantiasis got angry, and said to the people, "If you do not tell me at once where the hare is, I will jump on you and you will have to carry me for the rest of your lives." At this the people were frightened, as they knew the disease well, and did not wish to have it with them always, so they pointed out the heap of rubbish where the hare was hiding, and the Elephantiasis rolled off towards it.

Now all this time the hare had been listening, and when he saw the Elephantiasis coming towards him he jumped out of the heap and ran away as fast as he could go. He ran for some distance, and passed another farm, but did not go in, as he thought the same thing might happen to him there. He went on and on until he thought the Elephantiasis must be a long way behind, and it would be safe to stop for a time, so when he came to a small compound where the people were having their evening meal he went in and told them that he was being chased, and that the enemy were following him. When the people heard this they stopped eating, and having collected all their food they put it in the Egbo house and told the hare to stop there. They then armed themselves with bows and arrows to protect their homes from the enemy. The hare told them to go some little distance from the Egbo house, so that they should not be driven back upon him at once. He then sat down and eat the people's food.

For some time the people stood waiting for the enemy to appear, but they saw no signs of anyone until the Elephantiasis rolled up to them, when the hare called out "The enemy has come." At this one of the men raised his bow and arrow and was about to shoot when the Elephantiasis said, "Don't shoot, I am not your enemy; I am looking for my friend, the hare, and I want you to show me where he is." The people said he had not come that way, but the Elephantiasis replied that he had just heard the hare's voice, and again threatened to jump on one of the men if they did not show him where the hare was hiding. The people then called upon the hare to come out of the Egbo house, but instead of doing so, he ran away in the opposite direction, and went down to a stream where he knew a land crab

Stone ju-ju and carved wooden pillar. Egbo house in background.

lived. When he got to the hole he found the old mother land crab at the entrance, and told her his usual story, asking her to help him, as the men always gave him up, and he promised to reward her if she drove his enemy away or killed him. The mother crab agreed, but told the hare that she had young ones in one branch of the hole, and that he might go in and sit down in another part until the fight was over. So the hare went into the hole, and the old mother crab stood at the entrance with her large claws open ready and waiting for the enemy.

Not long after this the Elephantiasis rolled himself down to the stream, where he met the mother crab, looking very fierce, and asked her if she had seen the hare. The crab replied, "Yes, the hare is in my house, but I never give strangers up to their enemies."

When the Elephantiasis said he was a friend of the hare, the crab said, "I don't care whether you are a friend or an enemy, I am not going to give the hare up." This made the Elephantiasis very angry, and he threatened to jump on the crab. But the crab said, "I am not at all afraid of you. You can try if you like, and then you will see what will happen."

At this the Elephantiasis rolled himself back a few paces, and then went for the crab. The old crab was ready for him, and nipped him so severely with her sharp pincer-like claws that water came from his inside and he yelled with pain.

The hare then shouted out to the crab to fight well, and that when she had killed the Elephantiasis they would both make a good meal off him. When the Elephantiasis heard this he became more furious than ever, and rolled back again, and then made another attack on the crab. The crab then pinched him so severely that he burst and died, at which the hare was very glad.

When the mother crab told the hare that she had killed the Elephantiasis he told her to drag the body to the stream and wash it. Then the mother crab called for her knife, which the hare gave her out of the hole. The crab then dragged the Elephantiasis to the stream, where she cut him up and washed him properly. She then carried the meat back into the hole.

During the time the old crab had been fighting the Elephantiasis, the hare had been very busy, and had killed and eaten three of the crab's children, and then threw their shells behind the fireplace near to where the old crab used to keep her salt. When she returned the hare told her that they should cook and eat his dead enemy, so he made up the fire, and the flesh was put into a pot to boil. While the meat was cooking the crab went to get some salt, and to her horror saw the shells of three of her children on the ground where the hare had thrown them. Having put the salt into the pot she went into the next hole where she had left her children, to count them. But the hare, seeing that trouble was likely to come, and not liking the idea of being nipped by the crab's strong claws, with which she had just killed his enemy, took the pot off the fire and ran away with the meat.

When the mother crab returned vowing vengeance on the hare she found he had gone and had taken her pot with the meat in it; and although she shouted to him several times to come back she got no answer.

The hare ran on some distance with the pot of meat, on the road to his house and when he thought he was safe from pursuit he sat clown on an ant-hill, with his tail down a hole. Having looked round everywhere carefully to see that no one was following or watching him, he commenced to eat the flesh of his late enemy. All this time the ants were busy building their house, and while the hare was eating his food the ants had covered half his tail and had bitten it through.

When he had finished his meal the hare felt that something was wrong with his tail, so he jumped away from the ant-hill, and found to his disgust that he had left half his tail behind him where the ants had bitten it through. When he saw what had happened he did not like to return to his wife at once, as she might deny him so he waited until it was dark and then joined his wife. She was very glad to see her husband again, and asked him about the war party he was running away from.

The hare said, "All the trouble is now over, as I have gone through the ceremony of the war ju-ju , and the chief cut me on the tail so that in future I shall never die from war or fighting in any way." And as it was then dark the hare's wife lit the lamp,[10] but the hare hid his tail in the darkness so that his wife could not see it, as the wound had not healed up.

When the evening meal was over, the two hares retired for the night, but when his wife had put the lamp out, the hare told her that if she wanted to get up during the night or light the lamp she must wake him up first, as otherwise his war ju-ju would be spoilt.

Now the hare was tired after all his running, and very soon he was fast asleep, so when his wife was certain that he would not

---

10   The native lamp was of earthenware, with a fibre wick in palm-oil.

wake up easily, she got out of bed very quietly and lit the lamp, as she was extremely curious to know what the ju-ju man had done to her husband's tail. When she saw that the hare had lost half his tail, she was ashamed of him, and began to cry. Then the hare woke up and began to abuse his wife, saying that she had spoilt his ju-ju and would have to pay a great deal to make it right again. After a violent quarrel they eventually went to sleep; but in the morning at first cock-crow the hare's wife got up and packed up all her things, saying that she was going away to find another husband, as she could not possibly live with a hare who had lost half his tail, whether it had been cut by the ju-ju man or not.

The hare then said, "You have no sense. It will not help you at all to leave me, as all the other hares have had the same thing done to them on account of the war ju-ju. You had much better stay with me." But his wife was not satisfied, and told her husband that she should go out and see for herself whether what he had said was true; so she started off a long the path to the nearest hare's house.

Directly she was out of sight the hare ran through the bush as fast as he could to the house his wife was bound for, and as she was carrying a heavy load he got there some little time before her. He then told his friend that his wife had left him because he had lost part of his tail, and was on her way to see whether he had also lost his. The hare then asked his friend to step into his back room and allow him to speak to his wife from the door when she came. His friend gladly consented to help him, and soon after he had gone inside the hare's wife appeared and put down her load. The hare then stood up in the doorway, facing his wife, and calling her by name said, "Ekanga, where are you going with that load? Are you leaving your husband?" And his wife said, "Yes." The hare then said, "What is the matter?" and she replied, "My husband has lost his tail, and told me that it had been cut on account of the war ju-ju, and that all the other men-hares have also had their tails cut, so as I do not like to live with a hare who has no tail, I have come to see if he told the truth."

The hare then said, "We have all passed through the same ju-ju and had our tails cut off; look and see." He then turned round and showed her.

His wife then went on from one hare's house to another, but each time her husband went on in front of her and deceived her in the same way, until at last she got tired and turned back to go home. The hare then ran quickly home, and jumped into bed, and when his wife appeared he said, "So you have returned. You are a foolish woman, and you can go or stay as you please, I do not care." But his wife said that she was satisfied that her husband had spoken the truth, as all the hares she had seen had had their tails cut off, so she had resolved to turn back.

The next day the hare called all his company together, and told them that he had nearly lost his life the previous day on account of his long tail, as he had sat down on an ant heap with his tail down one of the holes, and some animal inside had caught hold of it and tried to pull him inside to kill him, but to save his life he had cut his tail off with a knife, and he strongly advised them to do the same. To this they all agreed, and cut their long tails off in order to escape from any enemy who might try to catch them by the tail, and ever since the hares have had no tails, as when the men-hares went home they made their wives and children follow their example, telling them that it was done for their good by the war ju-ju to prevent them from dying in battle. On account of the hare's wife lighting the lamp to look at her husband's tail and thus spoiling his war ju-ju, it has been a custom ever since that when men are going to fight they will never trust their wives with their war ju-ju, and they will not sleep with them or eat any food which they have cooked with their hands until the fighting is over.

Told by Ennenni, an Okuni woman. [26.7.10.]

XXVII.

How a cruel Inkum Chief was Poisened by his Slaves, and How his Son Hanged Himself on account of the Expenses of his Brother's Funeral

At Inkum in the olden days there dwelt a chief called Erim. He was very wealthy, having many slaves, both male and female, and a large farm. He was known throughout the country as a cruel man and a hard master. Most of Chief Erim's wealth was made by selling camwood and the large yams grown on his farm. The chief made a rule that each woman slave should bring him at the end of every seven days twelve balls or cakes of camwood. If any of them failed to do so, he tied them up to a tree and they were given fifty lashes on the back with a heavy whip made of twisted skin. They were also made to pay the value of the number of balls of camwoocl which they had failed to make. This meant that all the women slaves had to work very hard indeed, and they could get no help from their husbands in any way, as at first cock-crow all the men were sent off to the farm to work, and were not allowed to return until the evening.

Very frequently the men slaves were severely flogged by order of the chief, if he were not satisfied with the amount of work done on the farm, or if they annoyed him in any way. In consequence of his cruel treatment of them, all his slaves hated Chief Erim, and although they were much in fear of their master they often planned to kill him.

Now Chief Erim had only two wives; one was an Okuni wo-man, by whom he had a son called Odoggha Eyu, and the other was a native of Inkum, whose son's name was Oga Erim. The chief was very fond of both his sons, and never allowed them to do any work on the farm. He gave them plenty of food and good cloths, and they grew into strong young men. There was one thing, however, that vexed Chief Erim, and that was that Odoggha Eyu was his eldest son, and he knew that when he died Odoggha Eyu would return to Okuni, which was his mother's birthplace. The chief therefore made up his mind that his youngest son, Oga Erim, should inherit his property, and for several years taught him how to rule the people with a strong hand and to punish them severely if they did not work, as that was the way he had become rich.

When the two sons had grown up, the slaves made a plan to kill Chief Erim, whom they hated so much. The head slave waited until the day came for the women to bring their camwood to be counted, and then told his wife to keep back three balls of camwood, so that if the chief flogged her, he would be able to give a good reason to the other slaves why they should kill their master. When all the women slaves had brought their camwood, the chief told the head slave to count the cakes as usual. He did so, and told Chief Erim that his wife had only brought nine cakes of camwood instead of twelve, as she had been very busy in the house and hail had a lot of other work to do. The head slave also said that ever since he had been married his wife had always brought the right number of cakes, and as this was the first time she had failed to do so he begged the chief not to punish her. But Chief Erim was angry, and said that the head slave's wife ought to know better and should set a good example to the other slaves. He then had her tied up to a tree, and she was given fifty lashes, the blood running down her back on to the ground, the woman becoming unconscious from the pain. She was then released and water having been thrown over her she was carried to her house, where she was placed on the sleeping-mat.

The next day the woman was made to pay for the three missing cakes of camwood, and the chief told the other women slaves that the punishment the woman had received should be a warning to them and make them work harder.

The head slave washed the wounds on his wife's back, and put some mashed up leaves on the sore places to stop the bleeding and heal the cuts. When he saw what a terrible flogging his wife had received, his heart was full of rage against Chief Erim, so that very night he went to every slave, and they all agreed to kill their master. The head slave then went to a clever poisoner who lived not far away, and bought two powerful ju-jus; one would give the person against whom the ju-ju was made the "dry cough" (consumption), and the other would give him paralysis. He then hid the ju-jus, as they had decided to wait some time after the woman had been flogged before they gave the poison to the chief, so that no suspicion should be attached to them of having poisoned their master.

All the slaves went about their work as usual until the time arrived for the new yams to be dug, at which season it was customary for the people to give presents to their chiefs . The head slave then went into the bush and made a calabash of strong tombo. He then called Chief Erim's name, and having put the two ju-jus into the tombo, told the ju-ju to kill Chief Erim and not to harm anyone else. Having bought twenty-five yams and one cock, he took them, together with the calabash of tombo, and garn them to Chief Erim as his present. The chief thanked him for his dash, and told his small boy to pour out the tombo. The first glass was given to the head slave, who had brought the tombo, and he threw it on the ground, asking Ossorwor (God) to bless Chief Erim with plenty of wealth and long life. The "pourer-out" drank the second glass, and Chief Erim drank the next, the tombo was then passed round until it was finished, but the head slave poured the last glass, which had the remains of the poison in it, on the ground in front of the ju-ju, which was in the middle of the compound; this he did when the Chief Erim's back was turned so that he could not see.

About a month afterwards the ju-ju began to work, and Chief Erim felt sick; he coughed all day, and one side became useless so that he could not walk.

He wanted to go to the ju-ju man to ask him what was the cause of his sickness but being unable to move about he sent for his head slave and told him to go to the ju-ju man and tell him to come to his house so that he could consult him.

When the head slave came, he said to Chief Erim, "I have been your slave ever since I was a small boy. Surely you can trust me. Let me go and consult the ju-ju man on your behalf, and he will tell me what you should do in order to get well again. You have only to give me your loin-cloth, and then when he has seen it he will know what is the matter with you after he has cast lots."

Chief Erim agreed to this, and told his head slave to take two boxes of rods and some fowls as a present to the ju-ju man. The head slave kept the fowls and rods for him self, and did not go near the ju-ju man, but the next day he went to his master and said that he had consulted the ju-ju man, who had said that the chief's life was in danger; and that he had been poisoned by his Okuni wife, who wanted her son to inherit her husband's property. If Chief Erim wanted to get better, he should at once send the wife and her son to Okuni, as they were both witches, and that in three months' time he would be quite well again. The ju-ju man also said that if it had not been for the small ju-ju in the middle of Chief Erim 's compound, who had been fighting the witches for him, he would have been dead long before. The chief should therefore make a sacrifice of a white cock and a goat to the ju-ju for his help.

Chief Erim then told his wife to go back to Okuni and take her son with her. He also told the head slave to sacrifice the white cock and the goat to the ju-ju. This was done, but instead of getting better, chief Erim died in less than a month, and his son Oga Erim inherited his father's property.

When the chiefs of Inkum heard of the disease which Chief Erim had died from, they made an order that the body should be buried in a deep grave in the bush, that the funeral should not be kept as usual, and that no one was to mourn for the dead chief, as the sickness he had died from was a very dangerous one, and if any-one cried for him they would get the disease. The chief's body was therefore buried without any of the customary funeral rites, which saved Oga Erim a large amount of money.

It did not take the slaves long to realize that they were very little better off for the death of their late master, as Oga Erim carried on much in the same way as his father had. The first woman slave who failed to bring her twelve cakes of camwood was given forty lashes instead of fifty, but Oga Erim said that he was young yet, but that as he got older he would be much more severe and punish the people far more cruelly than his father had ever done, as he intended to be very wealthy, and they would have to work much harder than they had done during his father's lifetime unless they wished to be badly punished.

One day when he was vexed with a slave, he tied him up to a tree and led the driver ants to him, so that he died in great agony. After a time things became so bad that the slaves decided that they must kill Oga Erim, but they did not like to do so at once, as they thought that the Inkum people might suspect them, in which case they would be tortured in many different ways, so they resolved to wait two years before they revenged themselves upon their cruel master.

As the time went on Oga Erim became harder on his people, and some of the slaves were flogged and tortured almost every day; he seemed to take great delight in their sufferings, and spent much time in devising new forms of torture.

When Chief Erim had been dead two years, the head slave called all the other slaves together, and said that the time had arrived when Oga Erim must die, as he did not think that they would be suspected if they were careful. The slaves then discussed the best way to kill Oga Erim. One of them said, "Let us make him blind in both eyes," but the others would not agree, and said he should be killed at once, as if he were only blind he would know what was going on and would still be able to punish them. At last it was decided to poison Oga Erim, so the slaves brought a very strong poison made from the horns of a ram and some of the hair from the mane cut into small pieces. They then called Oga Erim's name and told the ju-ju to kill him and not to harm anyone else. The poison was then placed in Oga Erim's food and a few hours after he had eaten it he began to vomit and spit blood; so when the sun was going down he called for the head slave and asked him to get him some medicine to cure him. The slave advised his master to leave the compound and go to his farm-house until he got well, as he thought that someone must have put a ju-ju in the ground where he was lying, which caused him to be sick. As Oga Erim was unable to walk, the head slave ordered four slaves to carry their master to his farm. In the middle of the night Oga Erim died in great pain, and one of the slaves at once ran off and told the head slave what had happened. He told all the slaves to be quiet and not to tell anyone until he gave them permission, as the head slave knew that directly Odoggha Eyu heard of his brother's death he would at once come to Inkum to keep the funeral and take all the goods which were formerly his father's.

The head slave then went to the body of Oga Erim and got the keys of the houses where all the rods and other valuables were kept. When he got back to the town, he opened the store where all the rods were, and having called all the slaves together, he divided the rods amongst them all, and then locked the door again. He then went to the house where Oga Erim kept his walking-sticks, brass pans, pots and other expensive articles, and having opened the door, divided these things up and locked the door. After this the head slave divided up the cows, goats, sheep, pigs and fowls between them all, but he left five cows in the compound so that the funeral might be properly kept. He then told some of the slaves to carry their master's body to the town, but before this was done he warned all the slaves to be very careful not to keep any of their dead master's property in their own houses, as they might be accused of stealing, so he advised them all to send their things to their different friends' houses where they could be kept for them without anyone knowing.

A messenger was then sent to Odoggha Eyu to tell him that his brother was dead. The chiefs were also informed, and many people came to mourn, the women throwing themselves on the ground weeping.

When Odoggha Eyn heard that his brother Oga was dead, he called his company together to go with him to Inkum, and remembering how wealthy his father had been, he hired many slaves to carry the property back to Okuni. He also borrowed a large number of rods to provide a big feast at the funeral and to give his friends and the slaves he brought with him plenty to eat and drink.

When Odoggha Eyu arrived at Inkum, he asked the head slave to hand the keys of his brother's house to him, so that he could satisfy himself that everything was in order. But the head slave told him that it was the custom for him to bury the dead body first, and that after the feast the keys would be handed over; he also added that everything in the house was as his brother Oga had left it, and that all the doors were locked. Odaggha Eyu then bought five slaves, promising to pay for them after the funeral; these slaves he killed and placed in the grave with his brother. The five cows which remained in the compound were also killed, and their heads were put in the grave. The bodies of the cows were given to the people to eat.

Many men and women came to the funeral, as it was known that Oga Erim was rich, and Odoggha Eyu provided food and drink for them all, and the feasting, dancing and singing was continued for five days and nights. The grave was then filled in and beaten down, and the outside was polished. The head slave then handed the keys to Odoggha Eyu, who went first of all to the house where his father always kept his rods; when he opened the door and went inside there were no rods to be seen. Odoggha Eyu stood there silent for some time, wondering what had become of all his father's wealth and how he could manage to pay all the debts he had incurred on account of the funeral expenses. At last he asked the head slave what had become of all the rods which his father formerly possessed, and whether his brother had spent them all. The slave replied that he had received nothing himself, but suggested that the spirit of his late father had taken all the rods away.

After this Odoggha Eyu sent to the house where the brass pans, jugs, plates and other valuables used to be kept, and opened the door, only to find that it was as empty as the other house. Then he threw the keys down on the ground in despair and went away. He told his company what had happened, and advised them to go home at once, as he was unable to provide any more food and drink for them. Then the owners of the five slaves who had been killed went to him and demanded payment, and the other people to whom he owed money worried him all day, until at last he resolved to kill himself rather than go home in shame and debt.

Odoggha Eyu then asked where his father was buried, and when he was shown the place he went back to the house and sat down, waiting until it became dark. That night he got a rope and hanged himself on the branch of a tree overhanging his father's grave. His debtors, who were looking everywhere for him, could not find him, and thought he must have run away, but two days later his dead body was discovered hanging to the tree.

Ever since that time it has been a custom, whenever a person is absent when a sick relative dies and wishes to bury him, he first of all finds out how much property there is before he buys things for the funeral, so as to be quite certain that there will be enough to pay for all the expenses of the burial. If a man was poor, very few people would attend the funeral, but if he were rich many people would come. Hence the saying, "A small ju-ju has a small sacrifice, and a big ju-ju has a big sacrifice."

Told by Abassi of Inkum. [1.8.7.]

XXVIII.

How the Frog Beat the Bush Buck in a Race, and Won his Daughter as a Wife

Long ago, when the men, animals and birds were living together, there was a bush buck who was fine and strong; he was also a very quick runner. This bush buck had a daughter whose skin shone like a bright red stone. She was much admired by all the men and animals, and many of them wanted to marry her, and spoke to her father on the subject, but he placed such a high dowry on his daughter that no one was rich enough to pay it.

At last some of the young men, who were very anxious to possess the pretty daughter of the bush buck as a wife, asked the father to reduce the amount of dowry to such an amount as they would be able to pay. As the bush buck was very fond and proud of his daughter and did not want to part with her, he refused to reduce the dowry, but told the young men and animals that he would give them all another chance of winning his daughter, and that was, if any one could beat him in a race he would hand his daughter over to the winner as his wife without any dowry at all. In making this offer the bush buck thought he was perfectly safe, as it was well known that he was a faster runner than anyone in the country. A day was appointed for the races to be held, and a long straight course was cut. It was decided that the races should be run from one end of the course to the other and back again to the starting-point, and the first one to get back would be declared the winner.

When the day for the race arrived a large number of men and animals met, and the course was lined with spectators on both sides as far as the eye could see. Several young men who were noted for their speed and many swift-running animals competed for the bush buck's daughter, but they were all beaten by the bush buck. After several races of this kind had been held, the fame of the pretty daughter of the bush buck spread far and wide, and many other men and animals came from distant parts to try and win her, but without success.

One day, when the bush buck's daughter went down to the spring to get drinking-water, she met a young frog, who fell in love with her and decided to ask her father's consent to their marriage. But before he did so the frog called all his company, who were very numerous, together, and told them that he intended to try and win the bush buck's daughter, and that he would race her father. At this all the other frogs laughed, and said that the bush buck would have finished the course before the frog had jumped one pace.

The young frog allowed his companions to enjoy their laugh, and when they were quiet again he said, "I have a plan, and if you will all help me I am certain to win the race, and when I have got the bush buck's daughter for my wife I will give you a big feast, and it will be a great score to us to win her where everybody else has failed." He then said to his company, "Are we not all alike? "And they answered all together, with one croak, "Yes."

The young frog then told them his plan. As they all knew, the conditions of the race were that the two competitors were to start together and run to the end of the course, and then return to the starting-point, and the one who returned first would be the winner. All the young frogs were to go out in the early moming and hide themselves in holes at intervals along the whole of the course and one frog was to be at the turning point. Whenever the bush buck called out, one of the frogs was to answer him and pretend he had been running all the time.

All the frogs agreed that the plan was a good one, and promised to help their companion to win the race. When he had thus arranged everything to his satisfaction, the young frog went to the bush buck and challenged him to race for his daughter. But, although the bush buck laughed at the idea, he had to consent to run, and the race was arranged for the following day along the usual track, and the first home to be the winner.

Early in the morning all the frogs took up their positions along the course, and the young frog jumped on to the course where the starting-place was and waited for the bush buck to arrive. By this time many people had arrived to watch the race, and soon the bush buck joined the frog, and the signal to start having been given, they both jumped off together. But the frog returned to his hole, and the bush buck raced off alone as fast as he could go. When he had gone about half the distance the bush buck called out, "Where are you, frog?" and one of the frogs at once answered, "I am here, are you tired of running? "And the bush buck said, "Yes, I am tired. Let us run back, and the first in shall be the winner." So he turned round and started off again. When the bush buck got near the starting-place the frog came out of his hole and directly the people saw that he had got back before the bush buck, they declared the frog to be the winner, much to the disgust of many of the young men, who were watching the race, and who cursed the frog for his luck in winning such a fine wife. When the bush buck arrived he was much out of breath from running, and was greatly surprised at being beaten by the frog, but as he had passed his word that he would give his daughter to the winner, he handed her to the frog.

The frog then took his beautiful wife to his house near the spring, where they had a big play; and after the dancing was over the frog gave all the members of his company who had helped him to win the race quantities of food and tombo, which had been prepared for them. The young frog then went into the water, and tailed upon his wife to follow him. She went into the stream until the water came up to her neck, but, being naturally very timid, she was afraid to go further, and struggled back to the bank, where she said to her husband, "If you wish to live with me you will have to come on to the land, as I cannot live in the water." So the frog came out and joined his wife, but he only lived with her for a very short time, as the pretty bush buck walked so fast he could not keep up with her.

Very soon she strayed away into the forest, where she met a fine young bush buck, and, forgetting all about the frog, went off with her young lover. One day when she went to the spring to draw water the frog called out to her to return to him, but, as she refused to do so, the frog lost his wife for ever whom he had won so cleverly.

Told by Abassi of Inkum. [E.D., 11.8.10.]

XXIX.

Why a Python never Swallows a Tortoise

In the days when the elephant was king over all the beasts of the forest, it was the custom for all the animals to go once a year and make the elephant's farm for him. They cleared all the bush and planted his yams and plantains. On these occasions the elephant always entertained the animals, and when the work was finished the elephant gave them food. Now, although the python never did any work on the farm, he always attended the feasts and, being very greedy, eat more than his share of the food. This annoyed the tortoise so much that he stood up at the feast and abused the python before all the people, saying that he did not work, and then came and eat a large quantity of the food which had been provided by the king for the people who made his farm and planted his yams. The python was therefore compelled to leave the food and go home as he was unable to work, but he made a vow to revenge himself upon all the people. When the next season arrived and it was time for the farms to be made, all the people went as usual to make the elephant's farm and plant his yams, &c., but as the elephant had had such a very bad crop the previous year, he told the people he was very sorry, but that he was unable to supply them with food that year as he had no yams or plantains to give them. But in the evening, when the work was done, he gave them tombo to drink, and then told them to go.

When the python heard this he said, "Now the time is come when I can revenge myself upon the tortoise and the other people who would not let me eat the king's food last year." So he went off into the bush, taking his wife with him, and together they gathered large numbers of soft palm nuts. They also collected other nuts and fruit and made them into heaps by the wayside where they knew all the people would pass on their way home from working on the elephant's farm. Just before it got dark the animals began to arrive at the spot where the python had collected his nuts and fruit, and, being very hungry, they asked the python to allow them to eat some of his palm nuts. The python said, "Certainly, you can help yourselves, but remember if you do, when I am hungry I shall follow you and swallow you up when I catch you. When the animals heard this they were frightened, and although they were very hungry, they passed on and left the fruit untouched. The tortoise was the last to arrive, and when he saw the palm nuts he shouted out, "Hallo, python, I am hungry, may I have some of your fruit?" The python then reminded him how he had been insulted at the king's feast, but added, "If you are hungry you may take some palm nuts, but, when I am hungry I shall swallow you."

So the tortoise, not liking the idea of being swallowed by the python, passed along as the other animals had done. But he had not gone far when his hunger tempted him to return and eat the fruit. When he saw the python the tortoise said, "I want to eat the fruit as I am hungry, but, if you swallow me, my body is small and mostly shell so that your hunger will not be satisfied. If you will give me the palm nuts I will allow you to eat all the other animals except our king the elephant." So the python replied, "How can you give me all the animals for food, seeing that they do not belong to you?" The tortoise then told the python that he would go and stay with the different animals, and he would expect him every morning after rain had fallen during the night; he would then go off into the bush, so that when the python came to swallow him he would not be there, and he could satisfy his hunger with the animal he, the tortoise, had been staying with. The python agreed to this arrangement and allowed the tortoise to eat the palm nuts. When he had satisfied his appetite, the tortoise told the python he was going to stay the night with his friend the bush buck, and then went away. That night there was heavy rain. So in the morning the tortoise went off into the bush, leaving the bush buck to be eaten by the python. After this the tortoise went from one animal to another, and many of them were swallowed by the python, but the tortoise always escaped. And that is why pythons do not eat tortoises now.

Told by Abassi of Inkum. [E.D., 11.8.10.]

XXX.

The Game of Hide-and-Seek as Played by the Hawk and the Bush Cow

In the days when all the animals and birds lived together they were always on friendly terms, even the eagles and hawks did not molest the hens and ducks.

At that time the eagle was king over all the birds, and a very small grey-coloured antelope was made king of the animals. This antelope was appointed king because he was so cunning, and always knew when danger was near, having a very fine sense of smell and keen eyesight. The hunters were never able to kill him, because when they saw him, which was very seldom, it would be when he went to a pool to drink; then they would wait for the antelope to put his head down to the water, but this he never did, as he drank through small holes in his feet. He would then smell the hunters while they were watching him, and run away before they could kill him.

The eagle was elected king of the bird, because he lived higher up in the air than any of the other birds, and could thus direct them better. One day the eagle went to the antelope and challenged him to play at a game of hiding between the birds and animals. He chose the hawk to represent the birds, and the antelope selected the bush cow on the animals' side. They arranged that one should hide himself in the bush and the other should try to find him, but that if he failed to do so, the one hiding would be considered the winner and the loser would have to pay a large nmnber of rods as a forfeit.

The first day the hawk was told to hide in the forest and the bush cow had to find him. So in the early morning the hawk flew off to where he knew there was a very tall tree covered with creepers. He then hid himself in the densest part and went to sleep. All day long the bush cow wandered about trying to find the hawk, but without success, and when the evening came he was quite tired and went home and reported his bad luck to the antelope.

Later in the evening the eagle took the hawk to the antelope's house and said that as the bush cow had been unable to find him, he was the winner, to which the antelope agreed and paid over the rods to the eagle. The antelope was not satisfied, so they arranged to have another match; but the same thing happened and the antelope had to pay again.

On the third day the antelope said to the eagle, "It seems to be very easy to hide; let the bush cow go and hide and the hawk look for him." The eagle agreed to this, and the match was for the same number of rods. As soon as it was light enough to see, the bush cow went off into the forest until he came to a favourite swamp of his where he lay down and wallowed in the mud, leaving only a little of his head and back exposed to view. The hawk circled round and round and, knowing the habits of the bush cow and having very sharp sight, he very soon caught sight of the bush cow, so he swooped down and took a mouthful of hair and flew back to the eagle and reported that he had found the bush cow, and produced the hair as proof. That night the antelope had to pay again, and by this time he had lost quite a lot of money, so he arranged with the eagle that the hawk should hide the next day and the bush cow should try again.

When the eagle had gone, the antelope told the bush cow that he was very angry indeed with him, and that if he failed to find the hawk again he would make him repay all the money he had lost to the eagle. The hawk flew off the next morning, and very shortly afterwards the bush cow dashed off into the forest to look for him. As the hawk had always won so easily, he thought he would have some fun with the bush cow, so he left the shelter of his tree and circled up high in the air. The hawk very soon caught sight of the bush cow rushing about through the forest, so he flew down very quietly behind the bush cow and perched himself on the horns of the bush cow quite softly. For some time the bush cow ran about in all directions searching for the hawk, until at last, as he could not find him, he thought the hawk must have gone home, so he charged back again through the bush to the hawk's house and at times the hawk had to follow him by flying as the bush was so thick, but when the country was open he quickly settled quite softly on the bush cow's horns again.

As the bush cow went through the town he saw several different birds, and asked each of them as he passed whether they had seen the hawk about anywhere, but although they could all see the hawk perched on the bush cow's horns, no one answered him. When he reached the hawk's house, the bush cow searched everywhere for him, but finding he was not there he rushed out again and went round another part of the town to see if he could find him. On his way he passed several cocks and hens, and asked them where the hawk was, but they only laughed at him. The bush cow then asked them again, but they continued to laugh. At last he became so angry that he threatened to trample on them if they did not tell him. So the cock said, "What you are looking for is sitting on your head; if you wave one of your arms over your head you will find what you want."

The bush cow would not believe the cow at first and all the birds continued to laugh at him. At last, however, the bush cow did as the cock suggested, to find out if what he had said was true, and at once the hawk flew up and was seen by the bush cow, who at once galloped off and told the antelope that he had found the hawk and had very nearly caught him with his hoof. The eagle was then sent for, and, although he grumbled very much, had to pay the amount of the bet.

That night the hawk told the eagle that it was the cock and hens who told the bush cow to wave his aim over his horns, other-wise he never would have been found. So the eagle sent for them and said, "It was you who told the bush cow where the hawk was hiding and in consequence I have had to pay a large amount to the antelope as a punishment; for the future I shall allow the hawk to always kill your children whenever he can catch them."

Now at this time the cocks and hens, who were related to the bush fowls, used to live with them in the same place, and when the eagle told them that the hawk would kill their chickens, they made up their minds to go and live with the men. When the bush fowls heard this they begged the cock and hen not to do so, and told them that the men would kill and eat them, but the cocks and hens replied that they would rather take their chance with the men than have their chickens killed by the hawk in the bush.

The following morning, therefore, the cocks and hens set off with their children, carrying a piece of bark with them and told the other people they were going to get some fire. When they got to the men's houses they looked about and found that there was so much to eat and they were so comfortable that they at once decided to stay, and have lived with the men ever since, while their cousins the bush fowls live in the bush. The hawks still continue to kill the chickens, but the cocks and hens always run and take shelter when they see the hawk coming. In the early morning before the sun rises you can always hear the bush fowls calling to the cocks and hens to come back and live with them, and shortly afterwards you can hear the cocks answering them, saying that they prefer to live in safety with the men.

Told by Abassi of Inkum. [E.D., 4.1.11.]

XXXI.

Chief Kekong's Daughter 'Ndere
who married a Python

Chief Kekong was a very rich Okuni chief. He lived many years ago at the time when the Okuni people never eat the cat-fish, as they thought it was a part of the water ju-ju, having such a smooth skin.

Chief Kekong had a wife named Nyam, who was a fine woman, and they had a daughter called 'Ndere, who was much sought after by the Okuni chiefs and other rich men in marriage, partly on account of her beauty, and partly for her father's wealth. 'Ndere was very vain of her personal appearance, and although her parents frequently tried to get her to marry, she always refused.

About this time a python lived at Okuni. He was a very fine fellow, and wanted to marry 'Ndere so that he might inherit her father's property, but having no hands and feet he knew he would stand no chance of winning a girl who had refused so many offers. He therefore consulted another python, who advised him to go into a far country and try to borrow from different men a head, feet and hands, white teeth, and a fine face and nose, but that he should keep his own eyes. The friendly python told him that if he did this and returned to Okuni and asked 'Ndere to marry him, it was very likely that she would do so.

The next day the python set off to a distant country, where he was unknown, and went to a chief called Kaku. The python said that, although he was a stranger, he hoped the chief would help him as far as he could. Then Chief Kaku asked the python what he wanted and how he could assist him. So the python said, "I want to marry 'Ndere, the daughter of Chief Kekong of Okuni, but, as I have no hands or feet, she will not look at me. I therefore want you to lend me a face, teeth, arms and legs, so that I would appear to her as a stranger, and she would then marry me."

Now the python was not aware that Chief Kaku had already asked 'Ndere to marry him, and that she had refused to do so, as if the python had known this he would have gone to somebody else. The python promised the chief that if he would lend him the different parts of the body which he required he would return them all to him after he had married 'Ndere. Chief Kaku thought the matter over, and as he was very anxious to obtain 'Ndere as a wife for himself, he decided to do as the python asked, having determined that when the python returned the borrowed limbs he would have him killed and take 'Ndere as his wife, whether she liked it or not. The more Chief Kaku thought of the plan, the easier it seemed; so he sent for all his young men, and took a head from one, arms from another, legs from a third, and fine white teeth from a fourth, and so on, until at last the python was complete.

Chief Kaku gave the python one young hoy to accompany him back to Okuni, and the following day the python set off on his journey, wearing all his borrowed limbs.

When he arrived at Okuni he looked nicer than any of the other Okuni young men; his long neck and small eyes, white teeth and the fine colour of his body appealed to 'Ndere when she saw him, and she at once took a great fancy to him.

Very soon after his arrival the python asked Chief Kekona to allow him to marry his daughter 'Ndere, and when the chief asked him who he was and where he came from, the python replied, "I am the son of Chief Kaku, who lives over there," pointing to where the sun rose at the back of the house. Then Chief Kekong, who knew Chief Kaku, as he had tried to marry 'Ndere but failed, called for some palm wine, which was brought and given to the python. Chief Kekong said he would think over what the python had said, but warned him that 'Ndere had already refused his father. He said, however, that if his daughter agreed to marry him, he would allow her to do so. The python was then given food to eat and a room to sleep in during the night.

That night, when everyone had gone to sleep, Chief Kekong woke his wife up and called 'Ndere to come. He then told her that the python wanted to marry her, and asked 'Ndere what her wishes were. Although 'Ndere intended to marry the python, she did not wish her parents to know what her thoughts were, as she was an obstinate and disobedient girl. 'Ndere then said to her mother, "Tell me what you think I should do." 'Nyam replied, "I do not wish you to marry this man, and would prefer that you should marry an Okuni man, because if anything happened to you we should be near, and in the case of sickness we would try to help you, whereas if you marry this stranger you will go far away, and we shall not be able to do anything for you." 'Ndere said, "Yes, my mother, I hear what you say. Now what does my father say?" Chief Kekong replied, "If you love this young man, whom you have never before seen, and go away with him as his wife, you may be sold as a slave, as you are such a fine girl, or you might possibly be killed; and although I am Chief of Okuni, I have no power in Chief Kaku's town, and should not be able to help you. As you are my only child, I do not want you to marry this stranger, but I want you to remain at Okuni with me."

'Ndere then answered her parents as follows: "I have always refused, up to the present, to marry all the men you have asked me to marry, but I am going to marry this man. You must therefore hand me to Kaku's son as his wife, and I will go off with him to his country. If you refuse to do this, I will go outside into the bush and hang myself."

Her parents tried their best to persuade 'Ndere to change her mind, but she was obstinate, and continued to threaten to hang herself if they refused to do what she wanted; they therefore left her until the next morning.

When the morning came, the python went to Chief Kekong and asked him for his decision with regard to his daughter. The chief called 'Ndere to him and asked her what her wishes were on the subject. 'Ndere said, "I am willing to marry this young man, and will go with him to his country."

The python then sent the small boy who had come with him to Chief Kaku, asking him to send the dowry, and after a few days the boy returned, bringing with him rods, cloth, camwood, and palm-oil.

The chief then handed his daughter to the python, and after she had been rubbed all over with camwood and oil she was taken to the python's room. She was then circumcised and kept in a room for three days; after that she was able to walk, so 'Ndere told the python that she was then willing to go with him to his country, and the following morning they set off from the town, walking very slowly.

It was not until after they had walked for two days that they reached Chief Kaku's town and when he saw them he was so glad that he at once had a goat killed in front of 'Ndere and sprinkled the blood over her feet. The chief then had a plentiful supply of food brought, which was given to the python and his wife, and a room was appointed for their use.

When the evening came, all the men and women were called together to dance and sing, the chief giving them plenty of palm wine to drink and doing everything he could think of to show 'Ndere that the python was his son. As soon as the play had commenced, Chief Kaku told the python to come to his house, so that 'Ndere was left in the house which had been set apart for the use of her husband and herself. The chief then asked the python to return all the different limbs and other parts of the body which he had borrowed from the different young men of the town as he had promised to do. But the python begged to be allowed until midnight before he returned the things he had borrowed, saying, "My wife and I have only just arrived, and it would be a shameful thing if I have to join her crawling on my belly." The chief agreed to allow the python until midnight, and the python then went off to join his wife in their house.

When midnight came the python got up and went to the chief's house and returned the different portions of the young men's bodies which he had borrowed. He then returned to 'Ndere in his natural form of a python, but when she saw him she denied that he was her husband. During the remainder of the night the python tried to convince 'Ndere that he was the man she had married, but she sat up the whole night and refused to have anything to do with him.

As soon as it was light 'Ndere went with the python to the chief's house, and asked him whether the python was his son whom she had married. The chief answered her that the python was his son, and that she was his wife. He also said that his son was going to return to Okuni the following day, and that she would have to accompany her husband.

'Ndere was not at all pleased to see her husband going about on his stomach, and refused to sit near him all the day. When night came she went into a separate house and would not let the python in. That night Chief Kaka gave orders to four of his young men to arm them selves with sharp matchets, and to lie in wait on the road to Okuni. He told them to kill the python and to bring 'Ndere back to him. This the young men promised to do, and set off before it was light, telling no one where they were going.

After the python and his wife had had their early morning food, they started off for Okuni, but when they arrived at the first water outside the town where the road branched off to the farm, the python, remembering that 'Ndere had refused to marry Chief Kaku, thought it very probable that the chief would cause him to be waylaid and his wife taken away from him. He therefore determined to follow the farm road, which, althong much longer, he thought would probably be safer; he thus missed the four men who were lying in wait for him.

Towards the evening the four young men returned to the town and reported to the chief that 'Ndere and her husband had not passed along the road which they were guarding. Chief Kaku then guessed that they must have taken the farm road, and had probably arrived safely at Okuni. Although the python had escaped the trap which the chief had set for him, he had no intention of letting him go, and now that he had seen 'Ndere again he was more determined than ever to possess her for himself, and at once began to plan how he should kill the python and induce 'Ndere to marry him. As he could not send his young men to Okuni to kill the python and take 'Ndere away by force, as that would mean war between the two countries, for which he was not prepared, seeing that the Okuni people were very powerful, he determined to wait and lay another trap for the python.

The chief knew that 'Ndere was very dissatisfied at having a snake as a husband, and would probably be glad to marry him, although he was rather old, rather than continue to live with the python, providing the python could be got rid of. He therefore decided to wait until the dry season came round, when the python would go to his farm, and might be killed without causing any trouble. But the first thing he had to do was to get 'Ndere to agree to come to him, so he sent off two of his young men to watch the python's house, and told them to pretend they came from a distant country. He sent messages by these men to 'Ndere, telling her to do everything her husband told her to do, and that when the time arrived for making the new farms he would have the python killed, and she could then come and marry him.

The young men went to Okuni as they were ordered, and, after watching for some time, at last met 'Ndere alone at the spring, where she was getting water, and gave her the messages from the chief. 'Ndere, who hated the python, agreed to help, and said she would be glad to marry anyone who would get rid of the python; so the young men returned and told the chief what she had said.

When the time arrived for making the farms, the python took all his people out into the bush, but as they had no matchets or arms to use them with, all they could do was to roll themselves about in the grass and then burn it. Every morning when the python and the rest of his people went to the farm, 'Ndere followed later, bringing the foo-foo and soup in calabashes. The python would not allow her to go so far as the farm, as he told her she was such a fine girl that if the other pythons saw her they would certainly be so envious of him that they might kill him in order to get her for themselves. He therefore showed her a place where she was to bring the food; here he had made a string of snail shells hung on sticks, and told 'Ndere to rattle them when she brought his food, and that he would come to her.

The first day the pythons went to work on the farm 'Ndere brought the food and rattled the snail shells as she had been directed to do, and very soon afterwards the python came and took the calabashes away to the place where they were working, telling 'Ndere to wait until he had finished eating. When he had eaten all the food he returned to the place where he had left his wife, and found her waiting for him. He then said, "My good woman, you have done well, you hear my voice properly," and having given her the empty calabashes, 'Ndere returned to her home.

This was done for two days, and on the third day 'Ndere said she would like to go to the farm to see the people working, but the python would not let her, so she sent a word to Chief Kaku that the python went to the farm every day. The chief then sent four of his young men, who hid themselves at the place where 'Ndere brought the food for her husband. When she had shaken the string of snail shells, the python soon appeared, and the men who were ready sprang up, where upon 'Ndere ran away, in order to deceive her husband. The four men then attacked the python with sticks, and soon killed him; they then cut off his head and his tail, and carried them back to Chief Kaku, leaving the food on the ground where 'Ndere had placed it.

The other pythons who were working on the farm, missing their companion very soon, went to see what had become of him, and found his dead body with the head and tail missing, near the food. As they could not discover who had killed the python, they met together and decided that for the future they would not make any more farms or live in the towns, as the men were jealous of them on account of the python having married 'Ndere. They therefore now live in the bush and hide themselves.

When 'Ndere appeared before Chief Kaku, he received her quite calmly, without any feasting or dancing, as he did not wish his people to suspect that he had murdered her husband. But after a few days had passed, Chief Kaku sent privately to Chief Kekong and told him that he had caused the python to be killed, and intended to marry 'Ndere. He also sent a large amount of dowry to the chief.

Now in Chief Kaku's country there was a stream full of cat-fish (Akpambi), but no one ever caught them, and when the people went to the stream to get water the fish would look at them without any fear. 'Ndere, hearing of this, went to the stream with a basket, and the fish seeing her, came close, so she began to sing softly to them, when more fish came. Then 'Ndere caught two of the fish with her basket, and took them home and cooked them for food, but none of the girls in the house would eat them, as they all said that if they did so they would die.

'Ndere, however, was not afraid, and eat the fish, which she found to be good food, and the soup was very sweet. She also took some to Chief Kaku, and said, "If you love me, you will eat my fish; but if you refuse, then I shall know that you do not care for me, and I shall not marry you, but will return at once to my father at Okuni." But the chief said, "No one ever eats that fish, as it has a smooth skin and is part of the water ju-ju. If anyone eats that fish, he will surely die." Then 'Ndere said, "Yes, my parents also will not eat this fish, but there is always one man who starts back first from the farm, and then the other people follow. I have eaten the fish and found it good, and have not died. If you eat it with me you will not die, and if we live to see the next sunrise to-morrow, all the people will follow our example and will eat the fish."

The chief then agreed, and said, "I will eat the fish with you, and if we die we shall be treated as husband and wife in the spirit." They then sat down together and eat the cat-fish.

When the chief had finished his share he prepared himself for death, and having called his people together, told them what should be done in case he should die. 'Ndere and the chief then retired for the night, and the chief slept quietly, without any trouble, until the morning. When he woke up and found that he was quite well, he sent 'Ndere out again with her basket to catch more of the fish, as the soup was so sweet. So 'Ndere went down to the stream once more and caught a lot of fish, which she brought back to the house and cooked as before.

Then the chief called his friends together, and told them about the cat-fish and what good food it was. When the people heard that the chief had eaten the cat-fish and had not died, they thought they would like to try some for themselves, so they all had some of the fish which 'Ndere had cooked. When they had eaten it they found it so good that when they returned home they at once sent their wives out with baskets to catch some of the fish. And thus it became the custom for the women to go out in the dry season with their fishing-baskets to catch the cat-fish. This custom was started by 'Ndere.

Told by Ennenni, an Okuni woman. [E.D., 5.1.11.]

XXXII.

How Agbor Adam broke the Hunting Law of Okuni, and How He was Punished

In the dry season, many years ago, Chief Akum Alobi of Okuni ordered all his people to go out hunting. They were to surround certain portion of the forest and set fire to the bush, then, as the animals came out, they were killed. At the same time, the women were sent to bale out the pools in the streams and to catch the fish.

The hunting law was that, during the hunting time, the men might eat the meat of the animals they killed, but they were not allowed to eat any fish, and the women might eat fish only, and not eat any meat from animals killed hunting.

While the hunting was going on, a man called Agbor Adam went to his wife, Iza Kakem, and asked her to give him some fish to eat, as he was tired of nothing but meat. The woman refused to do so, saying that the hunting law was so strong that, if they broke it, they would certainly be killed. But Agbor Adam, seeing that there was no one within sight, told his wife that it would be quite safe, as no one would know, and that, if she gave him some of her fish, he would give her one of the animals he had killed. The woman then gave her husband a fish, and he told her to go to the place where he kept the animals he had killed and take whichever she fancied. So Iza Kakem, having looked over all the animals, selected a monkey, and took it to the bush shelter where she was sleeping, and cooked and eat it. Her husband also eat the fish.

Now, all that had passed between these two people had been observed by a bird called Aictor, who was sitting in a tree and could see everything that happened. Aictor was a native of the Ingor country, and could not speak the Okuni language, and, at that time, the Okuni people could not understand Ingor, as they were not on friendly terms with them, so that, when the bird sang in the Ingor language, no one could understand what he said.

After Agbor Adam had eaten the fish, he returned to the hunting shelter, where the men were all sitting down, not noticing that the bird had been following him all the time.

Aictor then perched himself on the chief's shoulder, and called out in the Ingor language, "Agbor Adam, Agbor Adam, you have broken the law made by Chief Akum Alobi between hunting-men and fishing-women, and you know that whoever breaks this law will be killed."

Aictor shouted so loud that the men, who had never heard a bird talking in their hunting camp before, began to ask among themselves what he was saying, but as they did not understand Ingor, they could not tell one another. They could only hear Agbor Adam's name being called out. They therefore went to the chief and asked him to tell them what the bird was saying, but even the chief himself was unable to explain, and told the men not to trouble about what the bird said, but to continue with their hunting, and that when they returned to the town he would call upon the lot caster for an explanation. The men then went out hunting again, but all day long Aictor followed them, calling out Agbor Adam's name, and saying he had broken the law.

When the hunters returned to the camp in the evening, they cut up the animals which had been killed during the day, and placed the meat in the smoke of the fires to dry. The skins were pegged out on the ground, and covered with wood ashes.

Later in the evening, the chief called Agbor Adam to him, and asked him if he could explain what the bird had been saying, but he could not do so, and said he would like the lot caster to be consulted when they returned to Okuni. The chief agreed, and said that they would all go back in three days' time.

Early the next morning, Aictor perched himself on the topmost branch of the highest tree in the hunting camp, and started to call Agbor Adam's name as loudly as he could. This so frightened Agbor Adam that, while the other men were hunting, he withdrew himself quietly from the party, and, having found his wife, told her that the whole of the previous day the bird had called his name and had started to call him again that morning. Agbor also said he was so frightened that he had come to ask her to run home with him, and he would then consult the lot caster as to what should be done before the chief arrived, as he felt certain the bird must have seen what they had done and would tell everybody.

His wife then began to pack up her smoked fish, but before she had finished, Aictor came and sat on a tree near to where they were standing, and called out "Agbor Adam! Agbor Adam! Yesterday l caught you breaking the chief's hunting law by eating fish, and now l find you running away from the hunting party." Although Agbor Adam could not understand what the bird said, he suspected something of the truth, so, having fitted an arrow to his bow, he aimed at the bird, thinking that if he could only kill him the trouble would be finished, but Aictor flew away.

When lza Kakem had packed the fish into a load for carrying, her husband helped her to place the load on her head, and they started off with the woman in front, Agbor Adam following close behind.

They walked on for some distance, until they arrived at a stream called "Keruba Ketor" ("deep hole, near the town," a place where women wash their bodies) and then Agbor suggested that they should rest for a while and wash. The woman placed her load in the forked branches of a tree near the stream, and, stepping into the pool, commenced to drink out of her hands. She had not finished drinking when they heard the bird calling out, "Agbor Adam! Agbor Adam! You are running away, but you will be found out."

When Agbor heard the now familiar voice of the bird, he looked round everywhere, but, as he could not see Aictor, he was frightened, and told his wife to pick up her load at once. Then they waded across the stream and began to run. They continued to run until they reached the second water, called "Ogboga Kedegha" ("the water with deep places"). Here the woman said she was going to wash, as she was so hot and tired. Aigbor also said he would wash, so they took off their cloths and stepped into the water, but they had only just started to wash themselves when the bird called out again, "Agbor Adam! Agbor Adam! Now you are half-way home, and, if you do not kill me, you will be found out."

Both Agbor and his wife were now thoroughly frightened, and, jumping out of the water, snatched up their cloths, and ran naked along the path until they reached the shade of a large tree, where they stopped and tied their cloths on.

Then the woman began to abuse her husband, saying, "You have been the cause of all this running and trouble," but Agbor told her that when he eat the fish and broke the hunting law he never thought he would be found out.

They then started off again, and walked as far as the third water, called "Ofat elikatt," ("the slippery water"; so called because the stream runs so fast over the stepping-stones that it causes a person's foot to slip).

Having rested for a little while, they started off again, but had only gone a few steps when the bird once more attracted their attention by calling Agbor's name. This time Aictor was saying, "Turn round and look at the little stream as it will be for the last time." As they did not understand what the bird said, they started off to run again, and did not stop until they reached the small stream quite close to the town, which is called "Ezi Ifom" ("the water where the cows drink").[11]

Here at last they managed to wash without any interruption from the bird, and when they were ready they walked on into the town, which they found almost deserted, as all the men and women were absent hunting and fishing.

---

11   The four streams mentioned in this story are still called by the same names, and are well known to the inhabitants of Okuni.

When they arrived at their house, however, they found that Aictor had got there before them, for they saw him sitting on the top of a palm-tree and when they came near they could hear him calling out, "Agbor Adam! Agbor Adam! Here shall I stay in the town until Chief Alobi and the hunters return, when I will tell them that you have broken their hunting law and you will be killed."

Agbor and his wife then ran into their house and shut the door carefully behind them. Agbor told his wife that when night came he would go and get a supply of food, but that she was not to let anyone in and not to answer anybody who called. He also said that when he got food he would return, and that if there was no one about outside trying to catch him, he would knock at the door and she could then let him in.

During the next two nights, Agbor went out as soon as it was dark and got as much food as he could into the house and then fastened himself securely in.

When the chief returned to the town with his hunters, he sent some men to call Agbor, but although they knocked at his door for a long time and called both Agbor and his wife by name, they received no reply.

When the morning came, the chief sent for the animals to come in, and, as the elephant was the biggest and strongest, he chose him. He then told the elephant that he was to get hold of Agbor Adam, but he did not wish him to be killed, as he only wanted to find out why the bird Aictor had been calling his name and why he had left the hunting party. So the elephant went to Agbor Adam's house and, having broken the door open, dragged him out with his trunk, and brought him before the chief.

Directly Aictor, who was sitting near the chief on a palm-tree, saw Agbor, he began to call his name, and said he had broken the hunting law.

As no one could understand the bird, the chief sent to Uman compound for a woman named Iman, who was a native of Abijon, and could therefore speak Ingor.

When she arrived, she told the chief and the people what the bird was saying, which was "Agbor Adam! Agbor Adam! Chief Alobi passed a law that women should not eat animals killed by the men in hunting, and that the men should not eat the fish caught by the women. But your wife eat a monkey which you had killed and you eat a fish caught by your wife, and then, when I called your name, you ran away with your wife and left the hunting party, but I followed you all the way and although you tried to kill me, I am here to give evidence against you as I promised."

When Chief Alobi heard this he rose up in anger, and stamped his foot on the ground, saying, "Surely Agbor Adam shall die this day. For, first of all, he disobeyed my hunting law, and then he deserted the hunting party. Is there anyone present who does not agree?" But no one answered.

Then Chief Aboli pointed to the palm-tree on which Aictor was perched, and told Agbor Adam that he should be hanged there, but, first of all, he should climb up and down the tree six times, and when he got to the top for the seventh time he should place his head in a noose and hang himself.

When Agbor's wife heard this, she ran and threw herself at

the chief's feet and, beating her breasts and tearing her hair, she implored him to spare her husband: but the chief walked away from her.

Agbor then climbed up to the top of the tree and came down again. This he did six times, but when he had got to the top of the tree for the seventh time, and was just going to hang himself, Chief Ossima 'nkom of Yammi appeared, and called upon him to stop, saying, "I am the oldest and biggest chief in the town, and am going to beg for you."

He then went to chief Alobi and said, "If a man kills another man he should be hanged, but if he breaks the hunter's law he disobeys a chief's order; he should be fined and not killed, and I think 260 rods would be a proper fine."

To this Chief Aboli agreed, and thus Agbor Adam's life was saved, so he climbed down the tree again and paid the fine.

From that time the people who disobeyed a chief were made to pay a fine in tombo, goats, or sheet, according to the order.

Told by Ennenni, an Okuni woman. [E.D., 6.1.11.]

XXXIII

How Essama Stole het Father's Goat in the Fatting-house, and her Brother was Punished for it

In the olden days at Okuni, when the women were circumcised, they were kept in the fatting-house for a long time and given plenty of food to eat. There was a wealthy chief at that time living in Okuni, called Okim. He had a daughter named Essama and a son called Ode. The chief was very fond of both his children, and when Essama grew up he bought a male goat and had it cut to make it grow bigger, so that when his daughter was circumcised and kept in the fatting house he would be able to give her the goat to eat. Both the goat and Essama grew up together, until the time arrived for the girl to be circumcised and kept in the fatting-house. Then Chief Okim told his son Ode that he was to be his sister's attendant while she was kept in the house, and that he was to look after the goat.

Essama stayed in the fatting-house for several months, until one day several of the girls of her company came to visit her. As she had nothing to give them to eat, she at last thought of her father's goat, which was being kept for her, but she dared not kill it while her brother Ode was in the house. She therefore sent him down to the river with a basket, and told him to fill it with water and bring it back to her. Ode did as his sister told him and took the basket down to the river, but he found that the water ran out of the basket almost as quickly as it went in; he therefore remained at the water-side some time. This gave Essama a chance to kill and cook the goat, which she ate with her company. Essama reserved a leg, some of the soup, and a yam, which she placed in a pot and hung over the fire to keep warm for Ode when he returned from the river.

It was late when Ode came back to the house, and he told his sister that he was sorry he could not fill the basket with water. He then asked her where the goat was. Essama replied that she had not seen the goat walking about anywhere since he had gone down to the river, and advised him to search everywhere for him. Ode did so, but failed to find the goat.

When he came back and told his sister, she pointed to the pot and said, "There is your food," so Ode took the pot down, but as he did so some of the soup fell over him out of the pot, as it was quite full. He then sat down and began to eat. While he was eating, his father returned from the farm, and, missing the goat, asked Ode what had become of it. When he heard that the goat could not be found, the chief made a great palaver with Ode, who began to cry. His father then said he was convinced that someone must have stolen the goat, and that all his people, including his son and daughter, would have to go through the ordeal of crossing over the river on a rope, to find out who had stolen the goat. So the next day all the people assembled, and the spider was called upon to settle the palaver, as he was the chief man who settled these trials. The spider went across the river, spinning his web as he went, and then returned to the side where the people were standing. The spider then told each man and woman to say before they started to cross the river, "If I stole Chief Okim's goat, let the rope break with me when I get to the middle; but if I am not a thief, let me cross over in safety."

One after the other the people crossed over the river on the spider's web quite safely, until at last there were only left Essama and her brother. Ode went before his sister, and when he reached the middle of the river the web broke, and he fell into the water, disappearing at once.

The chief then began to lament, saying his goat had been stolen, and now his son was drowned. He then told the people to go into the river and try to recover Ode's body. The young men at once dived in and searched everywhere, but could not find any trace of Ode.

As his son had been drowned, the chief would not allow his daughter to cross the river, and returned home with his people very sorrowfully. Chief Okim then ordered his people to tie up a bundle in a cloth to represent his son, and all people were ordered to mourn. A deep grave was then dug, and ten men were killed to accompany the Chief's son to the spirit-land. The bodies of the ten men were then put in the grave, and the bundle representing the dead Ode was placed on top. The grave was then filled in, whilst drums were being beaten and farewells to the chief's son were being shouted by the people. Several goats were killed, and a big feast was held, and the chief commanded all people to mourn for one year.

When the year of mourning was over, Chief Okim decided to build a new house, so he sent his boys to the river-side to get tie-tie. While they were engaged in drawing the tie-tie from the trees, one man named Oyonga heard a voice calling out, "Who is drawing the tie-tie there?" He stopped pulling and looked round everywhere, but as he could not see anybody, he went on pulling again at the tie-tie. The voice then called out again, saying, "Tell my father to bring a white goat, a white ram, a white cock, and a white chicken to the river-side and sacrifice them to the river ju-ju, and tell him that if he does this I shall be set free." Oyonga then asked the voice who it was speaking, and the voice replied, "I am Ode, Chief Okim's son who was lost, as when I took the pot down some of the soup made from my father's goat, which my sister had stolen, fell over me, so that when I tried to cross the river on the spider's web it broke by the ordeal and I was lost in the water."

Oyonga then ran back to the town and told the chief what he had heard. When Chief Okim heard what Oyonga had to say, he was vexed, as he did not believe him, so he ordered him to be tied up to a tree and given fifty lashes. Oyonga pleaded with the chief in vain, and he was flogged.

When Oyonga had sufficiently recovered from the flogging he had received, he begged the chief to go with him to the river where he had heard the voice; at first the chief refused to go, but after much persuasion he consented. When they got to the place Oyonga pulled at the tie-tie, and the voice at once called out, "Who is pulling there? Have you told my father to bring the white goat, ram, cock, and chicken to sacrifice to the ju-ju?"

When the chief heard his son's voice he went back to the town and got all the animals and birds as quickly as possible, and having brought them down to the water-side, sacrificed them to the river ju-ju. When the sacrifice was completed, the chief told all his young men to go into the river with a net; in case his son should not be able to get out of the water, they could then fish him out.

Very shortly the river ju-ju threw Ode up, and he tried to swim, but one of the men in a canoe pulled him out of the water and brought him to the bank. The people then beat drums and escorted the chief and his son back to the town, singing as they went.

As soon as they arrived, the whole of the townspeople came out with presents of various articles and gave them to Ode. Chief Okim then gave a great feast, and killed many cows and goats, and there was a big play and dancing in the town. When the play was over Chief Okim asked his son what he had found out while he was with the river ju-ju, and Ode replied that the river ju-ju made him understand that it was his sister Essama who stole the goat, but, as the ordeal found the scent of the goat on him, he disappeared in the water.

Then Chief Okim called out Essama's mother and told her what her daughter had done, nearly causing him to lose his son altogether. The chief and his wife had a quarrel, which ended in his fining her 1,200 rods, which was the price of a slave, and said that the whole of her family would have to help to pay. The rods were brought to the chief, and half the amount was given to Ode. The people then decided that it was because Essama was kept so long in the fatting-house which caused her to kill the goat, and they agreed that for the future girls should only stay in the fatting house for a few days, as they would then not be tempted to steal and bring shame upon their families.

Told by Ennenni, a dancing-woman of Okuni. [E. DAYRELL, 14.1.11.]

Quomodo evenit ut Penis primum cum Vagina coiit

Penis autem olim rure solus habitabat, haud procul a Testiculis, amico ejus, qui magus erat valde peritus, atque fundum proximum incolebat. Ultra tamen praedia Penis villam parvam habebat Vagina. Penis forte ad villam Vaginae vagatus, et fame afflictus, illam palmae nuces, quas nuper in horto coUegerat, rogavit, scilicet quod ipse totam diem in agro laborasset nec sibi cibum parare potuisset. Nec abnuit Vagina, sed se pauperem esse dicebat, et Penem debitum reddere alio tempore opportere. Quo pacto Penis cum nucibus abiit. Paullo postea Vagina haud procul ab aedibus Penis ligna capite ferebat, et, debiti memor, domum ejus aggressa, "Esurio" inquit "O Penis, cum totam diem haec ligna collegi, nec mihi cibum parare potui. Redde igitur nuces quas debes." Penis tamen noluit, et Vagina iterum vehementius nuces postulabat; deinde, cum se nihil profiteri sentiret, ligna in terram irata dejecit, seque insuper prostravit. Unum autem e lignis quod peracutum erat Vaginam inter crura altius vulneravit, gravique dolore afflixit. Quod visum Penis aegre ferebat, atque ligno extracto et vulnere aqua perluto Vaginam domum duxit. Haec tamen interdum, magno dolore pressa, lamentari non desinebat, quod maxime. Penem pigebat, qui eam penitus amabat, etiamsi nuces debitas reddere noluerat. Itaque Penis domum regressus servum jussit in villam Vaginae properare atque vulneri medicamenta adhibere. Quo facto servus, cum Vagina nihilominus inter gemitus vociferabat se vehementer dolentem sanari a Pene opportere, qui causa malorum fuisset, ad Penem regressus ea quae dixerat Vagina nuntiavit. Quae audita Penis diu meditatus statim ire amicum suum, Testiculos, consultum statuit, qui maxime sapiens diceretur. At Testiculi, de Vaginae vulnere certior factus, dixit Penem Vaginam sanare posse si verbis suis obtemperet; et Penis laetus se velle omnia facere quae necesse essent asseverabat. Eo autem tempore Penis nunquam erectus fiebat. Itaque Testiculi "Liquore" inquit "te implebo ita ut erectus fias; deinde i ad Vaginam teque in vulnus insere; quo facto te paene foras extractum iterum atque iterum in vulnus impelle, dum tandem liquorem quo te implevi in vulnus vomes." "At si quidam" inquit Penis "inimicus mihi gladio instabit jam in vulnere condito, inopinantem interficere poterit." "Bono animo es" inquit Testiculi "ego enim a tergo vigilabo pro te ne quid infaustum accidat." Itaque Penis ad Vaginam properavit et omnia quae amicus jusserat perfecit. At Vagina medicinam sibi magnopere profuisse dixit, et Penem precata est ut omni quaque nocte veniret eodem modo vulnus sanaturus. Paucis itaque diebus Vagina convaluit, sed rima alta in corpore manebat. Ex eo tempore etiam Testiculi et Penis in uno juncti sunt, ita ut Testiculi, quoties Penis Vaginam videat, eum liquore implet per quem validus fit. At si quid incommodi Vagina habeat, vel alio sit qui vehementius rixetur, tum Penis erectus non fit, nec rimam intrare potest.

(Translation)

How it happened that the Penis first united with the Vagina

Penis once lived alone on an estate not far from Testicles, his friend, who was a very knowledgeable wise man and occupied the estate next door. On the other side of the Penis' estate, however, Vagina owned a small estate. Penis, who happened to have wandered over to Vagina's manor and was ravaged by hunger because he himself had worked all day in his field and had been unable to prepare food for himself, begged her for the palm nuts she had recently gathered in her garden. And Vagina did not refuse this, but said that she was poor, and that Penis should repay the debt at another time. After this was agreed upon, Penis left with the nuts. Some time later Vagina was carrying some lumps of wood on her head not far from Penis' house, and, remembering the debt, she said, after she had approached his house, "O Penis, I am hungry, because I have been gathering these lumps of wood all day and have not been able to prepare food for myself. Therefore repay the nuts you owe me." Penis, however, would not do this, and Vagina again, with more emphasis, demanded the nuts; then, sensing that she was getting nowhere, she furiously threw the pieces of wood to the ground and threw herself upon them. One of the pieces of wood that was very pointed wounded Vagina rather deeply between her legs and plagued her with intense pain. Penis minded what he saw and brought Vagina home, after pulling out the piece of wood and rinsing the wound with water. She, however, overwhelmed

with great pain, did not stop moaning, which greatly saddened
Penis, who loved her very much, even though he had refused
to return the nuts she owed. Therefore Penis, after returning
home, ordered his slave to hurry to Vagina's house and tend
the wound with medicine. After this was done, the slave, after
returning to Penis, reported what Vagina had said, because Vagina
nevertheless continued to cry out in between wailing that since
she was in severe pain, she should be cured by Penis, who had
been the cause of her misery. After Penis had thought long and
hard about what he had heard, he decided to go at once to his
friend Testicles who was said to be particularly wise, and ask
him for advice. But Testicles, having been informed of Vagina's
wound, said that Penis could only heal Vagina if he obeyed her;
and Penis joyfully assured him that he was willing to do whatever
was necessary. At that time, however, Penis never became erect.
Therefore Testicles said, "I will fill you with liquid so that you will
become upright; then go to Vagina and thrust yourself into the
wound; after you have done this, after you have almost pulled out,
thrust yourself again and again into the wound, until finally you
spit out into the wound the liquid with which I have filled you."
"But if some enemy corners me with a sword while I am locked in
the wound just then, he will be able to kill me unsuspectingly," said
Penis. "Be of good cheer," said Testicles, "for I will have your back
so that nothing unfortunate happens." So Penis rushed to Vagina
and carried out everything his friend had instructed. Then Vagina
said the medicine helped her extremely well and begged Penis to
come over every night to heal her wound in the same way. And so

Vagina recovered in a few days, but the deep cut remained in her body. Since that time, Testicles and Penis have been connected so that whenever Penis sees Vagina, Testicles fills him with liquid making him potent. But if Vagina has some discomfort, or if there is someone somewhere who is arguing too violently, Penis does not become erect and cannot enter the cut.

(Told by Ennenni, a singing and dancing girl of Okuni. May 18th, 1911.)

Elphinstone Dayrell

Very little is known about the author Elphinstone Dayrell. He was a colonial administrator who worked as a district commissioner in Ikom, Eastern Province, Nigeria. He also was a *Fellow of the Royal Geographical Society* and *Fellow of the Royal Anthropological Institute.*

The first part of this VAMzzz Publishing compilation contains a volume which originally appeared as a notebook manuscript entitled *More Folk Stories from Southern Nigeria.* The author gathered his material from stories told to him by local people between May 25, 1910 and January 14, 1911. It was published as *Folk Stories from Southern Nigeria,* containing a collection of 40 folk tales, introduced by the folklorist Andrew Lang. Posthumely, one of the most well-known stories in the collection, *Why the Sun and Moon Live in the Sky,* has been turned into an award-winning children's book in 1995.

Dayrell's collection of tales was collected from the Efik and Ibibio peoples of South Eastern Nigeria. Dayrell also authored a second collection of folklore, this one entitled *Ikom Folk Stories from Southern Nigeria.* It was published by the *Royal Anthropological Institute of Great Britain and Ireland* in 1913 and fills up the second part of this volume.

Apart from these works Elphinstone Dayrell published an article (1911) on the ancient secret writing of Nigeria (Nsibidi): *Further Notes on 'Nsibidi Signs with Their Meanings from the Ikom District, Southern Nigeria,* which was explained to him by an elderly local woman. It was published in *The Journal of the Royal Anthropological Institute of Great Britain and Ireland,* Vol. 41 (Jul. - Dec., 1911), pp. 521-540.

Ekbo or Ekpo

Often in the Nigeria stories villagers refer to the *Ekbo* as a source of terror and repression. Therefore, to better understand the concept of Egbo, an explanation of this fraternity, which in West Africa usually had much more power than the country's political leaders, is indispensable.

Egbo is first of all a West African secret fraternity, related to the Ekpe or Ekkpe society of the *Efik* of Calabar - which was inspired by Ekbo - that was founded by the *Ekoi* in South Eastern Nigeria. In turn Ekpe inspired today's Cuban Abakua. The many-sided character of Ekbo may be judged from the immense powers which it has arrogated to itself in almost every direction. Under native rule it usurped practically all functions of government, made trade almost impossible for non-members, and exercised a deep influence on the religious and mystic side of the nation. The Ekbo Society rooted in centuries old traditions of totemism, centralized around the leopard totem. Hence the terms *Leopard Society* and *leopard men*, are often attributed to Ekbo and its members, but should not to be confused with the very violent *Human Leopard Society* which operated in the late 19th and early 20th century in Sierra Leone and Liberia or the more politically and anti-colonially engaged Congolese version. Because Ekbo was the first upgrade from totemism to fraternity, Ekbo Societies or Ekbo Clubs became a general term for West African fraternities, of which the Ekkpe or Ekpe Club of the Efik became the most powerful, due to their dominance in the most important trade center of the region: Old Calabar. Thus the Ekoi were more or less subjected to the Efik who held many trade monopolies the Ekoi were dependent on. Though a fraternity, sometimes rich and influential women were allowed to the Ekbo society. They could join every grade, yet they could never attain full membership. One great advantage to be gained from membership in the old days was the facility offered for the recovery of debts. A creditor brought his case before the Egbo Lodge in the debtor's town. The Council considered the matter, and if the claim was thought justified, the Club drum would be beaten through the streets, and the defaulter was ordered to pay. He was also bound to provide a *dash* for the Egbo Society. Should he be unable to comply with both demands, his goods were seized, and, other means failing, himself or some of his family reduced to the position of slaves, in order to make good all liabilities.

Egbo as the head of the lodge

The term *Egbo* is also used to denote the JuJu-head of an Egbo lodge. The head Ju Ju, or fetish man of each Egbo Society is disguised and frequently wears a hideous mask. There is a bell tied round his waist, hanging behind and concealed by feathers; this bell makes a noise as he runs. When the Egbo is out, no women are allowed outside their houses. They stay inside and pretend to be very frightened. The Egbo very often carries a whip in his hand, and hits out blindly at anyone he comes across. He runs around town followed by young men of his society beating drums and firing off guns. There is generally much drinking going on when the Egbo is playing.

Nsibidi

Before Ekbo emerged, a society existed of whom only chiefs could attain membership. This was the Nsibidi Club, who had the exclusive right to the execution of criminals and who used an ancient secret writing, consisting of symbols much akin to the sigils in Middle

Eastern and European magic. This secret language is also called
Nsibidi and survived the old club of chiefs.

Ekbo house

The importance of the society was obvious, even to the most careless
visitor to any land where it has gained a foothold, for the Ekbo house
was the principal building in every town. Even the smallest village
had its Egbo shed, and when a town decided to migrate the first thing
done, so as soon as the fresh site was cleared, before even new farms
were *cut*, or the land was divided up, was to fix the position of the
Ekbo house. A small shed, called Ekpa Ntan (the house without walls)
was erected to mark the spot where the Egbo house was to be build.
Inside the house are hung human skulls and the skulls of buffalo,
or bush cow, as they are called; also heads of the various antelopes,
crocodiles, apes, and other animals which have been killed by the
members. The skulls of cows and goats killed by the society are also
hung up. A fire is always kept in the Egbo House and in the morning
and late afternoon, the members of the society frequently meet there
to drink gin and palm wine. The rituals of Ekbo are very ancient, and
in it many JuJu cults are mixed. The name of Obassi is invoked before
every sacrifice, and an oblation of food and drink laid in front of the
Etai Ngbe (Leopard stone), the cut stone usually found before the second pillar of the Ekbo house.

Ritual

P. Amaury Talbot writes in his *In the Shadow of the Bush* (London,
New York, 1912):
"The ritual is certainly very ancient, and in it many JuJu cults are
mixed. The name of Obassi is invoked before every sacrifice, and an
oblation of food and drink laid in front of the Etai Ngbe (Leopard
stone), the cut stone usually found before the second pillar of the Club
house.
It is difficult to discover more than the merest fragments of the secrets
of Egbo, as any known informant would meet with a speedy death.

Still from what has been gathered – mostly as in the case already quoted, from snatches of song sung at different plays – there seems to be a close resemblance between these secrets and the Eleusinian and ancient Egyptian mysteries. Certainly a considerable amount of hypnotism, clairvoyance and spiritualism is taught, and only too many proofs have been given, that some of the powers of Nature are known and utilized by initiates, in a way forgotten or unknown to their white rulers. For instance, some of the esoteric members seem to have the power of calling up shadow forms of absent persons.

Once an exhibition of this nature given in the central court of the compound of one of the head chiefs of Oban, was described to me. It was midnight, and a bright moon was shining. Within the open space in the center of the compound a fire was burning. On this from time to time "medicine" was thrown, which caused clouds of smoke to rise. These died down, save for isolated "puffs," which after a time assumed definite shape. The spectators sat on the ground in a half-circle behind the fire, and facing a low mud wall, beyond which, against the background of the moonlit sky, dark silhouettes began to pass, each clearly recognizable as that of some person known to be absent at the time. There was no sign of any artificial means of producing these shapes, which continued to pass for about a quarter of an hour, at the end of which time they grew faint and at length faded. The Chiefs claimed to have the power of calling up the shadow shapes of white men, but no case in which this had actually been done was cited."

7 Grades of Egbo and the hierarchy

There are seven grades which the aspirant must pass before he can be admitted. All grades may be entered by young boys, should their fathers be rich enough to pay the necessary fees, but the secrets are not unfolded till middle age has been reached.

1. Ekpiri Ngbe. Small Egbo.

2. Ebu Nko. (An old word, the meaning of which is not known). At a dance given by this grade, members must always wear their best clothes. Aspirants to each of these are marked with white chalk on both arms.

3. Mbawkaw. (Old Ekoi word adopted by Efiks). Aspirants to this are marked on the forehead with Ekui (cam-wood dye). These three grades are called collectively *Abonn Ogbe,* i.e., children of the Egbos. They are neither important nor expensive to enter.

4. Ndibu. (Old word, meaning unknown, equivalent to Efik Nyampke). This is the second division, and one to which it is accounted a great honour to belong. It is often called *The Mother of the Grades.* Its president holds the second place in the whole society. If it was found necessary to expel a member who had reached this grade, death followed as a matter of course, lest any of its secrets should be revealed by the outcast. When a man joins Ndibu the head chiefs and officials stay in the Egbo house, while the young men dance and play round the town. The best friend of the aspirant brings forward a calabash containing a leg of meat, and two bottles of palm wine. The postulant then enters the Club house, and sits down before the Chief, who puts powder on his head, and recites all the names of the Egbo. The new member next rises and invokes the names in his turn, while after each the chiefs call out *Owe,* i.e., our own. He then goes out and dances with the young men. The play is carried on for about eight days, during which time palm wine and meat are supplied to all. In the early 20th century at Oban, entrance to this grade costed about £30, which must be paid before full membership is allowed.

5. Oku Akama. (The priest consents). This is not very expensive to enter, nor considered of much account, but it must be passed before further grades can be reached. The postulant is marked with yellow dye *(Ogokk)* on the abdomen and the back of his shoulders. The old Ekoi grade was called Asian, but when Oban adopted the Calabar Egbo, the Efiks insisted on this being suppressed.

6. *Eturi.* (Metal or brass rod), Efik Okpokgo. In the old days during a play, all fires had to be extinguished and no noise of any kind was permitted in the town. Formerly very few men succeeded in reaching this grade, but later it was usually passed on the same day as Nkanda.

7. *Nkanda.* The highest and final grade. Oban took this from the Efiks, who again insisted on the destruction of the old Ekoi equivalent *Isong* and of another old grade *Mutanda,* of slightly lesser importance. Nkanda is more expensive than any other grade, and most men only enter late in life. When a man has succeeded in joining this high grade, he is rubbed on head and chest with yellow powder *(Ogokk).* Five rings are made on front and back. Two yellow, one round each breast, a white one in the centre some few inches below, and, beneath this again, two more yellow ones, forming a square with those on the breasts. On the back the rings are arranged in the same way, but the central one is yellow and the four outer ones white. The arms are ornamented with alternate stripes of white and yellow, and till the last rite is finished, the man goes bare save for a long loin cloth which reaches from waist to feet.

The chief of Nkanda is the president of the Egbo Lodge, and by far the most powerful man of the town. His office is sometimes hereditary, and only free-born chiefs can aspire to it. A slave could not join Egbo, lest he should reveal its secrets to a new master. He could, however, be present at most of the ceremonies if his owner was a member of Egbo, and permitted.

One of the chief insignia of the Nkanda grade is called the Ekabe (Efik Ekarra) Nkanda. This is a kind of hoop, covered with bright-colored cloth. The attendant whose duty is to carry this, performs many curious evolutions with it. He is obliged to hold back the Okum (or "image") by its means if the latter, in a state of excitement, seems about to show himself to a non-member, particularly a woman, at a time when this is not permitted. Should the Okum succeed in evading the vigilance of the Ekabe bearer, a cow is killed, and a feast provided for the members at the expense of the defaulting official. Another symbol, used by Nkanda and Ebu Nko alike, is the Effrigi, a sort of wooden fan on which Nsibidi signs are inscribed. The head priest of the whole Egbo Society is called Iyamba, the old Ekoi equivalent for which was Musungu.

The Mariba

Other officials are Murua, who carries the rattle during "plays," and Isua, the master of ceremonies for the Abonn Ogbe. The head of each grade is called Ntui (chief) and acts as treasurer. Those who belong to the four higher grades, and have paid the fees in full, may join in another ceremony called Mariba, or Etem-I-Ngbe (the bush leopard). This is performed in the depths of the forest and with the greatest secrecy. It is during the "Mariba" that the successive mysteries are unveiled. The ceremony may also be performed at the funerals of very great chiefs. The danger run by non-members on such occasions, before the coming of white rule, may perhaps be better understood by the following case.

During the *Mariba* the sacred images, &c, are carried to a part of the *bush* where a little hut of green boughs has been built to receive them. Sentries are posted to keep all intruders from coming within a mile of this spot. P.A. Talbot reports of one occasion where two young girls, sisters, happened to have missed the patrol, and trespassed unwittingly within the sacred precincts, probably in search of nuts or bush fruits, which abound everywhere. They were caught by the sentries, brought before the Egbo, condemned to death, and hanged almost immediately. Their brother, who was a member of the highest grade of the society, was allowed, as a great favor, to be present at their death and afterwards to carry home the bodies to his family.

The Egbo "image"

Each grade has its particular dances and tunes, and each its own Okum Ngbe or Egbo "image," which is never supposed to come out and show itself unless under direct inspiration to do so.

The so-called "image" is a figure robed from crown to heel in a long garment, of the colour proper to the grade, and pierced with eye-holes. It usually bears on its head a wooden framework covered with skin and shaped like a human head, often with two faces, one male and the other female. This represents the omniscience of the Deity looking both ways, into the future and back to the past, as also the bi-sexual character shown in the oldest conceptions of Obassi Osaw and Obassi Nsi, Sky Father and Earth Mother.

Juju

The origin of the word Juju cannot be determined for sure. It is believed to be derived from the French joujou *(plaything)*, though other sources claim it is from the Hausa language, meaning *fetish* or *evil spirit.*

The term "Juju" – *Njomm* in the Ekoi-language – includes all uncomprehending, mysterious forces of nature. These vary in importance from elemental spirits, so powerful as to hold almost the position of demi-gods, to the magical aura of humans, animals, trees, herbs, stones or metals. In another sense the word also includes the means by which such forces may be controlled or influenced; secrets wrung from the deepest recesses of nature by men wise above their fellows, or mercifully imparted to some favored mortal by one or other of the Deities. Jujus vary in importance in different towns according to local opinion, but everywhere a dominant one is to be found, and whatever other attributes may be claimed for this, that of protection against witchcraft always ranks first. Each of the lesser Jujus presides over its particular department, though in many cases attributes overlap.

Thus Juju as a concept can only be understood as a *spiritual and magical scope* of overlapping forces, processes and things:

1. **Nature forces and entities,** also called *Ibokk* and *Ndemm.* The *Ndemm* dwell in or near rivers, pools, and springs, in trees, rocks,

and sacred stones, fairies, gnomes, salamanders, naiads, dryads, etc. They are male and female, their bodies built somewhat on the human model, but of more ethereal texture, varying in height from about six inches to four feet. Each race has its own particular work ; they are principally concerned with the growth of vegetation.

The *Ibokk* are natural or elemental forces which do not affect, or come into contact with, human beings – or in some cases do not even exist – until "made" by a native doctor or Juju-man.

2. A relion or magi-religious system with local variety. According to Isaiah Oke it is even a very large religion (as Juju keeps thriving in West Africa, below the surface of the Abrahamitic religions imported in West Africa, like Christianity and Islam).

3. West African magic, protection magic and medicine.

4. An object that has been deliberately infused with magical power.

5. The magical force itself, or the magical aura of objects, living things or persons.

6. An object used as a fetish or amulet in West African spiritual practices.

Juju is practiced in West African countries such as Nigeria, Benin, Guinea Bissau, Togo, Cameroon and Ghana, although its assumptions are shared by most African people. In the Americas Juju is still practiced among the Maroons of Suriname – and some other countries – who escaped their slaveholders in an early stage, took this African tradition with them and kept it alive.

Juju is principally applied for good and constructive purposes, but it is also used for for nefarious deeds, where in a contradictory way it resembles evil witchcraft. This switch to the dark side happens rather easily, as psychologically Juju is mainly based on pricipales of power and fear. Juju operates on the principle of spiritual contagious contact based on physical contact. The underlying belief is that two entities that have been in close contact, have similar properties even after being separated. It then becomes possible to manipulate one in order to reach the other. Thus, in that context, a person's hair, fingernails, a piece of clothing, a shoe, a sock, or a piece of jewel worn by them are all perfect candidates for Juju because they are believed to retain the spiritual aura of their owner.

Likewise, it is thought that spiritual similarity can be created by deliberately placing two things in physical contact. The underlying belief is that spiritual assimilation and fusion will take place, with one entity absorbing the qualities of the other. Thus Juju is seen as an important root of Voodoo magic in the Caribbean, while conversely Juju practitioners tend to perceive Voodoo magic as a very weak derivative of their system.

Amulets, charms, and mascots are all common forms of Juju. Usually worn for protective purposes, those objects have been infused with a particular type of energy, and wearing them is expected to create paths and possibilities for the wearer, as well as guard them against ill fortunes and evil spirits.

Specialists with extensive know-how and experience typically create Juju. The specialist may be a healer, because Juju is commonly used as treatment for physical and spiritual ailments – from healing insect and animal bites to counteracting and neutralizing curses. However, the specialist may also be a witch or a sorcerer, trying to harm someone through the casting of spells or curses, as well as placing Juju objects in their close contact so they may become spiritually contaminated and polluted. For instance, one may be offered spiritually poisoned food or drinks, which is thought to bring about disruption, trauma, or even death if not dealt with promptly and efficiently. A live animal may also be used as a Juju. It may be infused with a negative energy and then sent near someone. Once physical contact has been made, it is believed the person will most likely become ill.

The Ibibio

The Ibibio people are a coastal people, reputed to be the earliest inhabitants of the south southern Nigeria. It is estimated that they arrived at their present home around 7000 BC. They are mostly found

in Akwa Ibom and Cross River. The Annang, Efik, Ekid, Oron and
Ibeno share personal names, culture, and traditions with the Ibibio,
and speak closely related varieties (dialects) of Ibibio which are more
or less mutually intelligible. The Ekpo/Ekpe society was a significant
part of the Ibibio political system. They used a variety of masks to
execute social control. Body art played a major role in Ibibio art.
Mainly rain-forest cultivators of yams, taro, and cassava, the Ibibio
export mostly palm oil and palm kernels. They are noted for their
skillful wood carving.

Social structure

About 500 individuals made up the typical Ibibio village. Each village
consisted of compounds of rectangular buildings of several rooms,
arranged around a courtyard. Traditionally Ibibio society consisted
of communities that were made up of large families with blood
affinity, each ruled by their constitutional and religious head known
as the *Ikpaisong*. The Obong Ikpaisong ruled with the Mbong Ekpuk
(Head of the Families) which together with the heads of the cults and
societies constituted the *Afe* or *Asan* or *Esop Ikpaisong* (Traditional
Council or Traditional Shrine or Traditional Court). The decisions
of the Obong Ikpaisong were enforced by members of the Ekpo or
Obon society who acted as messengers of the spirits and the military
and police of the community. Ekpo members were always masked
when performing their policing duties. Although their identities were
almost always known, fear of retribution from the ancestors prevented
most people from accusing those members who overstepped their
social boundaries, by committing police brutalities. Membership was
open to all Ibibio males, but one had to have access to wealth to move
into the politically influential grades. The main purpose of Ekpo was
to protect its people and act as a defense against potential attackers.
The members participated in ceremonies concerned with ancestral
spirits and believed they could protect the community through magic
and religious ritual.

Religion

The Ibibio religion had two dimensions. The first dimension
centers on the pouring of libation, sacrifice, worship, consultation,
communication and invocation of the God of Heaven *(Abasi
Enyong)*, God of the Earth *(Abasi Isong)* and the Supreme Being
(Abasi Ibom) by the Constitutional and Religious King/Head of a
particular Ibibio Community, who was known from the ancient
times as the Obong-Ikpaisong. The word 'Obong Ikpaisong' means
King of the Principalities of the Earth' or 'King of the Earth and the
Principalities' or Traditional Ruler. The second dimension of Ibibio
Religion centered on the worship, consultation, invocation, sacrifice,
appeasement, etc. of the God of the Heaven and the God of the Earth
through various invisible or spiritual entities *(me Ndem)* of the various
Ibibio Division such as *Atakpo Ndem Uruan Inyang, Afia Anwan,
Ekpo/Ekpe Onyong, Etefia Ikono, Awa Itam,* etc.
Scattered throughout each village were sacred lands, *akai* (forest).
They were called akai because no one was permitted to clear them
for cultivation. All burial grounds, shrines for the village deities
and spots for secret societies such as Ekpo Onyoho, Ekpe, Ekoong,
Idiong, Ekong, and Obon, were sacred. Everything in these places
were equally sacred. Non-members of the secret societies were not
permitted to enter the spots set aside for such secret societies, even for
the collection of firewood, sticks, fruits (like *mkpook*), vegetables (like
afang and *odusa*) or snails, or to hunt the animals which abounded in
the forests. The explanation is simple. If non-members were allowed
to enter any secret society akai they might in due course discover the
secrets of their time-honoured society, and wicked people might even
desecrate the graves of their ancestors hence the ban.

The Soul and Life After Death

Like many Ibibio words, the name *Ukpong* (Soul) has four meanings.
First: ethereal body, secondly: soul, thirdly: spirit, and fourthly: over-
soul. The last always lives in the house of *Abasi Ibom* and it is quite
separate from the individuality which between incarnations stays in

the country of the dead. Though over-soul and spirit are combined, much of the Spirit is contained in that portion of the ego which is incarnated. According to P. Amaury Talbot, it is the soul proper that spends part of its time as a were-animal or in a bush-beast in the forest or water and is called *Ukpong Ikot*, or bush-soul. The shadow is not thought to be connected with the ethereal body but to be an emanation of the soul and therefore to be directly affected by any action on it. The majority of the Ibibio believe that a person's soul can be invoked into his shadow, which is made to appear in a basin of water. The shadow is then speared, his blood is seen in the water in the basin and the man dies. The Ibibio believe that after death the same kind of existence is led as during life on earth; for example, farmers, blacksmiths, hunters, and fishermen will continue with their former occupations while social intercouse and amusements will also proceed as before. The scenery, houses, crops and animals of the next world have the same appearance as in this world but only those beasts, plants and foodstuffs which have been sacrificed in honour of the dead are transported there. The land of the dead, like that of the living, is believed to be divided into various countries, towns, villages and lineages where different communities of people live as on earth.

The Efik

Efik people inhabit the lower Cross River in Cross River state, Nigeria. Their language is the main dialect and language of the Efik-Ibibio group of the Benue-Congo branch of Niger-Congo languages. It is widely spoken as a *lingua franca* throughout the Cross River region. The Efik, who are culturally and linguistically related to the Ibibio, migrated down the Cross River during the first half of the 17th century (though the date of that migration is contested by some) and founded Creek Town, Duke Town, and other settlements.
The Efik society consist of various clans which were originally known as *Esien Efik Itiaba* (English: Seven clans of Efik) and later known in the 21st century as *Esien Efik Duopeba* (English: Twelve clans of Efik).

The original seven clans are scattered between Cross River state and Akwa Ibom state and consist of Iboku (Duke town, Henshaw town, Creek town and Cobham town), Obutong, Adiabo, Mbiabo (Mbiabo Edere, Mbiabo Ikot Offiong, Mbiabo Ikoneto), Enwang, Usukakpa and Abayen. The last three clans had greatly dwindled in number and many of their members are believed to have been miscegenated into other Efik clans. Ibonda (an Efut clan) has sometimes been appended to Adiabo as one of the seven Efik clans. The bulk of the Enwang and Usukakpa are located in the present-day Akwa Ibom state.

Ethymology

Ethymologically the name *Efik* translates to Oppressors and is derived from the Efik-Ibibio verb root *Fik* (English: Oppress). The first letter of the word is correctly written as 'Ẹ' and denotes plurality. Several theories have been propounded on the origin of the word. One theory propounded by *Okon* and *Nkpanam Ekereuke* asserts that the term *Efuk* was a word of defiance and an expression used by the Ibibio man when in a fit of rage. The Ekereuke further assert that the word was later changed to Efik. Another theory states that the name Efik translates to Tyrants or *He who oppresses* and was the name of which the Efik called themselves after they had settled at Creek town.

Slave trade

Because of an European error in confusing their territory with that of the *Kalabari Ijo* (known as New Calabar), the Efik area became known as Old Calabar. Originally a fishing community, Old Calabar developed into a major trading centre from the 17th to the 19th century. Throughout the centuries, Efik traders traded with the Portuguese, Dutch, English and French and European ships had to pay a duty (comey) to Efik chiefs for the privilege of trading. The Efik were noted for their involvement in the slave trade were they acted as slave traders and middlemen between the inland slave traders and the Europeans. After the decline of the slave trade, the Efik transitioned into the business of exporting palm oil from the Cross river. Other trading items sold by the Efik included rubber, ivory, barwood and redwood.

Social structure

Households formerly consisted of a man, his several wives, and their children, but polygyny has become relatively rare. Once organized according to male descent, groups of households were formed into what is known as a House (not a structural reference), whose leader was chosen for ability rather than age. Related Houses occupied the wards into which settlements are divided.

The obong, or paramount leader, elected from among the heads of various Houses, traditionally exercised his authority as head of the Ekpe (Egbo), or Leopard, society. In addition to ritual propitiation of forest spirits – to ensure the well-being of the community – this graded secret male society made and enforced laws by fines, capital punishment, or boycotts, judged cases, maintained internal peace and served as the executive government of Efik society. The Ekpe was composed of the leading men of this community, and its higher grades were open only to those who could pay the heavy entrance fees. It also functioned as a force for tribal unity, as society members from one village were accepted by members in another village. The Ekpe continues to exist, but its dominant role in legislative, judicial, and economic affairs has been taken over by the state. Its putative supernatural powers also have waned.

Modern Efik society is a melting pot of people of diverse origin. Due to the rise of Calabar as a commercial centre since the 18th century, Efik settlements experienced a high rate of inward migration consisting of Sierra Leoneans, Lebanese, Cameroonians, Jamaicans and several other communities. Children of Efik maternal descent are still regarded as Efik and have contributed to the development of the Efik society. Due to the volume of cultural exchange, many other ethnic groups have often been regarded as being one with the Efik such as Kiong and Efut. During the 20th century a large part of the Efik population moved from the towns and settled in farming villages in the forest. The staple foods are yams and cassava, supplemented by taro, corn (maize), fruits and vegetables, and fish.

Religion

Traditional Efik religion included belief in a supreme creator god, ancestral and other supernatural beings, magic, sorcery, and witchcraft. However, the publication (1868) of an Efik-language Bible, the first translation of that scripture into a Nigerian language, had a significant impact, and in the 21st century most Efik identified themselves as Christians.

Calabar

Calabar, formerly Old Calabar is the town and port, capital of Cross River state, southeastern Nigeria. It lies along the Calabar River, 5 miles (8 km) upstream from that river's entrance into the Cross River estuary. Settled in the early 17th century by the Efik branch of the Ibibio people, the town became a centre for trade between Europeans on the coast and Africans farther inland. Fish, cassava, bananas, palm oil, and palm kernels were traded at Calabar for European manufactured goods, and the town also served as a major slave-trading depot. Duke Town (originally known as Atakpa or Akwa Akpa) and the other Efik settlements near Calabar – Creek Town, Henshaw Town, and Obutong (Old Town) – were forcibly united into the loosely knit state of Old Calabar by the Ekpe secret society, which was controlled by the towns' merchant houses.

The coast in this region was named "Calabar" by the Portuguese explorer Diogo Cao. His reason for choosing this name is unknown, since it was not used by the Efik people. But one theory states this region was the main source of the Calabar bean, a deadly poisonous bean that, when ingested, markedly affects the nervous system. When someone was accused of witchcraft or theft, the person was forced to eat the bean. It was believed that, if the accused survived this trial, she or he was innocent. Duke Town or Akwa Akpa was founded about

1650 by Efik families who had left Creek Town, further up the Calabar river, settling on the east bank in a position where they were able to dominate the slave trade with European vessels that anchored in the river. They soon became the most powerful people in the region. Duke Town became a center of the Atlantic slave trade, where slaves were exchanged for European goods.

Igbo people formed the majority of enslaved Africans which were sold as slaves from Calabar, despite forming a minority among the ethnic groups in the region. From 1725 until 1750, roughly 17,000 enslaved Africans were sold from Calabar to European slave traders; from 1772 to 1775, the number soared to over 62,000. In 1767, six British slave ships arrived in Calabar during a period when Duke Town and Old Town were in the midst of a feud. The leaders of Duke Town made a secret arrangement with the slave traders whereby the leaders of Old Town would be invited onboard their ships to settle the dispute; guarantees of their safety were made. When the leaders of Old Town came aboard the ships, they were seized, with some being kept as slaves while others were handed over to the leaders of Duke Town, who ordered their execution.

By the mid-19th century, after the waning of the slave trade, Old Calabar's economy had become based on the export of palm oil and palm kernels. After the chiefs of Duke Town accepted British protection in 1884, the town, which was called Old Calabar until 1904, served as capital of the Oil Rivers Protectorate (1885–93), the Niger Coast Protectorate (1893–1900), and Southern Nigeria (1900–06) until the British administrative headquarters were moved to Lagos. It remained an important port (shipping ivory, timber, and beeswax, as well as palm products) until it was eclipsed by Port Harcourt, terminus (1916) of the railroad, 90 miles (145 km) west.

The completion of roads from Calabar to Arochukwu, Ikom, and Mamfe (in Cameroon) and the Calabar–Itu–Expene highway (which provides easy access to the rest of Nigeria) contributed to Calabar's initial importance as a port. The port still exports some products, including oil, natural gas, palm produce, timber, rubber, cocoa, and piassava fibre. The town has a sawmill; rubber-, food-, and oil-palm-processing plants; and a cement factory. Wood carving is a traditional art of the Efik, and the town's artisans sculpt ebony artifacts for the tourist market in Lagos.

Calabar has long been an educational centre. Its first church school, established by the Rev. Hope Waddell of the Free Church of Scotland in 1846, helped influence the Ekpe secret society to pass a law (1850) prohibiting human sacrifice.

The protective spirit Efuk

Calabar is believed to have its own supernatural guardian or protective Juju. The *Ndemm* (nature elemental) *Efuk*, a male Juju, lived on Parrot Island in the Cross River till the mangroves were cut, when he descended into the water. His principal duty is to protect children, keep canoes from sinking, and help in trading ventures. He is represented by some large pots filled with water, a few Afia-Akuk rods, and a man's skull.

■

Recommended

Human Leopards
*An Account of the Trials of
Human Leopards Before the
Special Commission*
K.J. Beatty
210 pages, paperback
ISBN 9789492355492
www.vamzzz.com

The early 20th century showed an increase number of occult murders by the Human Leopard Society of Sierra Leone. The main reason for the killings was to obtain human fat for anointing a terrible fetish called the Borfima, whose black magic depended on the frequency with which it was "fed." These killings got mixed with ritual cannibalism, of which the first reports for this area date back to 1609.

Unlike other Leopards Societies an unexplainable social dissonant sticks to the Sierra Leone version: "The bush seemed to me pervaded with something supernatural, a spirit which was striving to bridge the animal and the human. Some of the weird spirit of their surroundings has, I think, entered into the people, and accounts for their weird customs. The people are by no means a low, savage race. I found many of them highly intelligent, shrewd, with more than the average sense of humor, and with the most marvelous faculty for keeping hidden what they did not wish to be known…" (W. Brandford Griffith, September 1915.)

This revised and illustrated edition comes with a Post Scriptum about other Leopard fraternities like the Congolese Anyota, the Nigerian Ekpe and it's offspring the Cuban Abakuá.

Paper books

VAMzzz Publishing creates new and revised editions of books in the categories Magic & Witchcraft, Secret Rites & Societies, Demonology, Celtic & Mythology and Astrology. These books are written by either highly qualified academic researchers, or experts in a special field of esoteric knowledge, craft or practice.

As a publisher, we deeply respect the author of any book we choose and strive to work our own kind of magic in such a way, that it would put a smile on the author's faces, should they be watching us from heaven. In most of our books we offer 'Post Scriptum', aditional information about the author and/or the subject.

In contrast to the current trend of digital screen addiction, we think, this variety of literature needs to be presented on paper. *No e-books, but real books!*

Apart from republications of valuable but forgotten books, we also offer regular interesting articles on our occult blog: www.vamzzz.com/blog

Previews of all books, including a complete table of contents, can be viewed on www.vamzzz.com. More books will be added to the list in due time.

VAMzzz Publishing

VAMzzz Publishing
P.O. Box 3340
1001 AC Amsterdam
The Netherlands
vamzzz@protonmail.com
www.vamzzz.com

Anansi
Jamaican stories of the Spider God
by Martha Warren Beckwith
494 pages, Paperback, ISBN 9789492355171

Anansi is both a god, spirit and African folktale character. He often takes the shape of a spider and is considered to be the spirit of all knowledge of stories. He is also one of the most important characters of West African and Caribbean folklore.

Voodoos and Obeahs
Phases of West India Witchcraft
by Joseph J. Williams
374 pages, Paperback, ISBN 9789492355119

This work goes into great depth concerning the New World-African connection and is highly recommended if you want a deep understanding of the dramatic historical background of Haitian and Jamaican magic and witchcraft, and the profound influence of imperialism, slavery and racism on its development. Williams includes numerous quotations from rare documents and books on the topic.

Spiritual Fetichism
A Study of West African Culture, Witchcraft, Magic & Demonology
by Robert Hamill Nassau
524 pages, Paperback, ISBN 9789492355188

Despite a nowadays anachronist and disturbing perspective, the book has remained most valuable for students of the occult, especially those interested in demonology, voodoo, hoodoo and its roots, African magick and religion, witchcraft, the classes of African spirits, and of course the spiritual and magickal use of a fetish.